The Students We Share

The Students We Share

Preparing U.S. and Mexican Educators for Our Transnational Future

EDITED BY

Patricia Gándara and Bryant Jensen

FOREWORD BY

Linda Darling-Hammond

Cover image from deeperlearning4all.org

Published by State University of New York Press, Albany

© 2021 State University of New York

All rights reserved

Printed in the United States of America

No part of this book may be used or reproduced in any manner whatsoever without written permission. No part of this book may be stored in a retrieval system or transmitted in any form or by any means including electronic, electrostatic, magnetic tape, mechanical, photocopying, recording, or otherwise without the prior permission in writing of the publisher.

For information, contact State University of New York Press, Albany, NY
www.sunypress.edu

Library of Congress Cataloging-in-Publication Data

Names: Gándara, Patricia, editor | Jensen, Bryant, editor.
Title: The students we share : preparing U.S. and Mexican educators for our transnational future / edited by Patricia Gándara and Bryant Jensen; foreword by Linda Darling-Hammond.
Description: Albany : State University of New York Press, [2021] | Includes bibliographical references and index.
Identifiers: ISBN 9781438483238 (hardcover : alk. paper) | ISBN 9781438483245 (ebook) | ISBN 9781438483221 (pbk. : alk. paper)
Further information is available at the Library of Congress.

10 9 8 7 6 5 4 3 2 1

To educators and teacher educators everywhere
who commit to learn from and build communities for
our children and youth.

*Con urgencia, trabajamos juntos para el bienestar
de los estudiantes que compartimos.*

Contents

LIST OF ILLUSTRATIONS — xi

ACKNOWLEDGMENTS — xiii

FOREWORD — xv
    Linda Darling-Hammond

INTRODUCTION
The Students We Share and the Teachers We Need — 1
    Bryant Jensen and Patricia Gándara

Part 1.
Teacher Preparation Across Borders

CHAPTER 1
Contrasting Realities: How Differences Between the Mexican and U.S. Education Systems Affect Transnational Students — 17
    Lucrecia Santibañez

CHAPTER 2
Binational Teacher Preparation: Constructing Pedagogical Bridges for the Students We Share — 45
    Cristina Alfaro and Patricia Gándara

CHAPTER 3
Normalista Perspectives on Preparing Mexican Teachers for American Mexican Students — 71
    Eric Ruiz Bybee, Bryant Jensen, and Kevin Johnstun

Part 2.
Transnational Teaching

CHAPTER 4
What Educators in Mexico and in the U.S. Need to Know
and Acknowledge to Attend to the Educational Needs of
Transnational Students   99
Edmund T. Hamann and Víctor Zúñiga

CHAPTER 5
Preparing Educators for Asset-Based Pedagogies: The Case of
Recently Arrived Transnational Students in Central Mexico   119
Sarah Gallo

CHAPTER 6
Equitable Teaching Enhances Achievement Opportunity for the
Students We Share   145
Bryant Jensen

CHAPTER 7
Mirroring Students' and Teachers' Classroom Experiences to
Address the Challenges of Transnationalism in Mexican Schools   175
Betsabé Román González and Juan Sánchez García

Part 3.
Bridging Policies

CHAPTER 8
Language and Cultural Skills of U.S. Teachers: Informing Policy to
Meet the Needs of Transnational Bilingual Students   201
Francesca López and Lucrecia Santibañez

CHAPTER 9
From *Plyler* to Sanctuary: U.S. Policy on Public School Access
and Implications for Educators of Transnational Students   223
Julie Sugarman

CHAPTER 10
Binational Policies for the Students We Share and the Teachers
We Need   249
    Patricia Gándara and Bryant Jensen

CONTRIBUTORS   269

INDEX   273

Illustrations

Figures

1.1	Average School Trajectory from Elementary to Higher Education in Mexico between 1990 and 2012.	24
3.1	Mural at *Amistad*.	77
3.2	Website Screenshot "El caso de Juan, el niño triqui."	85
8.1	Conceptual Framework Representing Teacher Preparation and Teacher Self-Efficacy as Mediators of Policy on DLLs' Achievement Outcomes.	204
8.2	Percentage of New Teachers with Bilingual and/or ESL Training over Time.	204
9.1	States with the Largest Numbers and Fastest-Growing Populations of Children of Immigrants.	227

Tables

1.1	Indicators of Bilingualism in Mexico and the United States	27
1.2	Basic Teacher Characteristics in Mexico and the United States	29
1.3	Primary Education Teacher Salaries and Working Conditions, Mexico and United States (2019, in US Dollars Converted by PPP)	30

2.1	Educational Attainment by Race for 25- to 29-Year-Olds, California, 2018	48
3.1	Research Participants at *Amistad* and *Cívica*	78
3.2	Key Term Frequency across Three Curricula (Emphasis Added)	79
6.1	Elements of Equitable Teaching and Associated Factors and Variables	150
7.1	Children Interviewed in the State of Morelos	178
7.2	Interviews with Teachers, Principals, and PROBEM's Director in the State of Morelos	179
8.1	Range of Language Instruction Educational Programs and Their Respective Language of Instruction and Goals	203
9.1	Nativity of Parents of U.S. Children Age 3 to 17—2016	225
9.2	Nativity of U.S. Children of Immigrants Age 3 to 17—2016	226
9.3	Citizenship and Legal Status of Children Age 3 to 17 Living with One or More Unauthorized Immigrant Parents—2016	228

Acknowledgments

We want to first extend our gratitude to former President of the University of California, Janet Napolitano for her commitment to the University of California-Mexico project, which brought many of the scholars in this book together under the Students We Share conferences hosted at the Casa de California in Mexico City. Thanks also to Veronique Rorive of UC-Mexico for her support and guidance over the last several years. The Ford Foundation provided critical funds to support this book and we thank Doug Wood for seeing the value in the project. Superintendent of Public Instruction for California, Tom Torlakson, provided critical funding for some of the work presented here and Mexican colleagues in Baja California, Yara Amparo López and Javier González Monroy, worked actively from the Mexican side of the border to support this work and continue to push for active collaboration to meet the needs of the students we share. We recognize and thank President Silvia Giorguli Saucedo of El Colegio de México, Felipe Martínez Rizo, founding director of the Instituto Nacional para la Evaluación de la Educación (now the Comisión Nacional para la Mejora Continua de la Educación), and Agustín Escobar Latapí of the Centro de Investigadores y Estudios Superiores en Antropología Social for their visionary leadership in migration and education scholarship and evidence-based policymaking. Sincerest gratitude to educators Ana Laura Peñaloza Urbina, Miriam de la Cruz Reyes, and Jorge Gerardo López Coutigno for supporting shared projects with teachers and students in the state of Morelos for over 15 years. Special thanks to Karen Janney, Diana Carberry, and Dan Winters of Sweetwater Union High School District in Chula Vista and Dr. Cindy Marten of San Diego Unified School District who opened their doors and provided invaluable assistance in gathering information to assess and meet the needs of transnational students. It is this kind of collaboration that moves us forward in the quest to support transnational students and their teachers. Finally, we acknowledge and thank each and every educator, parent, teacher educator, and student we share referenced in this book—for teaching us about hope, commitment, community, and joy. *Por ustedes, el futuro resplandece.*

Foreword

Linda Darling-Hammond

This book is about preparing educators to teach diverse students. But, more than that, it is about preparing teachers from two different school systems with different languages, norms, values, and practices to teach students who experience part of their educations in each of those systems. As the authors point out, this involves millions of students who move between Mexico (and increasingly Central America) and the United States, and often back again to their country of origin. In *The Flat World and Education, Empowered Educators,* and, most recently, *Preparing Teachers for Deeper Learning,* I have written about preparing teachers for a changing and global world, with an emphasis on meeting the needs of increasingly diverse students in the United States and other countries experiencing substantial immigration, noting the many considerations of language, culture, and equity that are critical for their learning.

These are the students of concern in this important book. Some come from Mexico and Central America to the United States for at least a portion of their educations, but many more, born and raised in the United States, find themselves in Mexico attempting to adapt to a schooling system that is foreign to them. Given that more than 600,000 of these students currently in school in Mexico are U.S. citizens, many will return to the United States to live and work. The kind of education they receive in both countries will determine the future that awaits them, and increasingly the future that awaits all of us, because they are part of this rich tapestry that is the United States, and we are all ultimately influenced by the level and quality of education every young person experiences.

Chapters in *The Students We Share* remind us that we are in this together—responding to challenges with projects, policies and practices meant to bridge two school systems by preparing teachers from both countries to sustain a binational pedagogy. But as the studies in this book show, neither U.S. nor Mexican teachers have been fully prepared to address the social, psychological, and learning needs of these "students we share." As a result, too many students fall through the cracks and end their educations prematurely. Some of the chapters in this book recount in heartbreaking detail the way students are made to feel invisible, or worse, as outsiders or interlopers in classrooms where their needs are not recognized. Our teachers, school administrators, and education system leaders all need support to understand the complexity of migration (see Chapter 4 by Hamann and Zúñiga), to enforce existing laws meant to protect children (see Chapter 9 by Julie Sugarman), and to implement more meaningful practices in classrooms (see Chapter 6 by Jensen).

The United States has always been an immigrant-receiving nation, but each wave of immigration has been different, and in recent decades the flow of immigrants has accelerated, resulting in increased percentages of students from Mexico and other Spanish-speaking nations in U.S. schools. However, while the composition of the K-12 student body in the United States has changed dramatically over the last half-century, the composition of the teaching force has been painfully slow to diversify. In 1970, about 80% of students were White as were about 90% of their teachers. By 2015, students of color were more than half of all students in the country, with the single largest percentage being Latinx, yet still 80% of the teaching force was White. This increasing mismatch between the backgrounds and experiences of students and their teachers is mirrored in the experience of U.S. students in Mexican schools.

This creates significant challenges for both teachers and students, and it has significant implications for how teachers are prepared in both countries to meet the needs of these students we share. Teachers must be prepared to teach students whose cultures, languages, and experiences are often very different from their own. This entails what I have called a "two-way pedagogy"—teachers must be prepared to learn from students about their lives and cultures so that they can, as Dewey said, bring the child to the curriculum and the curriculum to the child.

In my own work, I have noted that one of the most important aspects of effective teaching of diverse students is understanding their sociocultural context—how learning occurs and what is valued. In this way, teachers can know how to adapt the curriculum accordingly and what knowledge and experiential base to build on. Students do not arrive in our classrooms as blank slates. They come to us having already learned many things; it's up to us to assess what they already know and what will engage them in learning. Too often teachers assume that students have no knowledge of those things they cannot articulate in the language of the classroom, and they treat students as though they are starting from zero. This is both frustrating and demoralizing to the student who may have already mastered material in another language.

When students have already been educated in a different school system, they have experiences, expectations, and learned routines that may vary greatly from those of the school system they now find themselves engaged in. They are familiar with a different school culture, which has its own system of rules, implicit and explicit codes about language, pedagogy, social organization, discipline, missions and values, and other educational processes. Some of this is explained in Chapter 1 by Lucrecia Santibañez, in which she outlines the different preparation and expectations of teachers in the United States and in Mexico. This constitutes a lot of "knowing" that will be reflected in the ways that the student experiences schooling in the new context.

What teachers know, or don't know, about their students' experiences in another country can also affect the way they teach—and how likely they are to start where their students need them to. A perfect illustration of this is the "dictado" (dictation) that Sarah Gallo writes about in Chapter 5, in which the student arriving from the United States has no idea how to handle a routine expectation of students in Mexican schools. Of course, the teacher does not realize that the student, educated in the United States but speaking Spanish, has never been taught to read and write in Spanish and therefore is completely unprepared to take dictation in the language.

The challenge for teachers is to find ways to know and value who their students are, building on what they have already learned, and to envision and support their potential. Gloria Ladson-Billings calls this culturally relevant pedagogy. A sociopolitical consciousness may often be a motivator for the work of a culturally responsive teacher. Ana Maria Villegas and Tamara Lucas define this disposition as recognizing that people's ways of thinking are significantly influenced by race, class, gender, and language and by the hierarchical social systems in which they are located. Both Chapters 2 (Alfaro and Gándara) and 6 (Jensen) address the importance of teachers being critical observers of their own biases and products of their own experiences.

To be an equitable teacher in these circumstances requires knowing oneself as well as one's students. It also requires that we support teachers in this very demanding and uncharted work. Learning how best to educate diverse students who also have very different educational experiences requires a commitment that goes beyond what we have historically expected of our teachers. It is not fair or advisable to demand so much without also offering a roadmap for teaching in such a context and key supports along the way. Notably, several chapters address the teachers of teachers who often need to rethink their own pedagogy. We need much more work by researchers, designers, and teacher educators on the learning progressions of practicing teachers to implement desirable practices, as well as on the development of materials (e.g., instructive lesson videos, teacher inquiry protocols, formative measures of teaching/dispositions) needed to support teacher learning.

This book provides a roadmap with specific examples of good practice as well as the critical information that teachers need to serve students who straddle not only two languages and cultures but also two education systems. At the end of the day, improving students' opportunities to learn most fundamentally requires supporting their teachers—providing them with the resources and professional learning opportunities they need to be successful. Thus, improving teaching and learning for the students we share is a joint responsibility of policy makers, teacher educators, researchers, administrators, teachers, and community members.

Irrespective of walls and other barriers, the lengthy border between Mexico (and the rest of Latin America) and the United States is solely in the eye of the beholder. Millions of Americans live in Mexico, as do millions of Mexicans in the United States. One of five Mexicans spends some time in the United States, and millions more have family members on both sides of the border. The phenomenon of students being educated in both countries will continue, and probably increase, into the foreseeable future. Ironically, while this too often puts the students who are shared by both countries at an educational disadvantage, as this book points out, they are filled with potential. Their transnational and bicultural assets can make them invaluable bridges across nations that must work together but where language and cultural differences often get in the way.

This book challenges our notions of diversity beyond borders and our perspectives on how to prepare culturally responsive teachers in a binational context. It also challenges us to understand both the diversity of our students and the diversity of our educational systems, conceptualizing how we can better support the education of these students we share, thinking beyond our borders toward transnational teaching—a way to create a new, more expansive common ground in a world in which we are all, ultimately, interdependent.

Introduction

The Students We Share and the Teachers We Need

Bryant Jensen and Patricia Gándara

In an era of divisive debate about immigration and uncertainty for immigrants and their children, this book organizes contributions from U.S. and Mexican scholars to improve educator preparation and teaching and learning for the 9 million "students we share" from preschool to high school, from Oaxaca to Ohio. While immigrant students in the United States emanate from all parts of the globe, the shared border between the United States and Mexico accounts by far for the largest share of children of immigrants, and so this is our greatest challenge and also our richest opportunity. The book describes the diversity of transnational[1] students in the region and their experiences, including how geopolitics have altered migration flows over the past decade, and examines teaching qualities and teacher preparation policies to meet pressing curricular, linguistic, and cultural needs of transnational students in both countries. In the spirit of fostering greater binational collaboration, contributors recommend how actors in schools, communities, and state and federal governments can improve educator preparation and support as well as educational opportunities for the students and their futures that we share. Mexican-origin students, on average, have not fared well in the U.S. education system. They are the least likely of all racial/ethnic subgroups to complete a college education, and they have only recently begun to catch up with respect to high school graduation. Some of this problem is rooted in the limited educations they and/or their parents have received before coming to the United States. Some of it is due to the inadequacies of the U.S. education system to meet these students' needs. All of this suggests that we have a truly *binational* challenge. The challenge is becoming more complex every day with the increasing numbers of Central American children and youth arriving at the border, often with lower education levels and more interrupted schooling than their Mexican peers.

The coronavirus pandemic, moreover, has both exposed and exacerbated societal inequities in both countries, including in education. Employment pressures, lack of domestic space, limited access to devices, and faulty Wi-Fi have made distance learning from home incredibly challenging for many families, but especially in homes for the students we share. It is not clear how we will make up for lost instructional time.

Teachers are maxed out as well. Teaching virtually or in person under the pressure of safety protocols and accountability policies still in place in many schools creates tremendous stress, hardly ideal for high-quality or meaningful learning. Teachers will require a great deal of support and resources to hit the ground running to foster equitable learning opportunities for students once we resume normal school schedules.

The Students We Share focuses on teaching as a critical mechanism for change because 1) it is the most influential school factor associated with student success in the United States and in Mexico; and 2) the quality of teaching in PK-12 classrooms for students we share in both countries is woefully inadequate to meet the particular needs of these students. Highlighting the need to improve teaching is not meant to disparage U.S. and Mexican educators who work tirelessly day in and day out on behalf of the students we share. They work with limited resources and report a lack of preparation to respond to the needs, transnational experiences, and assets of students we share. Ours is a call for us all—researchers, administrators, teachers, policy makers, parents, and community members alike—to better understand the challenges and to seek more potent and durable solutions to enhance teacher preparation and teaching qualities to meet the pressing learning and developmental needs, as well as to take advantage of the assets, of the growing numbers of students we share between these two countries.

Contributors to this book summarize scholarship and provide specific and thoughtful recommendations. Our suggestions address what teachers need to know about transnational students, promising ways of forging a variety of binational education partnerships; specific policy and program improvements within each country; revisions to educator preparation, curricula, and standards; and the need for ongoing research investments in educator preparation. Critical to all of these suggestions, though, is the imperative that both nations share responsibility for these students who belong to both. Our intended audience for this book is teachers, teacher educators, school leaders, policy makers, migration and education scholars, and others who study transborder issues.

We share more in transnational students than common origins. We also share a common destiny. The students we share do not see their personal and professional futures as rooted in one country or another, but in both. This book provides a blueprint for improving teaching and teacher learning to prepare students for this future. Authors navigate complex research and institutional dynamics in Mexico and the United States to offer compelling and actionable recommendations to prepare educators for the students—and the future—we share.

The Students We Share

The "students we share" from preschool to high school between Mexico and the United States are a large and heterogeneous group (Hamann & Zúñiga, 2011a; Jensen & Sawyer, 2013). They include students who themselves have emigrated and, more commonly, children with immigrant parents whose origins span Baja California to Chiapas, and beyond. The schooling experiences of students we share are as diverse as they are. Their educational opportunities—i.e., access to high-quality schools—are stratified by socioeconomic status, language proficiencies, race, region (especially *within* countries), immigrant generation, and documented status (e.g., Bean et al., 2013; Galindo, 2013; Gándara, 2017; Jensen, Giorguli, & Hernández, 2018; Treviño, 2013).

In the United States

A majority (about 4 in 5) of the students we share are in the United States. Indeed, 40% of all U.S. children of immigrants have Mexican origins—nearly a million Mexican-born children and another 6.5 million second-generation[2] students (Urban Institute, 2016). Mexican Americans are the largest and the lowest-performing group of Latino students in U.S. schools (Gándara & Contreras, 2009; Reardon & Galindo, 2009).

The neighborhoods most Mexican immigrants live in are highly segregated, as are the schools that their children attend (Orfield, Kucsera, & Siegel-Hawley, 2012). These schools are underresourced, and the teachers of most Mexican American students are underprepared to meet their linguistic and academic needs (López, Scanlan, & Gundrum, 2013; Losey, 1995). The developmental assets of Mexican American children, born of family values and transnational experiences, tend to be underappreciated and largely unincorporated in U.S. classrooms (Jensen, 2013). Whereas bilingual instruction affords academic advantages (Cheung & Slavin, 2012; Gándara & Escamilla, 2017), most Mexican American students attend English-only schools and do not have access to bilingual teachers (Gándara & Hopkins, 2010).

These issues are complicated further by documentation status. More than a fourth of Mexican American children have an undocumented immigrant parent (Jensen & Bachmeier, 2015), and about half of Mexican-born children in the United States are undocumented themselves (Passel, 2011). Financial hardship, family separation, psychological distress, and the uncertainty associated with their own or a parent's undocumented status negatively affect their educational experiences and developmental outcomes (Bean et al., 2013; Yoshikawa & Kholoptseva, 2013). Growing numbers of U.S. students with origins in Central America (especially Guatemala, Honduras, and El Salvador, referred to as the "Northern Triangle") are affected by these matters as well. Of the nearly 2 million U.S. students with Central American origins, 40% have an undocumented parent (Jensen & Bachmeier, 2015). The analysis and recommendations that we provide in this book are relevant to these students as well, though the political and educational circumstances in the Northern Triangle are, in many ways, different and more dire than in Mexico. It is our hope that the programs and policies that are forged through this research can serve as a model for other students we share with Latin America as migration patterns evolve.

In Mexico

The fastest-growing group of "students we share" are in Mexico—U.S.-citizen children and youth with Mexican parents who, for one reason or another, find themselves living in and attending school in Mexico (Zúñiga & Giorguli, 2019). More Mexican immigrants are now leaving than coming to the United States (González-Barrera, 2015) because of deportations and voluntary returns. Increased employment opportunities in Mexico, coupled with the effects of the Great Recession as well as anti-immigrant rhetoric in the United States, have sustained relatively large flows of return migration to Mexico over the past decade. More often than not, migrants take their (mostly U.S.-born) children with them when they return. Currently there are more than 600,000 "American Mexican" PK-12 students in Mexican schools (Jacobo-Suarez, 2017; Jensen, Mejía Arauz, & Zepeda, 2017), more than 3% of the total enrollment. American Mexican students face several challenges in Mexican schools (Zúñiga & Hamann, 2013). Many have limited proficiency in Spanish, and much of the curricular knowledge and skills they gained in U.S. schools is undervalued in Mexican classrooms. A study in Nuevo León and Zacatecas found that American Mexican students were more than three times as likely as their Mexican-born peers to be retained a grade in school (Hamann & Zúñiga, 2011b).

There are another 650,000 or so Mexican children and youth with at least one emigrant parent in the United States.[3] These students "remaining behind" are often torn between schooling and their own migratory futures (Zenteno, Giorguli, & Gutiérrez, 2013). Parent migration exposure has led many Mexican adolescents to aspire to emigrate themselves, and more immediate plans to do so negatively affect their academic performance in school (Jensen, Giorguli, & Hernández, 2018). The situation for students remaining behind—as well as for American Mexicans, for that matter—is complicated further by the fact that migration disproportionately impacts rural and semi-rural communities in Mexico, where the quality of schools is markedly lower than in urban communities. Students in rural and semi-rural schools perform significantly lower (more than a full standard deviation) than their urban counterparts in Mexico (INEE, 2016). They have shorter school days, fewer resources, and less-prepared teachers than in urban schools (Schiefelbein & McGinn, 2008).

Teaching and Teacher Preparation

Among enrolled students,[4] teaching quality is the single most important school factor associated with the academic success of students we share (INEE, 2015; Rivkin, Hanushek, & Kain, 2015). The act of teaching involves not only what teachers do, but also what they know and who they are in terms of dispositions, identities, and backgrounds (e.g., Ball, Thames,

& Phelps, 2008; Borko, Liston, & Whitcomb, 2007). The role of teacher dispositions (e.g., social awareness, care, advocacy for students) for equitable schooling has become especially apparent during the coronavirus pandemic and the challenges of teaching virtually or hybrid. Teaching is "outrageously complex" (Shulman, 1987, p. 11). It includes daily lesson planning, organizing rich instructional activities, assessing students, fostering warm and respectful relationships, sustaining student interest, supporting socioemotional growth, and in some cases partnering with parents—all in ways that promote engaged learning for diverse students, including those with transnational lives.

A critical challenge in both countries is to prepare teachers (as well as school administrators and para-educators) to meet the teaching needs of transnational students in ways that respond rather than add to teachers' already-long list of demands, and to do so equitably. Equitable teaching not only provides students with adequate time and support for deliberate practice of academic knowledge and skills (Pianta & Hamre, 2009; Levin, 1984; Schiefelbein & McGinn, 2008), but does so in ways that connect with all students' everyday lives. Equitable educators seek to understand and incorporate the lived experiences, values, and practices of their students (see Chapter 6 in this volume). They embed instructional activity in the context of local community values and practices (Jensen, Pérez Martínez, & Aguilar Escobar, 2016).

This raises several questions about educator preparation in the United States and in Mexico for the students we share. What should educators know about the migrant experiences of students and their families? How does this knowledge enhance their instructional work? What should U.S. educators know about Mexican curriculum, and what should Mexican educators know about curricula in the United States? How do current policies in Mexico and in the United States address educator preparation for diverse learners like transnational children and youth? How do these policies vary within and across countries? What have we learned from successful bilingual educator preparation in the United States, and how might this be relevant to Mexican schoolteachers? How have Mexican and U.S. education institutions partnered in the past to meet the needs of students we share, and how can we build on these collaborations to improve students' opportunities for the present and the future? How can we design and implement curricular and instructional materials to enhance teaching and learning experiences for students we share, across institutional, linguistic, cultural, and political borders?

Purpose of *The Students We Share*

The purpose of this book is to provide critical knowledge that can help foster collaborations between U.S. and Mexican education institutions to improve educator preparation and teaching and learning for the 9 million and counting PK-12 students we share. Contributors include researchers and teacher educators from both countries who summarize what we know from extant research and binational experiences about teaching and preparing educators for students we share. The authors discuss how we should act on this knowledge to better prepare U.S. and Mexican educators for complex and expanding transnational realities. The book is also a call for creating truly binational teachers who understand and respond to the needs of those students who live at the border between these two nations, both literally and figuratively. Many of these students' futures will be in both countries.

We organize the book into three parts: 1) Teacher Preparation Across Borders, 2) Transnational Teaching, and 3) Bridging Policies. In the first section, we address institutional affordances and constraints in preparing U.S. and Mexican educators for the students we share. Contributors discuss teacher education policy contexts within and between countries, including the roles of Mexican normal schools and the teachers' labor union (*El Sindicato Nacional de Trabajadores de la Educacion*), as well as how U.S. states vary in their approach to preparing educators for culturally and linguistically diverse students. We review binational programs (Gándara, 2008; Martínez-Wenzl, 2013) that among other things seek to help prepare educators for transnational realities and provide policy recommendations to navigate the political terrain in both countries to improve educator preparation for the students we share. In Chapter 1, Santibañez describes the history and ongoing challenges of teacher education policy in Mexico, with a focus on preparing educators to teach transnational students. She begins with an overview of the education system in Mexico—how its history and operation affect the ways teachers are selected, prepared, and trained on the job and how Mexico has struggled recently to reform its teacher preparation and selection procedures. In Chapter 2, Alfaro and Gándara share long-standing experiences preparing bilingual teachers in California and Baja California that have resulted in a new effort to create a binational teacher workforce that is truly reciprocal, one in which teacher educators on both sides of the border teach each other. In Chapter 3, Bybee, Jensen, and Johnstun study *normalista* educators and students to examine how teacher education curricula in Central Mexico prepare teachers to meet the needs of the growing numbers of American Mexican children and youth arriving in that part of Mexico.

In the second section, we analyze what teachers should know and be able to do to meet the needs of transnational students in both countries, from preschool to high school. Authors address bilingual instruction, knowledge about migration, asset-based teaching, and student achievement opportunity within diverse classroom settings. They address implications for improving teaching for transnational students for a binational audience. In Chapter 4, Hamann and Zúñiga summarize research on transnational student experiences to specify what educators should know and acknowledge to meet the needs of students we share. They illustrate the complexity of circulatory migration of elementary and middle school students between countries, and argue that new challenges are emerging with the politics of U.S. immigrant expulsion. In Chapter 5, Gallo shares findings from a year-long ethnographic study of recently arrived American Mexican students in rural Mexican classrooms. She illustrates the advantages of asset-based pedagogies to teach Spanish literacy to these students, from elementary to high school in the state of Puebla. In Chapter 6, Jensen reviews research on the academic achievement of students we share between the United States and Mexico and advocates for "equitable teaching," a combination of generic and culturally situated classroom practices, to enhance their opportunities. Finally, in Chapter 7, Román González and Sánchez García contrast the perspectives of Mexican teachers with those of their American Mexican students on the challenges of transnationalism in classrooms.

The last section of the book addresses policy solutions to bridge teaching quality and learning opportunities for transnational students between both countries. In Chapter 8, López and Santibañez examine how well policies in Arizona, California, and Texas support the preparation of teachers to meet the developmental needs of emergent bilingual students, most of whom are of Mexican origin. They find marked differences in how well teacher education policies among states address the knowledge teachers need to support emergent bilingual students' development. In Chapter 9, Sugarman reviews the 1982 *Plyler v. Doe* Supreme Court ruling to clarify the legal requirements of schools and implications for educators to provide all students, regardless of immigration status, with a free and appropriate public elementary and secondary education. Finally, in

Chapter 10, Gándara and Jensen summarize the policy landscape during the pandemic as well as post-COVID to recommend ways of navigating the testy waters of immigration, language, and politics in both countries to achieve rational agreements to prepare the teachers we need for the students we share. They underscore lessons from past bilateral partnerships in education and emphasize mutual reasons for ongoing collaborations, not the least of which are the enormous assets that children of migration represent and the extent to which our futures are in their hands.

Notes

1. We use "transnational students" and "students we share" interchangeably throughout the book. Other labels (e.g., emergent bilinguals, Mexican American, American Mexican) are used by book contributors as well for particular reasons which they describe.
2. First-generation immigrant students refer to those who are foreign-born themselves (in Mexico, in this case), and second-generation immigrants are those with at least one Mexican-born parent. We do not include third-generation students—those with at least one Mexican-born grandparent—in our analysis and discussion in this book, though many of the issues we address are relevant to them as well.
3. The number is harder to estimate because the Mexican Census tracks family migration experiences "within the previous five years."
4. Equitable access to school is another problem for transnational students on both sides of the border. Only half of adolescents in general graduate from high school in Mexico (INEE, 2015). The high school graduation rate for Latinos in the United States is 81% (NCES, 2020).

References

Alfaro, C., & Quezada, R. L. (2010). International teacher professional development: Teacher reflections of authentic teaching and learning experiences. *Teaching Education, 21*(1), 47–59.

Ball, D. L., Thames, M. H., & Phelps, G. (2008). Content knowledge for teaching what makes it special? *Journal of Teacher Education, 59*(5), 389–407.

Bean, F. D., Brown, S. K., Leach, M. A., Bachmeier, J. D., & Tafoya-Estrada, R. (2013). Unauthorized migration for the educational incorporation of Mexican-Americans. In B. Jensen and A. Sawyer (eds.), *Regarding educación:*

Mexican-American schooling, immigration, and bi-national improvement. New York: Teachers College Press.

Borko, H., Liston, D., & Whitcomb, J. A. (2007). Apples and fishes: The debate over dispositions in teacher education. *Journal of Teacher Education, 58*(5), 359.

Cheung, A. C., & Slavin, R. E. (2012). Effective reading programs for Spanish-dominant English language learners (ELLs) in the elementary grades: A synthesis of research. *Review of Educational Research, 82*(4), 351–395.

Galindo, C. (2013). Math performance of young Mexican-origin children in the United States: Socioeconomic status, immigrant generation, and English proficiency. In B. Jensen and A. Sawyer (eds.), *Regarding educación: Mexican-American schooling, immigration, and bi-national improvement.* New York: Teachers College Press.

Gallo, S. (2017). *Mi Padre: Mexican immigrant fathers and their children's education.* New York, NY: Teachers College Press.

Gándara, P. (2008). A preliminary evaluation of Mexican-sponsored educational programs in the United States: Strengths, weaknesses, and potential. In E. Szecsy (Ed.), *Resource Book, Second Binational Symposium.* Tempe, AZ: Arizona State University.

Gándara, P. (2017). The potential and promise of Latino students. *American Educator, 41*(1), 4–11.

Gándara, P., & Contreras, F. (2009). *The Latino education crisis: The consequences of failed social policies.* Harvard University Press.

Gándara, P., & Escamilla, K. (2017). Bilingual education in the United States. In O. García, A. M. Y. Lin & S. May (Eds.), *Bilingual and Multilingual Education* (3rd ed.). Cham, Switzerland: Springer.

Gándara, P., & Hopkins, M. (Eds.). (2010). *Forbidden language: English learners and restrictive language policies.* New York: Teachers College Press.

García, O. (2009). Emergent Bilinguals and TESOL: What's in a Name? *Tesol Quarterly, 43*, 322–326.

González, N. (2011). *Immigration and migration in dynamic times and spaces.* Presented at Ethnography and Education Research Forum, Philadelphia, PA.

Gonzalez-Barrera, A. (2015). *More Mexicans leaving than coming to the U.S.* Washington, DC: Pew Research Center.

Hamann, E. T., & Zúñiga, V. (2011a). Schooling and the everyday ruptures transnational children encounter in the United States and Mexico. In C. Coe, R. Reynolds, D. Boehm, J. M. Hess, & H. Rae-Espinoza (Eds.), *Everyday ruptures: Children and migration in global perspective* (pp. 141–160). Nashville, TN: Vanderbilt University Press.

Hamann, E. T., & Zúñiga, V. (2011b). Schooling, national affinity(ies), and transnational students in Mexico. In S. Vandeyar (Ed.), *Hyphenated selves: Immigrant identities within education contexts.* Amsterdam: Rozenburg Publishers, UNISA.

Hamann, E. T., Zúñiga, V., & Sánchez García, J. (2018). Where should my child go to school? Parent and child considerations in binational families. In M. T. de Guzman, J. Brown, & C. Edwards (Eds.), *Parenting from afar: The reconfiguration of the family across distance* (pp. 339–350). New York: Oxford University Press.

Instituto Nacional para la Evaluación de la Educación (2015). *Los docentes en México: Informe 2015.* México, DF: INEE.

Instituto Nacional para la Evaluación de la Educación (2016). *Aprendizaje en tercero de secundaria en México. Informe de resultados.* México, DF: INEE.

Instituto Nacional para la Evaluación de la Educación (2017). *La educación normal en México: Elementos para su análisis.* México, DF: INEE.

Jacobo-Suárez, M. (2017). De regreso a "casa" y sin apostilla: Estudiantes mexicoamericanos en México. *Sinéctica, 48,* 1–18.

Jensen, B. (2013). Finding synergy to improve learning opportunities for Mexican-origin students. In B. Jensen & A. Sawyer (Eds.), *Regarding educación: Mexican American schooling, immigration, and binational improvement.* New York: Teachers College Press.

Jensen, B., & Bachmeier, J. (2015). *A portrait of U.S. children of Central American origins and their educational opportunity.* Washington, DC: MacArthur Foundation.

Jensen, B., Giorgulo Saucedo, S., & Hernández, E. (2018). International migration and the academic performance of Mexican adolescents. *International Migration Review, 52*(2), 559–596.

Jensen, B., Grajeda, S., & Haertel, E. (2018). Measuring cultural dimensions of classroom interactions. *Educational Assessment, 23*(4), 250–276.

Jensen, B., Mejía Arauz, R., & Aguilar Zepeda, R. (2017). Equitable teaching for returnee children in Mexico. *Sinéctica, 48,* 1–20.

Jensen, B., Pérez Martínez, G. M., & Aguilar Escobar, A. (2016). Framing and assessing classroom opportunity to learn: The case of Mexico. *Assessment in Education: Principles, Policy & Practice, 23*(1), 149–172.

Jensen, B., & Sawyer. A. (2013). Regarding *educación*: A vision for school improvement. In B. Jensen & A. Sawyer (Eds.), *Regarding educación: Mexican American schooling, immigration, and binational improvement.* New York: Teachers College Press.

Ladson-Billings, G. (1995). Toward a theory of culturally relevant pedagogy. *American Educational Research Journal, 32*(3), 465–491.

Levin, H. M. (1984). About time for educational reform. *Educational Evaluation and Policy Analysis, 6,* 151–163.

López, F., McEneaney, E., & Nieswandt, M. (2015). Language instruction educational programs and academic achievement of Latino English learners: Considerations for states with changing demographics. *American Journal of Education, 121,* 417–450.

López, F., Scanlan, M., & Gundrum, B. (2013). Preparing teachers of English language learners: Empirical evidence and policy implications. *Education Policy Analysis Archives, 21*, 1–31.

Losey, K. M. (1995). Mexican American students and classroom interaction: An overview and critique. *Review of Educational Research, 65*(3), 283–318.

Martinez-Wenzl, M. (2013). Bi-national education initiatives: A brief history. In B. Jensen & A. Sawyer (Eds.), *Regarding educación: Mexican American schooling, immigration, and binational improvement.* New York: Teachers College Press.

National Center for Education Statistics (NCES). (2020). *The condition of education: Public high school graduate rates.* Washington, DC: NCES. Retrieved from https://nces.ed.gov/programs/coe/indicator_coi.asp

Orellana, M. F. (2009). *Translating childhoods: Immigrant youth, language, and culture.* New Brunswick, NJ: Rutgers University Press.

Orfield, G., Kucsera, J., & Siegel-Hawley, G. (2012). *"E Pluribus" . . . separation: deepening double segregation for more students.* Los Angeles, CA: Civil Rights Project/Proyecto Derechos Civiles.

Passel, J. S. (2011). Flujos migratorios México-Estados Unidos de 1990 a 2010: Un análisis preliminar basado en las fuentes de información estadounidenses. *Coyuntura Demográfica,* 15–20.

Pianta, R. C., & Hamre, B. K. (2009). Conceptualization, measurement, and improvement of classroom processes: Standardized observation can leverage capacity. *Educational Researcher, 38*(2), 109–119.

Reardon, S. F., & Galindo, C. (2009). The Hispanic-White achievement gap in math and reading in the elementary grades. *American Educational Research Journal, 46,* 853–891.

Rivkin, S., Hanushek, E., & Kain, J. (2005). Teachers, schools, and academic achievement. *Econometrica, 73*(2), 417–458.

Schiefelbein, E., & McGinn, N. F. (2008). *Learning to educate: Proposals for the reconstruction of education in Latin America.* Paris: UNESCO & International Bureau of Education.

Shulman, L. S. (1987). Knowledge and teaching: Foundations of the new reform. *Harvard Educational Review, 57*(1), 1–23.

Treviño, E. (2013). Learning inequality among indigenous students in Mexico. In B. Jensen & A. Sawyer (Eds.), *Regarding educación: Mexican-American Schooling, Immigration, and Bi-national Improvement* (pp. 95–123). New York, NY: Teachers College Press.

Urban Institute (2016). *Demographic trends of children of immigrants.* Washington, DC: Urban Institute.

Yoshikawa, H., & Kholoptseva, J. (2013). *Unauthorized immigrant parents and their children's development.* Washington, DC: Migration Policy Institute.

Zenteno, R., Giorguli, S. E., & Gutiérrez, E. (2013). Mexican adolescent migration to the United States and transitions to adulthood. *The ANNALS of the American Academy of Political and Social Science, 648*(1), 18–37.

Zúñiga, V., & Giorguli, S. (2019). *Niñas y niños en la migración de Estados Unidos a México: La generación 0.5*. Mexico, DF: El Colegio de Mexico.

Zúñiga, V., & Hamann, E. T. (2013). Understanding American Mexican children. In B. Jensen & A. Sawyer (Eds.), *Regarding educación: Mexican American schooling, immigration, and binational improvement*. New York: Teachers College Press.

Zúñiga, V., Hamann, E. T., & Sánchez García, J. (2008). *Alumnos transfronterizos: Las escuelas mexicanas frente a la globalización*. México, DF: Secretaría de Educación Pública.

Part I

Teacher Preparation Across Borders

Chapter 1

Contrasting Realities

How Differences Between the Mexican and U.S. Education Systems Affect Transnational Students

Lucrecia Santibañez

There are currently more than 6 million children in the United States born to at least one Mexican parent (Urban Instituute, 2016). Population movements between Mexico and the United States flow in both directions. Between 2010 and 2015, U.S. immigration officials repatriated (either by deportation or voluntary repatriation) 1.4 million Mexicans back to Mexico (Lakhani & Jacobo, 2016). Since then, many more have been deported or left the country voluntarily. Many of those returning to Mexico take their families with them, including U.S.-born children. Estimates of 2015 census data suggest that close to 500,000 children, most of them U.S. citizens with prior experience in U.S. schools, had enrolled in Mexican schools (Giorguli & Gutierrez, 2011; Lakhani & Jacobo, 2016; Zúñiga & Hamann, 2015). An additional 800,000 children in Mexico have at least one parent living in the United States, further cementing the deep ties between families on both sides of the border (Jensen, Mejía Arauz, & Aguilar Zepeda, 2017).

In the journey between the two countries, children's lives are deeply disrupted. After spending the majority of their lives in the United States, U.S.-born children moving to Mexico face enormous cultural and language challenges (Lakhani & Jacobo, 2016). Three-quarters of U.S.-born children who moved to the Mexican state of Nuevo León because their parents were deported wanted to return to school in the United States (Zúñiga

& Hamann, 2008). Mexican children who migrate with their parents to the United States face similar difficulties. Navigating schools presents unique trials on both sides of the border. Both in the United States and Mexico, teachers face the exceptional task of helping these transnational students learn academic content, master a second language, and adapt to their new surroundings.

Several chapters in this book discuss teacher preparation both in Mexico and the United States and what teachers need to know to teach transnational students (see Chapter 2 on binational teacher preparation; Chapters 4, 5, and 8 on what educators need to know to teach transnational students). This chapter makes the central argument that the Mexican education system is different from the United States' in ways that fundamentally shape teacher practice and parental involvement and fail to meet transnational students' needs. To develop this argument, I describe three key aspects of the Mexican education systems that will determine how teachers on both sides of the border meet and address transnational student needs. First, I describe some of the system's main features, such as its organization and curriculum standards, as well as key policies around student assessment and accountability. Second, I discuss how teachers are prepared and selected in Mexico. Third, I describe how parents engage with schools in Mexico in ways that are uniquely different from the way parents interact with schools (or are expected to interact with schools) in the United States. The discussion seeks to illustrate why Mexican parents and their children may encounter difficulties navigating the U.S. school system and why children who return to Mexico with their parents after a deportation face a similar "culture clash." The chapter concludes with a summary discussion and recommendations for improvements in teacher preparation and support that take account of these contextual factors affecting education in Mexico. It is my hope that this discussion can lead to a better understanding of transnational students and their families and help eradicate deficit notions about this student population that unfortunately still pervade schools on both sides of the border.

Overview of the Education System in Mexico

Mexican children attend compulsory basic education from first to ninth grade. Preschool and kindergarten enroll children ages 3 to 5. Elementary school is composed of grades 1 to 6 and enrolls children ages 6 to 12.

Middle school comprises grades 7 to 9 and enrolls children ages 12 to 15. High school is grades 10 to 12, serving youth ages 15 to 18. High school was made compulsory in 2012. Almost 90% of basic education students attend public schools in Mexico. This is similar to the percentage of students enrolled in public schools in the United States. Twenty percent of high school students attend private schools, considerably higher than in the United States (INEE, 2018). This is mostly due to capacity (access) restrictions to public high schools in Mexico.

There are three types of public elementary schools: First, "general" schools are traditional schools akin to elementary and middle schools in the United States. Second, "Indigenous-intercultural and bilingual" schools exist in indigenous communities and teach using a bilingual curriculum. Some indigenous schools operate as "multi-grade" schools, i.e., the same teacher instructs two grades or more. A third mode of public elementary school provision is "community" schools. These schools exist in small rural and isolated areas and operate as multi-grade, one-room schoolhouses. Ninety-four percent of student enrollment at the public elementary level attends a "general" school.

At the Secundaria or lower secondary level, schools can be general, technical, or "Telesecundaria." Technical and general schools are basically the same type of school, except for some differences in school equipment and offerings (e.g., labs). They resemble U.S. middle schools. Telesecundarias are distance education schools where one teacher serves as a facilitator for all subjects, and students receive all or part of their education via videotaped content or televised broadcasts. Most Telesecundarias operate in rural areas and small towns. Almost 80% of students at the lower secondary level attend either a "general" or a "technical" middle school. The rest attend Telesecundarias.

Upper secondary, or high school, operates in a more fragmented way, with school types varying by governance (i.e., federal or state schools), autonomy (autonomous university-affiliated high schools or state-run schools), and topic (i.e., technical-professional programs or general, academic programs). Although high school is now technically compulsory, brick and mortar schools are not yet available throughout the country to meet the demand. Only 7 of 10 within the relevant age population (15–17 years old) are in school. This proportion is lower in rural and indigenous areas (6 of 10) (INEE, 2017). Many students drop out of high school after their first year, and only about half of Mexican youth graduate (INEE, 2018; Kattan & Szekely, 2015; OECD, 2018).

Students in Mexican elementary schools are taught by multiple-subject credentialed teachers; in secondary school, children are taught by single-subject credentialed teachers (middle school) or teachers with a subject matter specialization in their college degree (high school).

Brief Historical Background of the Mexican Education System

The modern Mexican education system was formally established in the early 20th century with the creation by President Porfirio Díaz of the *Secretaría de Instrucción Pública* (SIP). The year was 1905, and at that time, only about 10% of the Mexican population was literate. In those years, Mexico was mostly a rural country, with poor communications and infrastructure to cover a wide territory. Indigenous groups speaking dozens of languages concentrated in isolated rural areas, particularly in the southern states. The population was generally poor. An ambitious plan to modernize the country was implemented after the Mexican Revolution ended. In 1921, the SIP was rebranded as the *Secretaría de Educación Pública*.

The federal government's goal throughout most of the 20th century was to increase Mexicans' literacy levels. This was no small feat in a country devastated by civil war. Even though it took many decades to accomplish, Mexico ultimately succeeded. In 1895, more than 80% of the country's population of 16 years and older was illiterate, but by 1950 the illiteracy rate had fallen to 43%, and by 2010 it was 7% (INEGI, 2012). By contrast, in the late 19th century, only 20% of the White population of the United States aged 14 and over was illiterate—although close to 80% of the Black population was illiterate.[1]

Beginning in the 1970s, Mexican education began to look beyond basic literacy to developing higher-order skills in its population and improving learning outcomes. Three major reforms shaped the new vision, significantly altering how education in Mexico was delivered as well as strengthening the teaching profession. The first reform was implemented in the 1970s and involved "double-shifting" schools. The program added an afternoon shift to the majority of public schools in the country as a way to accommodate significant population growth as well as migration from rural to urban areas. Double-shift schools would operate in two 4.5-hour blocks, with a morning and an afternoon shift. In some cases, schools would operate a third night shift. Teachers at these schools could teach in the second shift under a newly created teaching position. This meant that almost overnight, teachers working two shifts doubled their salaries, and the school system doubled its capacity—without the need to build any new schools—or increase teacher hourly salaries. Double-shifting schools solved the short-term demand problem (and brought huge political gains to the ruling PRI party) but also brought its own set of complications. The reduced time-on-task and capacity constraints meant that students could not receive more than 4.5 hours of schooling per day. Moreover, double-shift schools generated inequities. The less preferred afternoon-shift schools enrolled more low-income children and reported worse learning outcomes and higher dropout rates than the morning-shift schools operating in the same school building (Cárdenas, 2011; Jensen, 2005). Double-shift schools continue to be the norm in most large towns and urban centers in Mexico, but slowed population growth has meant that many school buildings now have begun to operate as full-day schools.

The second important reform was decentralization. It happened in 1993 with the passage of the *Acuerdo Nacional para la Modernización de la Educación Básica* or ANMEB by the more technocratic, neoliberal administration of President Salinas de Gortari. This agreement was signed by all 32 states in Mexico, the national teachers' union (SNTE), and the federal government. This reform sought to give more power to the states. Scholars agree that while the reform decentralized some operational aspects of schooling (facilities, professional development), the federal government retained power over major matters such as curriculum, collective bargaining, and funding (Ornelas, 2004). To this day, the more than two-thirds of the education budget that is used to fund schools across the country still comes from the federal government. The federal government continues to set the national curriculum, develop and publish (free) textbooks, and set teacher credentialing requirements. Importantly, collective bargaining continued to take place between SNTE and the federal government—although after 1993 SNTE took advantage of being able to hold a second negotiation with state authorities.

The third key reform in Mexico was a controversial, large-scale teacher accountability reform known as "*Reforma Educativa*." It was enacted in in 2013, and even though it touched on almost all aspects of education, from curriculum to school-based management, the most controversial aspect had to do with teacher contracts and evaluation. Two of its provisions fundamentally changed how teachers were recruited and promoted. The first provision instituted competitive selection, via a standardized screening test, for all teaching positions at the entry level and for all promotions into administrative positions. New teacher positions could no longer be sold or inherited. Principal or other administrator positions would no longer be handed out at the discretion of educational authorities or union officials, but would now be open to all who wished to apply. The new process made teacher promotion and selection transparent and more meritocratic, but there were doubts among some academics and teachers that screening exams were a good way to select teachers (Gil Antón, 2018). The single published study of the effects of the new form of teacher selection on students found that this kind of screening led to higher student test scores (Estrada, 2019).

The second key element of this reform was and remains the most controversial. Teachers in Mexico, by law, receive tenure after six months on the job. Under the new law, teachers were required to take a performance evaluation test at least once every four years. Failure to pass the test after three attempts would lead to loss of the position. This effectively would have eliminated teacher tenure, although in practice fewer than 1,000 teachers lost their jobs (from more than 200,000 who were evaluated since 2015).

In 2019, to fulfill a campaign promise, President Andrés Manuel López Obrador revoked the *Reforma Educativa.* Most of its evaluation provisions, including both teacher and student evaluations, were canceled. Although there's little hard data to support these claims, the generalized sentiment on the part of teachers was that the performance evaluation component of the *Reforma* was not well implemented and was generally unfair. Even though very few teachers lost their jobs, they felt that losing tenure protections was contrary to the labor agreement that had sustained the teaching profession throughout its history.

The Teachers' Union

The *Sindicato Nacional de Trabajadores de la Educación en México* or SNTE is the largest union in Latin America, with more than 1 million members (Santibañez & Jarillo, 2007). It was formed in 1944 as a way to combine all existing teachers' union groups into one single institution (Muñoz Armenta, 2008). Since its creation, SNTE has held a monopoly over teacher labor relations in the country. SEP is not allowed to bargain with any other union, and, by law, all public-sector teachers have to belong to the union (Muñoz Armenta, 2008). Mandatory union membership dues (about 1% of base salary automatically deducted from each paycheck) and the minimal accountability it must give to its members or the public over the use of these funds give its leadership enormous financial and political power (Santibañez & Jarillo, 2007).

Education Quality in Mexico

Students in Mexican public schools report worse learning outcomes than students in U.S. schools. Much of this is related to the fact that most Mexican students are low income. The average educational attainment of Mexican parents (adults aged 25 and over) is 9.2 years, with large variations across the country: 6.7 years in rural areas and 10.2 in urban areas (INEE, 2016). As a comparison, the average educational attainment for the adult population in the United States is 13 years. In addition, Mexican schools are seriously underresourced. The school day is short (4.5 hours in elementary school, 7 hours in middle and high schools). Mexican classrooms have limited technology and lack basic learning materials, including books (Puryear, Santibañez, & Solano, 2012). Extracurricular and enrichment offerings are limited, and most schools do not offer gifted programs, special education services (i.e., individualized education plans), counseling, and other support services. There is some evidence to suggest that many teachers also lack key pedagogical content knowledge themselves. There isn't a great deal of evidence to support this assertion, but a recent study of pre-service teachers in six countries (South Korea, Taiwan, the United States, Bulgaria, Germany, and Mexico) found that Mexican teachers showed the lowest scores of mathematical knowledge and mathematical pedagogical content knowledge (Schmidt et al., 2007). For years, scholars have decried the low levels of academic rigor, poor resources, and the outsized role the teachers' union plays in selecting faculty and governing existing teachers' colleges (Santibañez, 2007; Tatto & Velez, 1999). Teachers in indigenous intercultural schools, while indigenous themselves, often speak an indigenous language that is different from their students' (Santibañez, 2016). In many rural areas, education is delivered via television ("*Telesecundaria*") or in community settings where teachers have only a high school degree and teach multiple grades at the same time.

It is therefore not surprising that Mexican students score low in most international tests of student achievement (OECD, 2012).[2] There are wide variations by region and socioeconomic background, but even the richest students in Mexico score only slightly higher on the international PISA test than the poorest students in the United States. While one-quarter (25.8%) of students in U.S. schools scored below the basic level (Level 2) in the PISA mathematics exam, more than half of students in Mexico scored at this level (54.5%). Low indicators of educational preparation and competency mean that these students will not develop the necessary competencies to be successful in higher education and the labor market (OECD, 2012).

As is the case in the United States, average country-level outcomes mask enormous variation within and across states. Some states do fairly well (Mexico City, Querétaro, or Nuevo León). In states like Tabasco or Morelos, however, more than half of students do not meet minimum competency standards in language, and more than 65% do not meet minimum standards in mathematics.[3] Despite these variations, even in the highest-scoring states, like Nuevo León or Mexico City, close to 40% and 50% of students do not meet minimum standards in language and mathematics, respectively.

Mexico also faces high levels of high school dropout. Almost all Mexican children attend elementary school, but about half do not finish high school (INEE, 2018; Kattan & Szekely, 2015; OECD, 2018). In the United States, this figure is closer to 8%. The majority of dropouts in Mexican schools occur in the middle-to-high school transition (after ninth grade) and during the first year of high school (10th grade) (see Figure 1.1).

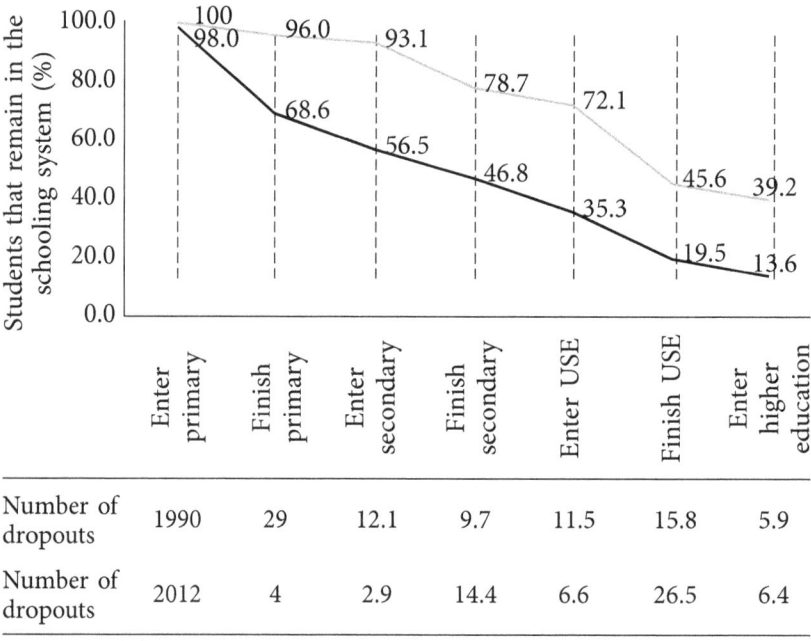

Kattan & Szekely (2015).

Figure 1.1. Average School Trajectory from Elementary to Higher Education in Mexico between 1990 to 2012.

High school dropout rates are mainly due to demographic and economic factors: not being able to afford staying in school, becoming a household head (i.e., teenage pregnancy or losing the breadwinning parent), living in a large household, or belonging to an indigenous group (Kattan & Szekely, 2015; INEE, 2017). Among girls, a significant proportion of those who drop out (20%) report doing so because of teenage pregnancy (INEE, 2017). School-related reasons reported for dropping out include low-quality schooling, low academic performance, such as repeating a grade, or not liking school (Kattan & Szekely, 2015; INEE, 2017).

Educational Funding

Education spending in Mexico as a proportion of GDP is close to 5%, similar to the proportion in the United States.[4] Spending in Mexico has followed an increasing trend, yet absolute levels of spending per student are much lower than the OECD average. In 2014, Mexico spent about US $2,000, adjusted for inflation (constant dollars) per student in public education. The United States spent about $18,000 per student, although there are dramatic differences by state. A child finishing his or her entire K-12 education trajectory costs Mexican educational authorities about U.S. $30,000 (constant prices), and U.S. states about $235,000. Even though these estimates are not adjusted for purchasing power parity, the difference is staggering.[5] Teacher and staff compensation has been the main driver of this increased spending—more than 90% of national expenditures on education go toward paying staff payroll (OECD, 2013). Nationally, in the United States, about 80% of school funding goes to paying staff salaries (57%) and benefits (23%) (U.S. Department of Education, 2019).

The way Mexico funds public schooling is complicated and, some claim, dysfunctional (México Evalúa, 2011). Despite the 1992 decentralization reform, three types of schools continue to exist in each state: fully federally funded schools (*"Sistema Federal"*), dual-funded schools (*"Sistema Estatal"*), and fully state-funded schools (also part of *"Sistema Estatal"*). The decentralization reform gave states the power to run these schools on a day-to-day basis, but the funding still comes primarily from federal resources. Differences among the various systems are related to health care (federal or state funded) and pensions. Also, local districts or regions (*"Zona Escolar,"* each with a *"Supervisor"* or superintendent) will only include schools within their system. The distinction is meaningful for teachers and staff, but not for students who in most cases see no difference between federal- and state-funded schools.

As previously mentioned, about two-thirds of education spending on all types of schools (except fully funded state schools, which are a small number) comes from the federal government. Only 14% of education spending in Mexico is funded by state resources, and the rest is funded by private sources (households and businesses). Some states spend as much as half of their own funds (from state taxes) on education (e.g., Jalisco, Baja California, Yucatán) and some states spend less than 5% (e.g., Hidalgo, Chiapas) (México Evalúa, 2011). A key reason for states' reliance on the federal government to finance their education systems is that most of the taxes paid by Mexican taxpayers go directly to the federal government. Even though states as well as the federal government can set taxes, all states in Mexico have signed away their powers to spend these resources directly in favor of the federal government.[6] Local property taxes do not fund schools in Mexico—as they do in many parts of the United States. This gives taxpayers in Mexico less leverage over educational decisions and governance than is the case in the United States.

Curriculum Standards, Student Assessment, and Accountability

Mexico has a national curriculum that all public schools in the country, grades first through ninth, must follow. The curriculum is contained in the national *"Planes y Programas de Estudio"* or curriculum standards. The curriculum was last updated in 2017. The curriculum is not designed around standards, as it is in the United States (Díaz-Barriga, 2005), but around broad themes and subject areas. Contrary to the case of the United States, Mexico does not have sheltered or immersion Spanish programs or any services geared toward developing Spanish fluency among Spanish Learners (SLs) and helping them either retain their bilingualism or transition into a mainstream curriculum. For decades, Mexico has had bilingual and intercultural programs designed for Mexico's linguistic minority children living in indigenous communities. Even these long-standing programs have serious implementation challenges such as lack of trained bilingual teachers and limited resources (Santibañez, 2016). In Mexico, all national and state assessments are conducted in Spanish with no accommodations for speakers of other languages. The strategy most often used to improve Spanish proficiency among U.S. children of parents returning to Mexico is to retain them in a grade (Zúñiga & Hamann, 2009), a strategy often used in the United States as well (Callahan et al, 2019).

Mexico also has an extensive English as a second language (ESL) program for all public-school students, although its implementation is weak. Table 1.1 shows data on bilingualism in Mexico and second language learning.

A recent report by the Mexican NGO *Mexicanos Primero* found that 79% of ninth graders who have received nine years of English instruction in school had no working knowledge of English and placed in the lowest competency level on a test of English language skills (O'Donoghue & Calderón Martín del Campo, 2015). Mexican public-school teachers who teach ESL are woefully unprepared and in many cases are not fluent themselves (O'Donoghue & Calderón Martín del Campo, 2015). Eighty-eight percent of English teachers in Mexico scored below a seventh grade level in a standardized test of English skills (O'Donoghue & Calderón Martín del Campo, 2015). Similar data for teachers' second language skills do not exist in the United States.

Table 1.1. Indicators of Bilingualism in Mexico and the United States

	Mexico	United States
Population that speaks English (Mexico)/Spanish (U.S.)[1]	10%	18%
Public elementary schools offering foreign language instruction (2007)[2]	100%	15%
Weekly hours learning a second language[3]		
Elementary school	2.5	0
Middle school (secundaria)	3	0

[1] U.S.: Includes all people in the country (not just adults). Source: *Forbes* magazine, retrieved from http://www.forbes.com/sites/collegeprose/2012/08/27/americas-foreign-language-deficit/#413be1ad382f. Similar figure is given by *Instituto Cervantes*, retrieved from https://www.theguardian.com/us-news/2015/jun/29/us-second-biggest-spanish-speaking-country (16.5%). Mexico population speaking English: INEGI, 2012. Refers to population 18 years or older.

[2] Source: For Mexico: SEP (Mexican Curriculum) and O'Donoghue & Calderón Martín del Campo (2015). For U.S., *Forbes* magazine (ibid).

[3] Source: For Mexico: O'Donoghue & Calderón Martín del Campo (2015). For U.S., *Forbes* magazine (ibid).

Contrary to the case in the United States, state-sponsored assessment of student achievement is not commonplace in Mexico. Before 2006, Mexico did not test all students in all grades. Student assessment was mainly done for international testing programs such as TIMSS or PISA, and for a group of teachers participating in "Carrera Magisterial," the national merit-pay teacher program that began in 1993. This program had a student achievement component. In 2002, Mexico created the autonomous *Instituto Nacional para la Evaluación de la Educación* (INEE) to evaluate the quality and results of the Mexican education system. INEE administered a series of sample-based "NAEP-like" tests under its EXCALE program. In 2006, Mexico created "ENLACE," which tested all students in grades 3 to 9 every year. Students received their results on a yearly basis. ENLACE results were used for all teachers participating in Carrera Magisterial as part of their "student achievement" evaluation component.

In 2014, claiming that ENLACE had become corrupted because of its use for high-stakes teacher evaluation (i.e., *Carrera Magisterial*), SEP and INEE canceled the test. As of 2014, there is no longer a censal exam in Mexico (i.e., all students, all grades). In 2015, a new test was designed and administered called "PLANEA." It is given yearly to sixth, ninth, and twelfth graders. In 2018, the INEE was dismantled by the new presidential administration, and some of its evaluation functions were absorbed by the Ministry of Education.

The cancellation of the ENLACE program and the disappearance of INEE has dealt a blow to external accountability efforts for Mexican schools. While critics of ENLACE contended that parents and schools did not use the information in the first place (Martínez Rizo et al., 2015), the immediate result of ENLACE's dissolution was that parents, students, activists, and other civic groups have less information to understand their children's progress in school and to compare schools and classrooms within schools for the purpose of improvement.

Teachers in Mexico

The teacher workforce is different between Mexico and the United States. Table 1.2 shows basic teacher demographic and other characteristics for elementary teachers in both countries. In Mexico, teacher statistics usually refer to teaching positions, not individuals. However, for the sake of

Table 1.2. Basic Teacher Characteristics in Mexico and the United States

	Mexico	United States
Female	67%	89%
Teachers with MA or more	10%	55%
Teachers with BA only	51%	41%
Teachers with Normal Superior or Normal Primaria	26%	3%
Teachers with HS only	3%	0%
Median age (years)	39	42
More than 15 years experience	43%	41%

Sources: U.S.: SASS, 2011/12. Mexico: CEMABE, 2013—in INEE, 2015.

simplicity in this chapter, I refer to both individual teachers and teaching positions as "teachers."[7]

In Mexico, teaching is a powerful engine for social mobility (Santibañez, 2016). Data from standardized exams taken by all students in their last year of teachers' colleges reveal that close to 60% of teacher candidates in Mexico live below the official poverty line. Their families earn around $1,179 pesos, or U.S. $92 per month, per capita. Among candidates to be an indigenous teacher, the proportion living in poverty is even higher, 87%. Upon entering the teaching profession, these individuals also enter the Mexican middle class.

Table 1.3 shows teacher working conditions, including salary levels in both countries. Starting teacher base salaries in the United States are almost twice what they are in Mexico, about $40,000, compared to close to $20,000. However, Mexican teachers also receive significant bonuses (i.e., Christmas bonus "*Aguinaldo*," vacation bonus "*Prima Vacacional*"), which depending on the state can amount to two to six months of extra pay. The difference, nevertheless, is significant even when adjusted for purchasing power parity. Of course, if they choose to work two shifts, and many of them do, their salaries can approximate those of beginning

Table 1.3. Primary Education Teacher Salaries and Working Conditions, Mexico and United States (2019, in U.S. Dollars Converted by PPP)

	Mexico	United States
Average Starting Teacher Base Salary[1]	$19,893	$39,183
Hours worked (contract hours)[2]	25	38
Hours in front of the classroom[2]	20	31
Average length of school day (hours)[2]	4.5	6.5
Average length of school year (days)[2]	200	180

[1] Source: OECD (2019), Education at a glance: Teachers' statutory salaries, OECD Education Statistics (database), retrieved from https://doi.org/10.1787/b43a4622-en (accessed February 25, 2019). Salaries are in U.S.$ converted using purchasing power parity (PPP) for private consumption.

[2] U.S.: SASS, 2011/12. Mexico CEMABE, 2013 & INEE, 2015. Sources for hours of school day, and length of school year: U.S.—retrieved from http://www.theatlantic.com/education/archive/2014/05/extended-school-days/371896/. Mexico—retrieved from http://www.excelsior.com.mx/nacional/2016/01/26/1071208

U.S. teachers. In this case, however, Mexican teachers would be contracted to spend 40 hours per week in front of the classroom (teaching)—more than is the case in the United States.

The main driver of the salary difference between teachers in the United States and Mexico is the number of hours worked. The elementary school day is 4.5 hours in Mexico, and a teacher's contract is 25 hours per week—20 in the classroom. In the United States, teachers are hired on full-time contracts (i.e., minimum of 38 hours per week).[8] As previously mentioned, because schools in Mexico operate in two shifts, teachers may hold two teaching positions, doubling their hours worked and their pay. While their school shift may be shorter, Mexican teachers work 200 days, however, compared to 180 days worked by teachers in the United States.

Factors Affecting Teacher Effectiveness

In this section, I highlight three factors affecting the ability of teachers in Mexico to deliver a high-quality education: (1) teacher skills, preparation, and qualifications; (2) teacher mobility; and (3) teacher incentives for improvement and accountability. These factors affect teachers' ability to teach all students and will also affect transnational students, given that their needs are greater than those of non-transnational students.

Teacher Selection. For most of the 20th century, teacher preparation, recruitment, and selection were done centrally by the federal government. To obtain a teacher position, teachers had to graduate from a normal school. Until 1984, individuals holding only a middle school diploma could enroll in a normal school to obtain a teaching degree. After 1984, normal schools awarded bachelor's degrees and required a high school diploma to enroll. Close to 80% of public elementary and middle school teachers in Mexico have the equivalent of a BA (INEE, 2016). Before the 2013 *Reforma Educativa*, teachers would apply to their state's educational authorities to obtain a teaching position. New teaching positions were created when new schools/classrooms were built or whenever a current teacher retired. Upon retirement, teachers could recommend someone to take over their post, and these people usually were granted the position. This created a black market where positions could be "bought" from current owners or current owners could pass on these positions to their children or other family members. Anyone named by the current owner of the post would get priority in the application process. The cancellation of the 2013 *Reforma* may mean that this is once again how some teachers are selected in Mexico.

Teacher Mobility. Whenever teachers have to leave a school for any reason, whether temporary, such as taking maternity leave, or for an extended period, such as taking an administrative position in the central office, they continue to hold their teaching position or *"plaza."* Their positions will be filled by substitute teachers with a "temporary" contract. Sometimes these substitute teachers can remain in schools for years until the rightful owner of the "plaza" decides to return.

Teachers see mobility as a fundamental labor right (Olvera, 2010). When a new teaching position opens up, teachers who have requested to transfer from their current school to the new school will get priority rights based on seniority. Because everything is done centrally (at the state level) and can happen *at any point in the academic calendar*, a new position in School A can set off an entire chain of events: Teacher in school B requests to move to school A, teacher in school C requests to move to school B, and so on. This creates an enormous amount of disruption for students who may see two or more teachers in the same school year (Loera, 2006). Of course, teacher mobility is also a major problem in U.S. schools serving low-income and immigrant students: These schools experience twice the rate of teacher turnover as more affluent schools (Goldring, Taie, & Riddles, 2014)—although in the United States, this tends to be after the school year ends, and not necessarily mid-year, as is frequently the case in Mexico. In Mexico, teacher mobility will be more likely to affect schools in disadvantaged communities and rural areas, which are seen as less desirable for teachers wanting to move up the school food chain (Sánchez, 2009; Santos & Carvajal, 2001). These are also the schools more likely to be attended by transnational students.

Teacher Incentives for Improvement and Accountability. In general, teachers in Mexico have little external incentive to make changes to their classroom practice or to upgrade their skills based on pressures from parents, students, or the school administration staff. There are several reasons for this. First, teaching is a highly secure occupation in Mexico. Teachers receive tenure after just six months on the job and are almost never fired. Before the *Reforma Educativa* passed in 2013, most of the important moves for a teacher career (i.e., moves to more desirable schools, promotions to administrative posts, additional teaching positions) were based on decisions made by the teachers' union, the state education authorities, or both. Now that the *Reforma* has been revoked, the process has largely reverted to the teachers' union. School principals do not formally hire teachers, nor do they decide by themselves when teachers can move or should move to another school. They play a limited role in selecting professional development and in teacher appraisal (Santiago et al., 2012).

Second, the double-shift under which most schools operate means hectic working conditions for teachers and little time for planning, collaborating with other teachers, or meeting with parents. Teachers in cities and larger towns often must rush from their morning school to their afternoon school. Elementary teacher contracts specify that of the 4.5 hours of the school shift, 4 must be spent teaching in front of the classroom. At the secondary level, teachers are hired on hourly contracts. Frequently, these contracts are spread across two or more schools: 10 hours here, 15 hours there, 5 hours at yet another school (Santiago et al., 2012). This makes professional learning and collegial work very difficult. It also limits the amount of time teachers can spend at school to meet parents, school administrators, and other teachers. Occasionally, teachers get planning periods or planning days, for example for the monthly meeting of the "*Consejo*

Técnico Escolar." Teachers working two shifts have been noted to claim that there is "little time to work with students" and that the "intensity" of the time spent in front of students (40 hours per week) generates an "environment unfavorable toward learning" and negatively affects teachers' "commitment" to teaching and even their health (Cárdenas, 2011).

Third, the Mexican education system has little external accountability. This was made even worse after the elimination of standardized testing in all grades for all students. Parents and school administrators have little information, beyond bimonthly grades, to monitor and intervene when they see students performing poorly. Formative assessments are rare, and when they exist, they are seldom used to tailor a teacher's practice (Martínez Rizo et al., 2015; OECD, 2012). Teachers are not formally observed and monitored (in terms of classroom practice) by school administrators or district staff. Most monitoring is done for basic compliance: teacher attendance, punctuality, etc. And even then, several studies have found extensive absenteeism and late arrival on the part of some teachers (OECD, 2009; Santibañez, 2016). It must be noted, though, that some of this lateness and absenteeism is due to tough rural/isolated conditions in some regions (Santibañez, 2016).

Parents in the Mexican School System

Parents on both sides of the border place a high value on education as a way for children to move up the social ladder and access a better quality. They have high expectations for the education of their children (Goldenberg, Gallimore, Reese, & Garnier, 2001; Halgunseth, Ispa, & Rudy, 2006; Nieto, 2005; Valdés, 1996). How parents view their role in promoting educational success, however, is different in Mexico and the United States. In this section I focus on two very different ways parents get involved in their children's education in the United States and Mexico: participation in school activities and participation through school governance. I argue that these cultural misunderstandings are partly the result of how parents in Mexico are expected (or not expected) to interact with schools. In fact, parents in Mexico are not expected to play a central role in schools, and their participation is directly constrained by education law and common practices (Santizo, 2011). I argue that this often results in cultural misunderstandings between Mexican parents and U.S. schools.

Participation in School Activities

The mainstream American view of parental involvement places high value on activities that are specifically tied to academic outcomes and school resources—such as reading to children, developing vocabulary and numeracy skills, or fundraising and volunteering to help in the classroom or more broadly at the school. It should be acknowledged that this traditional view or model of parental involvement in the United States, described by Epstein (2001), has important limitations. It is by no means all-inclusive or representative of the experiences of all parents in U.S. public schools. Many parents, particularly immigrant and non-English speaking parents, feel excluded by this model of parental involvement. They face real, strong barriers to engage with schools and teachers in this way (Olivos, Jimenez-Castellanos, & Ochoa, 2011; Valdés, 1996). For example, though some Latino parents may not read books to their children, they foster literacy in other ways, such reading the bible or other prayer books, playing "Lotería," or learning and reciting poems (Zentella, 2015). Latino immigrant parents face real challenges to engage with schools in other ways, such as volunteering or participating in school activities. Scholars attribute these challenges to language communication barriers, deficit-views of the families themselves that are (consciously or unconsciously) transmitted by schools, and inflexible work schedules (Tarasawa & Waggoner, 2015; Valdés, 1996; Wasell, Hawrylak, & Scantlebury, 2015; Zárate, 2007).

These limitations notwithstanding, many teachers and school staff in the United States, most of whom are not themselves bilingual, bicultural, or have an immigrant background, internalize this mainstream model of parental involvement. Teachers and staff often view Mexican-immigrant parents as "caring less" than White or middle-class parents about their children's education (Halgunseth, Ispa, & Rudy, 2006; Valdés, 1996). U.S. teachers report that Mexican-immigrant parents don't come to school as often, don't respond to communications, don't help with homework, and don't read to their children. Teachers criticize the fact that parents "take their children to Mexico for almost anything throughout the school year" and that they prioritize family matters over academic matters (Quiocho & Daoud, 2006, p. 260). In her classic ethnography of 10 Mexican American families at the U.S.-Mexico border, Guadalupe Valdés documented the cultural misunderstandings around education and how the apparent "lack" of Mexican-immigrant parents' involvement in schools stemmed from different conceptions of what it meant to be "*educado*" or educated. These concepts are profoundly different in American and Mexican schools.

Valdés argues that Mexican-immigrant parents place a high value on the concept of "respect" or to be respectful to teachers and other adults. Parents in Mexico consistently rate behavioral skills as just as important as cognitive skills, something that is different from other parents in the United States. See Chapter 6 by Jensen in this book for more on this topic.

Parental participation in Mexican schools is considered to be high for aspects that involve volunteering for school cleaning duties and maintenance and repair (Huerta-Velásquez, 2010; Santibañez, O'Donoghue, & Abreu, 2014). Mexican parents are less likely to participate in education-related activities such as interacting with teachers and school staff, participating in school events and monitoring evaluation results (when Mexico had a censal testing program), or being part of parent associations (Murrieta et al., 2009; Sanchez-Escobedo et al., 2010; Santiago et al., 2012; Solís & Aguiar, 2017). As in the United States, higher-income, more educated parents participate more. Studies in the states of Sonora and Yucatán found that parental participation was higher in schools with higher achievement levels, when parents had more schooling, and in private schools (Murrieta et al., 2009; Sanchez-Escobedo et al., 2010; Solís & Aguiar, 2017).

Another way that schools can engage the community in the United States is through policies that keep school grounds open after school for community use. School playgrounds and facilities all over the United States are used in the afternoons and evenings as places where youth can practice sports and other activities. In Mexico, by contrast, schools are not usually open to parents and the larger community. First, when schools operate in double-shifts, it leaves no time for schools to be used for athletic, play, or other purposes. Second, even when schools are not operating on double-shifts, concerns about safety and liability mean that most schools shut their doors when the principal or other responsible staff member is not on the premises. This prevents families from seeing and using schools as gathering places for community-building purposes and could be one reason why parents consistently report not being connected to the school and not engaging in much communication with school staff (Murrieta et al., 2009; Sanchez-Escobedo et al., 2010).

Parental Participation in School Governance

In the United States, parents can sometimes take part in important governance aspects of their schools such as selecting school principals or making funding decisions through their local school councils. Parents who are U.S. citizens can vote in school board elections—an important way they can make their voices heard. By contrast, Mexican parents are prevented by law from intervening in decisions around curriculum, teacher and administrator selection (hiring/firing), teacher evaluation and classroom practice, and funding levels (Ornelas, 2004; Santiago et al., 2012; Santibañez, O'Donoghue, & Abreu, 2016). Educational authorities at the state and federal levels set these rules and make these decisions. There are no elected school boards making decisions over how schools are run. School-level parent councils or "*Consejo de Participación Social*" have some role and responsibilities under education law, but these have not been fully implemented. Schools are not funded by local property taxes, and municipalities cannot raise funds through bonds or other voter-approved tax measures for schools. Therefore, there is little influence in schools by other local actors, such as municipalities and local elected officials.

Parents in many schools, particularly those in rural areas, see teachers as authority figures because they are often the most educated (schooled) people in the area. This limits their participation, because many parents in Mexican public schools often feel it is not their place to question teachers or engage in the academic aspects of schooling—even informally. In this situation, parents tend not to initiate contact, demand accountability, or intervene in classroom matters from them (Guzmán & Martín del Campo, 2001; Santizo, 2011). And parents in low-income and rural areas are often unable to support their children at home. In 2008, only 36% of ninth graders surveyed for a national profile reported that their parents helped them with homework (Santiago et al., 2012). Teachers and school leaders in Mexico consistently report low levels of parental support received by children in their education, including a lack of academic support at home for homework or reading (Santiago et al., 2012; Valdez, Martín, & Sanchez, 2009). However, this low participation of parents in schooling matters appears to be concentrated in low-income communities. This suggests that some of the structural barriers to this type of parental involvement in the United States, such as working around inflexible schedules or holding deficit views of families, are also present in Mexican schools. The second kind of parent engagement through governance (school board elections) or parent associations is not prevalent (or not even allowed) at all. This may not be unique to educational settings. Other research has found low levels of participation in organized civic associations in Mexico as well (Houtzager & Acharya, 2010).

Discussion

This chapter describes several key ways in which education in Mexico is fundamentally different from the education system in the United States. These differences have implications for how teachers are able to meet the needs of transnational students. Key differences among the two systems around how education is funded and governed, the role of the union, teacher working conditions, and parental involvement have implications for how families interact with teachers and schools and, ultimately, how their children fare in school. The different roles that teachers and parents are expected to play in U.S. and Mexican schools can have real consequences for students' academic trajectories. In the United States, academic goals are central to the purpose of education, and parents are expected to be actively involved—even if in reality, mainstream expectations and practices place real constraints on low-income and immigrant parents' abilities to effectively engage with schools. In Mexico, the education system is set up in a way that ensures parents and other local actors have little to no participation in central aspects of education, including school administration, policies, and curriculum. Even though public education is funded through their income and other taxes, parents have no formal voice over educational matters.

Teachers are often the most educated people in a community, creating tension between how parents and teachers interact: Teachers are seen (and act) as authority figures, and parents often feel they have little to contribute beyond monetary or labor donations. Central delivery of public education is justified by the necessity of developing a more equitable and cohesive society out of a multitude of different groups, some with non-dominant ethnic and linguistic identities. This centrality is convenient for political and labor matters. The government has only one union to negotiate collective agreements with, and this union is given monopoly power in return. The union uses this power to its advantage, particularly after it began playing an active role in national elections and promoting its own candidates for state elected positions (Larreguy, Montiel Olea, & Querubín, 2017). Of course, while teachers' unions in the United States do not wield anything like the political power of the union in Mexico, they are also a powerful voice in American politics.

Mexican-immigrant parents who have been exposed to this kind of education at home have a hard time navigating a very different, more democratic educational system in the United States. These difficulties are compounded by the fact that their economic and legal situations often prevent them from fully engaging in their school's community (i.e., not speaking English, being undocumented, having to work multiple jobs and thus being unable to attend functions and meetings during the school day, etc.) (Morales, 2019).

The differences and conflicting definitions of the school actors' roles and expectations extend also to teachers. South of the U.S.-Mexico border, teachers are authority figures and expect parents to play a limited role in their schools and classrooms, and expect educational authorities to play an outsized role. North of the border, teachers and parents are expected to participate intensely in children's education and are seen as co-participants, though this is far more true at the elementary level than at the secondary level, where teachers rarely see parents, and teachers often comment that they prefer it that way. Parental roles are sometimes played out in shared formal governance and participation structures, local funding structures, and informal (cultural) norms and expectations. However, in reality, immigrant and low-income parents have much less opportunity to participate formally in the education of their children in the United States than middle-class, native-born, and English-speaking parents. In Mexico, teachers are mainly accountable to the educational authorities and to the *Sindicato*. They are not accountable to parents, as parents aren't likely to play any significant role in key aspects of their job: tenure, assignment, selection, curriculum, pay, evaluation, etc.

Students who are moving between the two countries have to contend with these two very different realities of what is expected of them, their teachers, and their families. The growing number of transnational students moving between both countries and "returning" to Mexico is likely to put pressure on an already stressed Mexican education system, where teachers work in tough conditions and have lower qualifications, support, and financial compensation. Currently, there are few mechanisms for teachers to meet the needs of these students. Contrary to the United States, which has civil rights legislation regarding linguistic minority children (Gándara, Moran, & Garcia, 2004), Mexico only recognizes the rights of indigenous-language students (i.e., the original peoples of Mexico) to be schooled in their own language and/or in transitional bilingual programs (Santibañez, 2016). There are no programs to transition children moving from the United States who speak English into Spanish-only environments. Teachers do not receive specialized training at the pre-service or in-service level to help them teach these students and foster an inclusive classroom. The experience for students can be extremely taxing as they struggle to negotiate their identity and cultural citizenship; they are seen as neither Mexican nor American, and in the eyes of their teachers they struggle and can be seen as a challenge to teach (Kleyn, 2017).

What can be done to ensure teachers in Mexico are better prepared to attend to the needs of transnational students and to take advantage of the assets they bring with them? First, it would be important that teacher preparation programs educate future teachers to be able to recognize biculturalism and bilingualism as an advantage that can be beneficial for all students in their classroom. Just as is the case in the United States, deficit views of linguistic-minority, low-income, and immigrant children must be eradicated from the classroom. Fostering inclusive classrooms should be a goal of all teacher preparation programs in Mexico.

Second, some states and regions are likely to concentrate an influx of transnational students (i.e., border areas, rural and highly inequitable states with large proportions of migrant populations). Teacher professional development efforts could be targeted in these regions to incorporate strategies and knowledge that enable teachers to be able to integrate these students better into the daily routine and avoid discriminatory, exclusionary, or otherwise negative behaviors and biases related to the children's immigrant status. See Alfaro and Gándara, Chapter 2 for a discussion of such efforts in the California–Baja California region.

Third, Mexico could take advantage of the influx of "returning" children who can speak English to establish public school dual-language immersion programs in the country. This would serve both English-dominant and Spanish-only students well.

Last, Mexico could build on current programs that seek a greater parental involvement in schools, such as the "Programa Escuelas de Calidad," to engage transnational families more broadly in these efforts and take advantage of the fact that many have been exposed to a more inclusive model of parent involvement in U.S. schools and may have developed skills they can share with other parents.

Notes

1. Mexico source: INEGI http://www.inegi.org.mx/RDE/RDE_07/Doctos/RDE_07_Art1.pdf. US source: NCES, https://nces.ed.gov/naal/lit_history.asp

2. OECD (2012). PISA 2012 Results in Focus: What 15-year-olds know and what they can do with what they know. Source: http://www.oecd.org/pisa/keyfindings/pisa-2012-results.htm

3. PLANEA results for 2015. Retrieved from http://www.seslp.gob.mx/consejostecnicosescolares/PRIMARIA/4-3aSesionOrdinaria/RESULTADOSPLANEA.pdf

4. World Bank data, retrieved from https://data.worldbank.org/indicator/SE.XPD.TOTL.GD.ZS

5. Source: World Bank Data, retrieved from data.worldbank.org

6. The "*Sistema Nacional de Coordinación Fiscal*" is a system whereby states agree to transfer all resources from tax collection to the federal government. The federal government then transfers back resources to the states, according to a set of rules and regulations around public spending. Source: PRODECON. "Lo que todo contribuyente debe saber." Retrieved from https://www.gob.mx/cms/uploads/attachment/file/64513/Lo_que_Todo_Contribuyente_debe_de_saber.pdf

7. There are more than 1 million teaching positions in Mexican public schools. These don't represent necessarily 1 million people, because individual teachers in Mexico can have two (or more) teaching positions.

8. Elementary school teachers report working 52 hours weekly on average, but this includes time during school, before or after school, and on weekends (Coppersmith, 2013).

References

Callahan, R., Figlio, D., Mavrogordato, M., & Ozek, U. (2019, February 28). "Authors of a splashy new ELL retention study urge "great caution" *Education Week*.

Cárdenas, S. (2011). Escuelas de doble turno en México: Una estimación de diferencias asociadas con su implementación. *Revista mexicana de investigación educativa*, 16(50), 801–827.

Díaz Barriga, F. A. (2005). Desarrollo del currículo e innovación: Modelos e investigación en los noventa. *Perfiles educativos*, 27(107), 57–84.

Epstein, J. L. (2001). *School, family and community partnerships: Preparing educators and improving schools*. Boulder, CO: Westview Press.

Estrada, R. (2019). Rules versus discretion in public service: Teacher hiring in Mexico. *Journal of Labor Economics*, 37(2), 545–579.

Gándara, P., Moran, R., & Garcia, E. (2004). Legacy of Brown: Lau and language policy in the United States. *Review of Research in Education*, 28(1), 27–46.

Gil Antón, M. (2018). La reforma educativa. Fracturas estructurales. *Revista Mexicana de Investigación Educativa*, 23(76), 303–321.

Giorguli, S. E., & Gutiérrez, E. (2011). Niños y jóvenes en el contexto de la migración internacional entre México y Estados Unidos. *Coyuntura Demográfica*, 1, 21–25.

Goldenberg, C., Gallimore, R., Reese, L., & Garnier, H. (2001). Cause or effect? A longitudinal study of immigrant Latino parents' aspirations and expectations, and their children's school performance. *American Educational Research Journal*, *38*(3), 547–582.

Goldring, R., Taie, S., & Riddles, M. (2014). *Teacher attrition and mobility: Results from the 2012-13 Teacher Follow-up Survey* (NCES 2014-077). U.S. Department of Education. Washington, DC: National Center for Education Statistics.

Guzmán, E., & Martín del Campo, S. (2001). Caracterización de la relación familia-escuela y sus implicaciones en la interacción psicopedagógica. *Educar, 18*(1), 8–21.

Halgunseth, L. C., Ispa, J. M., & Rudy, D. (2006). Parental control in Latino families: An integrated review of the literature. *Child Development, 77*(5), 1282–1297.

Houtzager, P. P., & Acharya, A. K. (2011). Associations, active citizenship, and the quality of democracy in Brazil and Mexico. *Theory and Society, 40*(1), 1–36.

Huerta-Velásquez, E. H. (2010). Formas de participación parental en las escuelas secundarias Mexicanas de altos y bajos resultados académicos. *Revista Iberoamericana de Educación*, (54), 167–185.

INEE (2016). *Panorama Educativo de Mexico 2015*. México, D.F.: Instituto Nacional para La Evaluación de la Educación.

INEE (2017). *Directrices para mejorar la permanencia escolar en la educación media superior*. México, D.F.: Instituto Nacional para La Evaluación de la Educación.

INEE (2018). *Panorama Educativo de Mexico 2017*. México, D.F.: Instituto Nacional para La Evaluación de la Educación.

Jensen B. (2005). Culture and practice of Mexican primary schooling: Implications for improving policy and practice in the US. *Current Issues in Education, 8*(25).

Jensen, B., Mejía Arauz, R., & Aguilar Zepeda, R. (2017). Equitable teaching for returnee children in Mexico. *Sinéctica* (48).

Kattan, R. B., & Székely, M. (2015). Patterns, consequences, and possible causes of dropout in upper secondary education in Mexico. *Education Research International*.

Kleyn, T. (2017). Centering transborder students: Perspectives on identity, languaging and schooling between the US and Mexico. *Multicultural Perspectives, 19*(2), 76–84.

Lakhani, N., & Jacobo, M. (2016, July 13). Uprooted in Mexico: The US children "returned" to a country they barely know. *The Guardian*.

Larreguy, H., Marshall, J., & Querubín, P. (2016). Parties, brokers, and voter mobilization: How turnout buying depends upon the party's capacity to monitor brokers. *American Political Science Review, 110*(1), 160–179.

Loera, A. (2006). *Caja de Herramientas para colectivos escolares: buenas practicas de gestión escolar y participación social en las escuelas públicas mexicanas.* SEP, UPN, HE, México, 2006, pp. 148–149.

Martínez Rizo, F. (Coord.). (2015). *Las Pruebas ENLACE Y EXCALE. Un Estudio de Validación*. México: INEE.

México Evalúa (2011). "10 Puntos para Entender el Gasto Educativo en México: Consideraciones sobre su eficiencia." México Evalúa, Centro de Análisis en Políticas Públicas, A.C. Serie "¿Gastamos para Mejorar?" México D.F.

Morales, M. (2019). *Parent involvement in contested times: A brief analysis of the effects of anti-immigrant policies*. Unpublished PhD Dissertation. Claremont Graduate University. Claremont, CA.

Muñoz Armenta, A. (2008). Escenarios e identidades del SNTE: entre el sistema educativo y el sistema político. *Revista mexicana de investigación educativa, 13*(37), 377–417.

Murrieta, M. U., Ibarra, L. M., & Ruelas, C. S. T. (2009). Participación de los padres de familia en dos escuelas secundarias de Ciudad Obregón, Sonora. In X Congresso Nacional de Investigação Educativa, área 16: sujetos da educação.

Nieto, S. (2005). Public education in the twentieth century and beyond: High hopes, broken promises, and an uncertain future. *Harvard Educational Review, 75*(1), 43–64.

O'Donoghue, J., & Calderón Martín del Campo, D. (2015). Sorry: El aprendizaje del inglés en México. Mexicanos Primero, Mexico D.F.

OECD (2012). PISA 2012 Results in Focus: What 15-year-olds know and what they can do with what they know. Paris: OECD.

OECD (2018). Mexico country note. Education at a glance 2018: OECD indicators. OECD Publishing: Paris.

Olivos, E. M., Jiménez-Castellanos, O., & Ochoa, A. M. (2011). *Bicultural parent engagement: Advocacy and empowerment*. New York: Teachers College Press.

Olvera, A. (2010). Movilidad docente. *Revista Latinoamericana de Estudios Educativos (México), 40*(1).

Ornelas, C. (2004). The politics of privatisation, decentralisation and education reform in Mexico. *International Review of Education, 50*(3–4), 397–418.

Quiocho, A. M., & Daoud, A. M. (2006, September). Dispelling myths about Latino parent participation in schools. *The Educational Forum, 70*(3), 55–267. Taylor & Francis Group.

Puryear, J. Santibañez, L. & Solano, A. (2012). Education in Mexico, a new vision for Mexico. In C. Loser & H. Kohli (Eds.), *A new vision for Mexico 2042: Achieving Prosperity for All* (Chapter 3, pp. 87–108). Emerging Markets Forum.

Rodríguez, L., Oramas, A., & Rodríguez, E. (2007). Estrés en docentes de educación básica: estudio de caso en Guanajuato, México. *Salud de los Trabajadores, 15*(1), 5–16.

Sánchez, L. A. (2009). La movilidad laboral de los docentes de telesecundaria de zonas rurales marginadas, en el cotidiano escolar, y su repercusión en los alumnos de tercer grado (Doctoral dissertation, UPN-Ajusco).

Sánchez Escobedo, P. A., Valdés Cuervo, Á. A., Reyes Mendoza, N. M., Martínez, C., & Alonso, E. (2010). Participación de padres de estudiantes de educación primaria en la educación de sus hijos en México. *Liberabit, 16*(1), 71–80.

Santiago, P., McGregor, I., Nusche, D., Ravela, P., & Toledo, D. (2012). *OECD reviews of evaluation and assessment in education: Mexico 2012*.

Santibañez, L. (2007). Between said and done: Preparation and professional development of middle school teachers in Mexico. *Revista Mexicana de Investigación Educativa, 12* (32), 305–335.

Santibañez, L. (2008). Educational reform: SNTE's role. *Revista Mexicana de Investigación Educativa, 13* (37).

Santibañez, L. (2016). The indigenous achievement gap in Mexico: The role of teacher policy under intercultural bilingual education. *International Journal of Educational Development, 47,* 63–75.

Santibañez, L., & Jarillo, B. (2008). Muscle, timing and priorities: Teacher unions and education quality in Mexico. *Well-Being and Social Policy, 3* (2), 21–40.

Santibañez, L., Abreu-Lastra, R., & O' Donoghue J. L. (2014). School-based management effects: Resources or governance change? Evidence from Mexico. *Economics of Education Review, 39,* 97–109.

Santibañez, L., Martínez, J. F., Datar, A., McEwan, P. J., Setodji, C. M., & Basurto-Dávila, R. (2007). *Breaking ground: Analysis of the assessments and impact of the Carrera Magisterial Program in Mexico*. Santa Monica, CA: RAND/MG-141.

Santibañez, L., Saavedra, J. E., Kattan, R. B., & Patrinos, H. A. (2018). Comprehensive private school model for low-income urban children in Mexico. World Bank Working Paper No. 8669.

Santizo Rodall, C. (2011). Gobernanza y participación social en la escuela pública. *Revista Mexicana de Investigación Educativa, 16*(50), 751–773.

Santos, A., & Carvajal, E. (2001). Operación de la Telesecundaria en zonas rurales marginadas de México. *Revista Latinoamericana de Estudios Educativos (México), 31*(2), 69–96.

Schmidt, W. H., Tatto, M. T., Bankov, K., Blömeke, S., Cedillo, T., Cogan, L., Han, S. I., Houang, R., Hsieh, L. P., Santillan, M., & Schwille, J. (2007). *The preparation gap: Teacher education for middle school mathematics in six countries. MT21 Report*. East Lansing: Michigan State University, *32*(12), 53–85.

Solís Castillo, F., & Aguiar Sierra, R. (2017). Análisis del papel del involucramiento de la familia en la escuela secundaria y su repercusión en el rendimiento académico. *Sinéctica*, (49).

Tarasawa, B., & Waggoner, J. (2015). Increasing parental involvement of English language learner families: What the research says. *Journal of Children and Poverty, 21*(2), 129–134.

Tatto, M. T., & Vélez, E. (1997). Teacher education reform initiatives: the case of Mexico. *Latin American education: Comparative perspectives*, 165–218.

Urban Institute (2016). *Demographic trends of children of immigrants*. Washington, DC: Urban Institute.

U.S. Department of Education (2019). *The condition of education 2019* (NCES 2019-144). Retrieved from https://nces.ed.gov/programs/coe/indicator_cmb.asp

Valdes, G. (1996). *Con respeto: Bridging the distances between culturally diverse families and schools: An ethnographic portrait*. New York: Teachers College Press.

Valdés Cuervo, Á. A., Martín Pavón, M. J., & Sánchez Escobedo, P. A. (2009). Participación de los padres de alumnos de educación primaria en las actividades académicas de sus hijos. *Revista electrónica de investigación educativa, 11*(1), 1–17.

Wassell, B. A., Hawrylak, M. F., & Scantlebury, K. (2017). Barriers, resources, frustrations, and empathy: Teachers' expectations for family involvement for Latino/a ELL students in urban STEM classrooms. *Urban Education, 52*(10), 1233–1254.

Zarate, M. E. (2007). *Understanding Latino parental involvement in education: Perceptions, expectations, and recommendations*. Tomas Rivera Policy Institute.

Zentella, A. C. (2015). Books as the magic bullet. *Journal of Linguistic Anthropology, 25*(1), 75–77.

Zúñiga, V., & Hamann, E. T. (2008). Escuelas nacionales, alumnos transnacionales: La migración México–Estados Unidos como fenómeno escolar. *Estudios Sociológicos de el Colegio de México, 26*(76), 65–85.

Zúñiga, V., & Hamann, E. T. (2009). Sojourners in Mexico with U.S. school experience: A new taxonomy for transnational students. *Comparative Education Review, 53*(3).

Zúñiga, V., & Hamann, E. T. (2015). Going to a home you have never been to: The return migration of Mexican and American-Mexican children. *Children's Geographies, 13*(6), 643–655.

Chapter 2

Binational Teacher Preparation

Constructing Pedagogical Bridges for the Students We Share

Cristina Alfaro and Patricia Gándara

I was born and raised in Santa Ana, California but last year my parents were deported so now we are here in Tijuana, Baja California, Mexico. My younger brother is still in California living with my tía (aunt). I am waiting for my tía to come for me so I can return to my school. The plan is for me to return by January 2020, if all goes well. I don't speak Spanish "very well" and since my teachers know that I intend to return to California, I feel that they don't have any idea of what to do with me while I am here. Es como que estoy en "limbo" y siento que estoy muy atrasada, esto me preocupa bastante (It is as if I am in "limbo" and I feel that I am very behind, this worries me so much)—hmmm, because I want to go to college, this is my dream.

In this quote, Paloma, a seventh-grade student, eloquently describes the social-emotional struggles of many students whose life trajectories and academic realities are often invisible, not understood, and go unaddressed because of politics, bureaucratic challenges, language barriers, low levels of communication, and inadequate and unequal educational opportunities on both sides of the border (Gándara & Contreras, 2009; Hamann,

2008). And yet she is eloquent in two languages—an asset that is often overlooked among the *students we share*. She speaks for the estimated 2 million students who have experienced some part of their young lives in both the United States and Mexico, often going to school in both systems. All of these students are considered the students we share. Not included in these numbers are the U.S. students who accompany their families to Mexico only to end their schooling prematurely because of the challenges they face in trying to enroll, or the immediate need to help support the family. That number is potentially large but not known.

Today, there are more than 53,000 U.S. citizen students in Baja California's schools alone (Piña, 2018). Some have grown up on the Mexican side of the border, but many have been displaced, mostly from California, and have lived part of their lives in the United States and now part in Mexico. Many intend to come back to the United States to study and to live, like Paloma. However, their futures depend greatly on how well we are able to educate these students on both sides of the border. Mexican-origin students do not fare well, as a group, in California, nor do English Learners (ELs), more than 80% of whom are Spanish speakers. One of the reasons identified as contributing to the low levels of education completed is the inability of teachers on both sides of the border to adequately teach and meet the needs of the students we share. The common denominator between Mexican and U.S. schools is that teachers on both sides of the border are underprepared to educate these students. This is neither fair to the teachers who come to feel ineffective and frustrated nor to the students whose very lives depend on the education they are able to obtain.

This chapter analyzes what has been learned from an earlier program to prepare teachers binationally to better understand, and meet, the educational needs of immigrant students to the United States, and how that learning has been applied to a new project model—*Formadores de Docentes Binacionales* (FDB) (Binational-Bilingual Teacher Education)—that aims to equip teachers with the knowledge and skills necessary to welcome, teach, and learn with and from immigrant students who are often racialized. The key purpose of this reciprocal binational teacher education project is to focus on the faculty who prepare the teachers in both California and Baja California with the prospect of preparing many more teachers ready to meet the challenges and build on the wealth of our binational context.

In California, almost 228,000 students have received their Seal of Biliteracy as of June 2018. This is significant because the Baja California educational system initiated its own version of *el Sello de Biliteracidad* as a way to honor and value students' bilingualism and biliteracy. Additionally, under the leadership of former State Superintendent of Instruction Tom Torlakson, the California Department of Education affirmed its commitment to binational educational partnerships by launching Global California 2030. Moreover, Baja California Secretary of Education Miguel Ángel Mendoza González initiated *Proyecto 2030* for Baja California Mexico to mirror Global California 2030. The FDB Project goals align well with California statewide initiatives as well as the current work undertaken by Baja California, where efforts to design bilingual teacher preparation programs and to open the state's first public bilingual school are underway. Given this, our collective and collaborative binational work and research are designed to inform their development and implementation.

We begin with the contextual binational realities and continue with what has been done to address this issue in the past, the literature that supports the need to transform what we are currently doing, and end with recommendations for future work and research.

Our Contextual Reality

The state of California assesses its students annually and disaggregates data by English Learner (EL) and other categories. Unfortunately, it does not disaggregate the EL test scores by language, but because more than 80% of ELs in California are Spanish speakers, the EL test score category is a fair proxy for Latinx ELs generally. At the eighth-grade level, just before entering high school, only 6% of ELs could meet state standards in math compared to 40% of non-EL students (CAASPP, 2018). One in five Latinx students (overwhelmingly of Mexican origin) does not graduate with her or his class, and of those who do graduate, only 42% are able to complete the required courses to enter a four-year college or university. This compares to 55% of White American students who complete these courses, and 76% of Asian Americans (Dataquest, 2017). This non–college bound pipeline problem results in enormous disparities in college completion by race and ethnicity (see Table 2.1).

Table 2.1. Educational Attainment by Race for 25- to 29-Year-Olds, California, 2018

	Percent of total pop.	Percent BA Degrees + Above
Latinx	39.4	15.3
Black	5.8	22.0
White	36.6	46.0
Asian	14.7	62.1

Note: Authors' calculations based on data from the American Community Survey, 2018.

In California, half of all students are the children of immigrants, and overwhelmingly they are of Latinx background. For decades, these students have been encountering schools and teachers who are not adequately prepared to educate them (López, McEneaney, & Nieswandt, 2015). Surveys of teachers in California note that inability to communicate with students and their parents is a primary concern of teachers of ELs (Gándara, Maxwell-Jolly, & Driscoll, 2005; Santibañez & Gándara, 2017). A study by Hopkins (2013) conducted in California, Arizona, and Texas with about 600 bilingual and non-bilingual teachers of immigrant students found that teachers who spoke only English were much more likely than bilingual teachers to expect parents to reach out to them, rather than the reverse. Thus, there was very limited communication between the two. This lack of connection between schools, students, and their parents is certainly a factor in low academic achievement for many Latinx children of immigrants because parents often do not know how to support their children's schoolwork, and the schools have little knowledge of the resources or challenges faced by these families.

Baja California has what is considered in Mexico to be one of the highest education attainment levels among the 32 Mexican states, at 9.7 years, on average. That is barely one year of high school or *preparatoria*. Moreover, only 17% of Mexicans between 25 and 64 had attained a college degree (*licenciatura*) by 2016 (OECD, 2017). While Mexico has been deeply engaged in education reform over the last several years and both teacher pay and preparation have been increasing (see Chapter 1), and compulsory education through high school (*preparatoria*) is the law as of 2012 (INEE, 2018), it still lacks the infrastructure to fully realize this goal in the immediate future. For example, in 2017, 12,000 students in

Baja California were unable to access a public high school because there simply were not enough seats (Reyes, 2017). The students most likely to be left out are those students we share who do not know how to navigate the Mexican school system. In Mexico, schools and teachers have little understanding of these U.S. students' educational history, experiences, or expectations (Jacobo & Jensen, 2018). If teachers notice them at all, as they tend to blend in with other students, it is often to see them as lazy or intellectually inferior. The teachers, especially in the upper grades, are also challenged by—and sometimes resentful of—the idea that they need to be teaching these students basic Spanish reading, writing, and academic forms at a grade level in which Mexican students have long since mastered the material.[1] Moreover, education systems that do not communicate with each other often derail students' aspirations when they are denied credit for courses they have taken and passed in the other country or are placed in lower grades with younger students "to catch up" (Zuñiga & Vivas-Romero, 2014).

Unless there is a strategic and organized manner of helping educators on both sides of the border understand each other's cultures, educational systems, languages, and grade level requirements, students will continue to fall through the cracks—with the potential of their deferred dreams leaving a permanent scar on their development. Moreover, the loss of talent and productivity by these students will have long-term impacts on both countries. Hence the necessity for educators on both sides of the border to work together to support these students in accomplishing their academic and personal goals.

International Teacher Education Program

The International Teacher Education Program (ITEP) was established as a California State University (CSU) system-wide bilingual (Spanish/English) credential program for elementary multiple-subject teacher candidates with the goal of preparing bilingual teachers with the cultural and linguistic knowledge needed to meet the needs of the large immigrant Spanish-speaking student population in California. The program, administered through the CSU International Programs Office, was approved in 1994 by the California Commission on Teacher Credentialing (CCTC) and authorized to credential teacher candidates seeking a multiple-subject (elementary) credential with a Spanish/English bilingual authorization.

First originated in Mexico City, the program was moved in 1998 to the colonial city of Querétaro, with approximately 1,500,000 residents located about 125 miles north of Mexico City. In addition to San Diego State University (SDSU), where the program was initiated, nine other CSU campuses participated, including San José, Fresno, East Bay, Long Beach, San Bernardino, Sacramento, Sonoma, Bakersfield, and Fullerton.

The ITEP was implemented for 15 years and focused on preparing culturally and linguistically competent teachers with a high level of academic Spanish and a strong knowledge base about the Mexican educational system to be better prepared to receive immigrant students in U.S. schools. The program brought CSU students from throughout the state to SDSU for one partial spring and two partial summer "bookend" sessions of coursework and student teaching. The other part of the summer, fall, and spring sessions were spent in Mexico. Participants engaged in methods courses alongside Mexican *normalistas* (see Bybee et al., Chapter 3) and taught for a total of nine months in Mexico and three months in the San Diego area in bilingual classrooms with large Spanish-speaking student populations in schools situated in close proximity to the Tijuana, Mexico, border.

Candidates who completed the credential program received a multiple-subject elementary Bilingual Cross-Cultural and Language Academic Development (BCLAD) credential from the CCTC. This program represented the only international credential program in California approved by the CCTC. The program was initially designed for teacher candidates who had intermediate written and oral fluency in Spanish, although Spanish was their heritage language, or who were developing Spanish as an additional language and desired to become bilingual teachers. However, shortly after the inception of the program, many fluent Spanish speakers chose to participate to further professionalize their Spanish "academic language" and develop deeper cultural knowledge.

The program developed a partnership with the *Secretaría de Educacíon Pública* (Mexico's Secretariat of Education), which allowed U.S. bilingual teacher candidates to student teach in public schools in Querétaro. After a program orientation at SDSU, 30 teacher candidates each year spent nine months studying at the *Escuela Normal del Estado de Querétaro* (Normal State Teachers College of Querétaro) and the *Universidad Tecnológico de Monterrey, Querétaro* campus. Additionally, candidates student taught in three distinct settings: private, public, and indigenous schools. Their indigenous experiences included schools throughout Mexico from Oaxaca,

Puebla, Toluca, Amealco, and Atlacomulco. Teacher candidates participated for eight weeks in public schools, two weeks in private schools, and three weeks in indigenous schools during their student teaching practicum while also taking education methods courses taught by Mexican professors and university supervisors. Upon their return to the United States, teacher candidates completed their teaching methods courses at SDSU and engaged in 10 additional weeks of student teaching in a dual-language setting with cooperating bilingual teachers (Alfaro, 2008a).

During their nine-month stay in Mexico, teacher candidates lived with host families, or sometimes with families of program faculty, and interacted with other Mexican national teacher education candidates in educational, cultural, and language workshops. Thus, teacher candidates learned both the California State Standards as well as the Mexican Education Standards through various situated learning and teaching opportunities with Mexican *normalistas*. The opportunity to teach in different sociocultural contexts with culturally heterogeneous students forced teacher candidates to experience cultural, pedagogical, and ideological dissonance, an experience that promotes increased ideological and pedagogical clarity (Alfaro, 2008b). The pedagogical experiences were structured in such a manner that compelled teacher candidates to juxtapose their personal belief systems with those of the dominant society in both the visiting country (Mexico) and the United States. As a result, teachers were prepared to critically examine the political and ideological dimensions of education for racialized communities on both sides of the U.S./Mexico border.

Program Impact

Throughout a decade of ITEP implementation, with a cohort of 30 students per year, approximately 300 teacher candidates graduated from ITEP. Currently, 85% are teaching or in leadership roles in biliteracy settings and 15% are in sheltered English classrooms in the United States. Certainly, this is not to imply that every candidate was automatically transformed through these experiences. However, the experiences gained played a large part in their elevated Spanish proficiency and cultural learning and, importantly, the reason they stayed in the field (Alfaro & Quezada, 2010; Cushner & Brislin, 1996). According to Block (2002), critical experiences and learning opportunities are "periods of time during which prolonged contact with a new cultural setting causes irreversible destabilization of the individual's sense of self" (p. 4). For ITEP program graduates, these critical experiences embodied critical learning opportunities where program graduates developed their sociocultural and linguistic identities as bilingual-binational educators.

Understanding Borderland Psychology

In this section, we share two statements from ITEP graduates (Alfaro, 2008a) that exemplify the impact of their binational teaching and learning experience. Alina states:

> I was born and raised in Orange County, California in a White upper-middle class community and had never crossed the border to Mexico until I participated in ITEP. My experience in this program helped me to understand the similarities and differences between our educational systems—more significantly I recognized the importance of teacher agency in advocating for immigrant students that are constantly negotiating multiple languages and identities. I am currently a school principal in Southern California where I have created a safe academic space for borderland students and their families. One immigrant parent told me "*oiga para ser gringa usted de veras nos entiende y valora nuestras vidas, culturas, e idiomas, por eso la queremos tanto*"—I consider this a great compliment and a tribute to what I learned in ITEP.

In this quote, Alina highlights the importance for educational leaders to understand and value the strengths and challenges of "borderlands" students and their families, where being from the borderlands incorporates those who cross borders and live with multiple identities. Romo and Chávez (2006) characterize the borderland as a hybrid space in which individuals are constantly negotiating multiple languages and identities, which also complicate a sense of identity and belonging. They maintain that "the geopolitical border between Mexico and United States represents the beginnings, endings, and blending of languages, cultures, communities, and countries" (p. 142). In their work on border pedagogy, Cline and Necochea (2006) argue that teachers working in borderland communities require certain dispositions in order to serve their students effectively. To be effective, this requires that their teachers understand the border psychology as well—what it means to be a person with one foot in each of the two countries. The current political context suggests that the number of binational students will increase as more U.S.-born children move with their parents to Mexico, even as others enter or return to the United States, with California being a primary destination.

Developing a Sense of Belonging

The ITEP, far more than being a teaching experience, became an approach for humanizing student realities. The statement below demonstrates how Javier, an ITEP graduate (Alfaro, 2008a), not only connects his personal immigration experience to those of the students he teaches, but also, through this journey, ascertains the importance of a sense of belonging.

> I was born in Mexico City and immigrated to San Francisco, California as a young teen and personally experienced what many of my students in my "Newcomer Classroom" experience. However, it was not until I participated in ITEP that I realized the emotional trauma that immigrant children and their families experience when they come to the U.S., especially under the perpetual anti-immigrant ideologies and politics. During my time in ITEP I worked in public and indigenous schools in Mexico where I was able to learn from family *testimonios* about students' back and forth trajectories between borders and their lack of belongingness to either country, but what I found even more pressing was the lack of knowledge U.S. teachers have about immigrant students' stories, their linguistic and cultural capital and the challenges they face when crossing physical and ideological borders and their critical need to belong.

In this statement, Javier clearly depicts immigrant students' need to belong, which too often goes unrecognized by educators on both sides of the border. Gibson, Gándara, and Koyama (2004) found that a sense of belonging is one of the most critical characteristics of Mexican-origin youth who adapt well to schooling in the United States as opposed to those who do not. Students with supportive peer relations in school tend to like school more and remain engaged in schooling. By contrast, those who do not develop those relationships are more likely to disengage from school and drop out altogether (Osterman, 2000). Therefore, it is critical for teachers to be aware of this and to support the development of a sense of belonging in their students.

Whether racialized immigrant students are in Mexico or in the United States, it is important to know what their prior schooling experiences have been and what their and their parents' expectations are of the school. It is also important to understand the cultural features associated with the prior schooling experience—flag ceremonies, saying of the Pledge of Allegiance, celebrating holidays, even what is considered proper dress and behavior. These things are critical for students to feel accepted and have a sense of belonging. Belonging is complicated for students who may come and go, and it is bound up with identity: What am I? American, Mexican, both, or neither? As Morcheday and Alfaro (2019) quote Camila, a recently deported fifth grade student, "Ahorita siento que no soy de aquí ni de allá" (p. 30). In this statement, Camila describes a state of socioemotional disequilibrium and lack of belongingness that all educators must learn to address in the most humanistic manner.

In this binational context, it is important to note that for immigrants and students learning a new language, a key issue is the extent of use of the primary language in instruction. It is obvious that if students were educated bilingually wherever they attend school, their transitions would be greatly facilitated and a sense of belonging would likely increase. However, most teachers of immigrants do not currently speak the language of their students (Hopkins, 2013; O'Donoghue & Calderón Martín del Campo, 2015), so there are limits to the use of primary language in instruction. This is especially true in Mexico, where very few teachers are strong in English, and even half of the English teachers do not meet the standards their students are expected to achieve (Calderón, 2015). Yet the research is consistent in finding clear benefits for bilingual education in ultimately attaining higher levels of English proficiency (Umansky & Reardon, 2014), better performance in English Language Arts (Steele et al., 2017; Valentino & Reardon, 2015), as well as higher levels of college attendance and higher earnings in the labor market (Callahan & Gándara, 2014). Given the pecuniary advantages associated with bilingualism and biliteracy, Agirdag (2014) has even questioned whether not providing bilingual instruction for the children of immigrants is tantamount to stealing from them. Developing strong bilingual teachers remains an acute challenge for both countries.

Teacher Preparation and Professional Learning

Across the nation, institutions of higher education, in particular colleges of education, typically prepare preservice teachers with a repertoire of what are considered to be best teaching practices. These practices are aligned to state standards for the teaching profession. In the case of wanting to ascertain the highest level of what is considered to be an accomplished teacher, another set of standards exists, those outlined by the National Board for Professional Teaching Standards. Sadly, neither set of standards speaks to the importance or necessity for teachers to develop sociopolitical, cultural, and linguistic competence. Given our highly diverse cultural and immigrant populations, we argue that it is imperative that teachers develop the knowledge, disposition, and skills (KDS) necessary to teach and learn with and from their immigrant students and their families (Alfaro, 2018).

There are two bodies of literature that are especially relevant to the teaching of the students we share: (1) the knowledge, dispositions, and skills needed by teachers to help ELs succeed and join the mainstream; and (2) the knowledge, dispositions, and skills necessary to meet the needs of students who are immigrants. While these two areas of research are clearly related and relevant to the same students within the United States, the needs they address can be quite different. Spanish as a second language (SSL) is not well developed in Mexico as is English as a second language (ESL) in the United States, so it is necessary to extrapolate the ESL literature to the Mexican context and to keep in mind that many of the students we share are having to learn Spanish in order to succeed in their new Mexican school and community. As such, Mexican-origin students, when in the United States, are referred to as "heritage Spanish speakers," and when they move to Mexico, after a few years they may switch to become "heritage English speakers."

Research on teaching students defined as ELs in the United States tends to focus on pedagogical knowledge about teaching "special populations" and the teaching of language. Teachers of immigrant students, however, are expected to acknowledge and value the cultural backgrounds and life *testimonios* of students in their teaching and to introduce students to different expectations and procedures of schooling than they may be familiar with. Today, the teaching of ELs and immigrant students (which the U.S. literature often treats as one and the same) must also take into account the current attacks being made on immigrant families by the federal administration and the extent to which immigrant communities are living in fear, and the schools that teach immigrant students are reeling from related pressures (Ee & Gándara, 2019; 2020).

Teaching Language to Racialized Students

Setting aside social conditions such as poverty, segregation, social-emotional trauma, and linguistic isolation, which are unfortunately common to many immigrant students pushed to the margins in both the United States and Mexico, one explanation for the low achievement of these students rests with teacher preparation (Mordechay & Alfaro, 2019). There is a body of evidence to suggest that teachers need a specialized set of skills and dispositions to effectively teach language learners (Faltis & Valdés, 2016; Lucas, Villegas, & Freedson-Gonzalez, 2008; Menken & Antunez, 2001; Santos, Darling-Hammond, & Cheuk, 2012), and that teacher preparation programs are not equipping new teachers with critical skills (Alfaro & Bartolomé, 2016; Coady, Harper, & de Jong, 2016; de Jong & Harper, 2005). Santibañez and Snyder (2018) divide the skills needed to adequately educate language minoritized students into three categories: (1) scaffolding, the skills to support learning in the second language; (2) pedagogical knowledge, skills in teaching content to students who do not have a command of English; and (3) cultural knowledge and social justice orientation. In order to implement this knowledge, however, teachers must understand the complexity of language teaching and learning (Bunch, 2013). Santos et al. (2012) outline four critical components teachers must fully grasp to effectively teach language learners: (1) language progressions: How do students learn language, both in terms of general language acquisition and in terms of the acquisition of discipline-specific academic language?; (2) language demands: What kinds of linguistic expectations are embedded within specific texts and tasks with which students are being asked to engage?; (3) language supports: How can classrooms and schools be organized to support students in continually building a deep understanding of language and content?; (4) language scaffolds: What specific representations and instructional strategies can be used to help students gain access to the concepts as well as to the language they need to learn? Scaffolding and supporting instruction can include making language objectives clear and consistent by explicitly designing and implementing both designated and integrated language development teaching and learning opportunities and safe spaces, modifying dense texts to make them comprehensible, or using the primary language to create comprehensible, relevant, and purposeful cognitive learning opportunities.

In all cases, the teacher must be adept at eliciting language and creating an innovative, language-rich classroom environment. In order to do this, teachers must have an explicit understanding and ability to recognize students' language of ideas and language of display as they prepare and implement lessons (Alfaro & Bartolomé, 2016; Bunch, 2006; Flores & Rosa, 2015). Pedagogical knowledge, according to Santibañez and Snyder (2018), includes skills such as knowing how to teach content and language simultaneously. One example is the teaching of science in a way that fosters language learning by creating projects that require students to interact verbally (Feldman & Flores Malagon, 2017). Teaching reading in first and/or partner languages also falls in this category. Finally, cultural knowledge and social justice orientation include framing the students as having valuable assets, reaching out to parents in culturally appropriate ways, and advocating for students (Alfaro, 2018). Some researchers argue that teachers need to combine all three of these areas seamlessly to assess their ELs' linguistic, academic, and cultural characteristics and to use this knowledge to adapt instruction (Coady et al., 2016; de Jong et al., 2013; Faltis & Valdes, 2016; Hernandez, 2015; Lucas et al., 2008; Lucas & Villegas, 2013). Santibañez and Snyder (2018) conclude that there is little evidence that teacher candidates in California are actually being taught all, or even most, of these critical skills. It is important to note that ITEP afforded these teaching and learning opportunities through science and other methods courses in Spanish—learning content and elevating their academic Spanish. Given this, teacher candidates were challenged to learn content area academic Spanish while teaching Mexican students in public Mexican schools and guided by content area Mexican professors from the *Universidad Pedagógica Nacional* in Mexico. Through ITEP, teacher candidates learned to teach and learn from students with a cultural wealth approach (Yosso, 2005). ITEP teacher candidates experienced, firsthand, the process of learning content and language in their methods courses to then develop their own lessons that focused on developing language while teaching content to their students.

Many transborder collaborative efforts have been implemented with the intent to better prepare teachers to teach culturally and linguistically diverse immigrant student populations, but few if any programs have been established with sustainable infrastructures to continue beyond certain individual leadership efforts, undependable funding, and the impact of political changes on both sides of the border. In the case of ITEP, when the CSU and federal funding ended, so did the program. Nevertheless, there were many lessons learned from more than a decade of program implementation that are being applied to a new project to effectively prepare teachers with the KDS to educate bilingual-binational students.

What We Learned

Through our collective research and experience in developing and implementing transborder education programs, we have learned that most, if not all, transborder program efforts and scholarship focus on preparing bilingual teachers through engagement in study abroad or teacher exchange programs, with an emphasis on the experiences of U.S. teachers who travel to Mexico (Alfaro, 2008; Alfaro & Quezada, 2010; Hamann, 2008; Kasun & Saavedra, 2016; Olmedo, 2004; Ruiz, Baird, & Hernandez, 2016; Santamaria, Santamaria, & Fletcher, 2009; Sawyer, 2014). Similar to the results we found in more than a decade of the ITEP implementation, this body of research indicates that such experiences inform U.S. teacher candidates' personal and professional development by shaping understandings of the circumstances facing immigrant students and ELs and increasing empathy toward them; enhancing cultural competence and a sense of global interconnectedness; and furthering appreciation for multicultural inclusive pedagogy and a desire to create transformative classroom spaces (Alfaro, 2008b; Hamann, 2008; Kasun & Saavedra, 2016).

Because there was no attempt to create a *reciprocal* program that also benefited Mexican teachers who would be teaching U.S. students, a principle lesson we have learned is that teaching in an era of binational students requires that we engage in authentic collaboration between both U.S. and Mexican educators. The goal must be to prepare teacher educators and public-school teachers on both sides of the U.S.-Mexico border in a manner that equally serves both countries. In other words, not a "one-way" program where U.S. teachers learn about Mexican schools and return to teach in their U.S. classrooms with enlightened knowledge. Instead, the most critical lesson we have learned is that in order to have the greatest and most sustainable impact, we must create a "two-way" reciprocal teacher preparation program where teacher educators learn about each other's educational systems. Of course, this is especially necessary given the two-way movement of students from one country to another. This major lesson is what informs the new model of binational teacher education discussed in the section below titled *Formadores de Docentes Binacionales*. This is a teacher educator collaboration among the Baja California Secretary of Education, the Superintendent of Public Instruction for California, San Diego State University, the University of California, and the California Association for Bilingual Educators.

The following are six key lessons that are being applied to this two-way reciprocal teacher education program to meet the demands of the thousands of students we share along the Mexico and California border (and beyond):

1. *Identify binational teacher knowledge, dispositions, and skills (KDS)*—This first lesson revolves around the necessity for colleges of education to identify and come to an agreement about the KDS required to prepare teachers to effectively teach immigrant populations on both sides of the border. Accordingly, teacher educators must determine what curriculum, hands-on experiences, and assessments will ensure educator competence for teaching culturally and linguistically diverse *binational* and often indigenous students. This must be reflected across programs' mission and vision, syllabi, methods courses, and field practicum.

2. *Develop trust relationships*—Authentic trust relationships must be developed, nurtured, and maintained with educational leaders across the border in order to gain access to work with and in Mexico's public school system as well as in the U.S. schools. Education officials and leaders in Mexico must be fully convinced that in addition to the benefits for children in U.S. schools, there is also a sincere and concerted effort to improve the opportunities and conditions for Mexican students and communities. Many times they are skeptical, rightfully so, of U.S. researchers' intentions and feel they must protect their schools and communities from any potential exploitation. Similarly, U.S. schools are equally wary of researchers and often loathe to invest the time and resources required to run special programs in their schools. Deep trust must also be developed and nurtured in U.S. schools. Because the SDSU teacher preparation program already enjoyed good relations with local districts, this was made easier, but as programs grow beyond these select districts, new trust relationships must be developed and nurtured.

3. *Acknowledge teacher educator expertise*—It must be clear to Mexican colleagues that U.S. partners possess the expertise needed to inform and guide the proposed project in collaboration with them. For instance, in addition to bilingual and teacher preparation expertise, they

need to see clarity of intent and possibilities based on potential partners' previous research and work with international communities. And U.S. colleagues must be cognizant of the important work of Mexican partners and acknowledge their expertise.

4. *Navigate la política*—U.S. teacher educators must learn to work with, through, and around Mexico's political bureaucracy and administrative ebbs and flows. This requires flexibility, collaboration, and explicit communication and understanding about Mexican systems of operation and ways of conducting business. Mexican educators must be made aware of the unique challenges and rules that govern teacher education at the state level in the United States given that U.S. schooling is highly decentralized and very state specific. These differences are often not fully appreciated by Mexican educators.

5. *Emphasize authentic collaboration*—In a review of the literature on transborder/international programs, Alfaro and Quezada (2010) found that the focus is typically one-sided in favor of preparing U.S. teachers abroad to work with immigrant students with no reciprocity or intent to prepare the teachers in the visiting country to better serve that country's students and communities, or the U.S. students who find themselves abroad.

6. *Increase the scale of our endeavors*—To meet the needs of the large and growing population of students we share, it is not enough to prepare 30 teachers a year. It is critical to find ways to scale up our efforts, and one important way is to prepare the faculty who prepare the teachers so that they can impact the hundreds of teacher candidates they educate each year.

7. *Forefront social justice and equity*—The heart of a binational project must include an authentic collaboration around social justice and equity in education practice. Hence, the collaboration must engage teacher educators in a process to deconstruct, construct, and reconstruct the manner in which we typically prepare teachers. In this manner, teacher educator teams work closely to learn with and from each other others' work and research to co-construct a pedagogical social justice framework to inform collaborative work and efforts to address a critical theme(s). We have found very little work reported in this area in the existing literature.

Given these important lessons and building on previous research, we set out to create and pilot a project that would have teacher educator collaboration, from both sides of the border, at the core of a transformative binational program with a sustainable infrastructure that benefits both countries and stands the test of time. Moreover, the project explicitly addresses the gaps in previous programs and research with a binational curriculum and program that can ultimately be shared as a "two-way" reciprocal teacher preparation model with other institutions of higher education on both sides of the border.

Formadores de Docentes Binacionales Project: *Students We Share*

Both Mexico and California are in need of bilingual teachers who have well-defined understandings of each other's sociopolitical structures, cultures, languages, teacher preparation standards, and school systems, as well as the KDS to teach and learn with and from binational students who have attended school on both sides of the border. In a concerted effort to develop a sustainable infrastructure, the *Formadores de Docentes Binacionales* Project (FDB Project) is a teacher educator collaboration between San Diego State University, University of California, Baja California Secretary of Education, California Superintendent of Public Instruction, California Department of Education, *Universidad Pedagógica Nacional,* and *escuelas normales* (Tijuana, Mexicali, and Ensenada). This project engages teacher educators and teacher candidates on both sides of the border in learning opportunities through a series of curriculum modules collaboratively developed by teacher educators from participating universities and *escuelas normales* (teacher education institutions). Additionally, teacher candidates, alongside their professors, engage in situated transborder experiences. A critical aspect of the program is the "scaling up" of teacher preparation. While 300 teachers were prepared over a 10-year period in the ITEP program, the FDB project forecasts that between 2018 and 2020, it will prepare about 300 teachers in one year. This is because the project does not just focus on teacher candidates, but is developing capacity among teacher educators on both sides of the border who will use the curriculum with their teacher candidates.

Other key purposes of the project are to develop, implement, and evaluate teacher education curriculum that will create opportunities for bilingual teacher candidates to (1) develop critical consciousness related to the sociopolitical, sociocultural, sociolinguistic, and social-emotional dimensions of binational education; (2) understand how these dimensions shape students' educational experiences; (3) advance their pedagogical approaches to build on binational students' assets and academic challenges; and (4) develop a sense of agency and advocacy for the education and well-being of immigrant students and their families. Taken together, we create binational learning spaces at each of our institutions to shape teacher candidates' KDS across diverse institutional and geographic contexts. Unlike previous programs discussed in the literature, instead of privileging the teaching and learning of U.S. teacher candidates studying in Mexico, the FDB Project offers a unique opportunity for U.S. and Mexican teacher educators and teacher candidates to engage in joint curricular experiences with the aim of facilitating binational sociopolitical understandings and pedagogies. It also represents a unique opportunity for faculty within the UC and CSU systems, and in San Diego and Tijuana, to collaborate around a very complex and joint problem of practice: "students we share." The FDB Project is built on the very distinctive strength that teachers in border regions inhabit unique physical and cultural spaces, as their lives are shaped by a borderland that is "highly diverse, volatile, and ever in constant flux" (de la Luz Reyes & Garza, 2005, p. 155). Hence, U.S. and Mexican teachers who reside in the border region often have more in common with one another than with teachers in the interior of their countries (Alfaro, 2008b; Alfaro & Quezada, 2010; Suarez-Orozco, 2001). This pilot, however, is also meant to teach us how to extend such a program into the interiors of both countries through a binational teacher preparation and professional development curriculum to be disseminated by the *Secretaria de Educación Pública* of Baja California and the California Department of Education as well as in colleges of education in institutions of higher education.

The FDB team includes 15 teacher educators across institutions that are piloting the curriculum at participating universities along with a series of complementary transborder hands-on activities to bring the teacher candidates together for critical experiences and dialogues. The project activities and experiences include observations in K-12 schools and universities in San Diego and Tijuana, Ensenada, and Tecate (all of the Baja California border region) as well as virtual learning opportunities. The participants' coursework and practicum are focused on teaching and learning theories and practices where culture, language, and sociopolitical issues are central, and include culturally and linguistically responsive teaching, English or Spanish as a partner language, the centrality of culture in human experience and ways that culture and cultural difference influence learning and teaching, and community-based and culturally diverse field experiences for teacher candidates. The program's immediate mission encourages teacher education candidates not only to embrace the philosophies behind bilingualism and biculturalism, but also to learn how to engage in a process wherein individuals learn to function in their primary cultural community and that of the dominant mainstream in which they now live (Alfaro, 2008b). Several scholars have called the process biculturalism because of the interaction between two cultural systems, the individual's ensuing state of mind, and response to this process (Block, 2002; Darder, 2012; Ramirez, Castaneda, & Herold, 1974).

The FDB Project requires teacher candidates to go beyond reading the additional multicultural chapter or listening to a guest speaker who merely offers a basic understanding of the changing ethnolinguistic and sociocultural context in which they will be teaching. Rather, prospective teachers in this program engage in a collaboratively created curriculum and situated learning experiences that position them in contexts that allow them to negotiate their *own* sociocultural, linguistic, and political position in a binational context. It asks teacher candidates to take the opportunity to understand the students they will soon educate and to critically interrogate the ideological and political dimensions that influence their classroom practice before undertaking to guide their students through this binational educational space.

In the broader society, much attention is paid to the social, political, and economic issues in the border region, but with very little emphasis on the serious educational issues that result. In order to address the critical educational demands of the students we share across borders, FDB curriculum is grounded in four dimensions that lie at the intersection of these issues: (1) sociopolitical—the sociopolitical dimension acknowledges the complexities of educating binational students in the context of shifting immigration and economic policies (Jensen, Mejía Arauz, & Aguilar Zepeda 2017); (2) sociolinguistic—the sociolinguistic dimension attends to whether and how binational students are afforded opportunities to develop bilingualism and biliteracy, and the extent to which teachers acknowledge language as a resource rather than a problem (Ceballos, 2012; Hamann, 2008; Olmedo, 2004; Yosso, 2005); (3) sociocultural—the sociocultural dimension considers the funds of knowledge embedded in binational communities and how teachers attend to them in culturally sustaining ways (Alfaro & Bartolome, 2016; Alfaro & Quezada, 2010; de la Piedra & Araujo, 2012; Hamann, 2008; Serna-Gutierrez & Mora-Pablo, 2018; Sawyer, 2014); (4) socioemotional—the socioemotional dimension recognizes binational students' feelings of not belonging and identity confusion that may be related to effects of detention and deportation (Brabeck, Lykes, & Hunter, 2014) or feelings of invisibility (Hamann, 2008; Sánchez

García, Hamann, & Zuñiga (2012). We view these dimensions as distinct but interconnected, as they interact to shape the experiences of binational students, classroom teachers, and teacher educators.

Conclusion

To date, minimal research exists, and very little attention is given to the area of binational teacher preparation with the readiness to teach a generation of students we share. Next steps for teacher preparation programs and professional development efforts should include a focused attention on designing and teaching instruction and assessments for students in binational contexts—these efforts should consider surfacing the issues and challenges specific to the complex relationships between education, economics, race, culture, and language for students on the border and beyond.

Given what we have learned from 10-plus years of the ITEP implementation, we conclude that the FDB is a project whose time has come. Through this project, we implement what we know from the literature and lessons learned in previous efforts. In order to move the needle toward the benefit of the students we share, we must strategically and authentically address the sociocultural, sociolinguistic, and socioemotional tenets as well as understand the sociopolitical climate that has created these conditions for immigrant students and their families, and we must scale up the production of teachers with these skills. It is expected that the impact of the FDB teacher preparation curriculum and practicum activities will provide critical social justice–oriented and asset-based learning spaces for project participants to effectively work with both English and Spanish language learners. Additionally, we expect that because we are attacking this problem jointly (across borders), we will create a sustainable infrastructure. We conclude with what we consider *nuestro sueño* (our dream)—to create a strong and sustainable movement that prepares an abundance of bilingual-binational critically conscious teachers to teach in research-based public dual-language schools on both sides of the border. In this manner, when students traverse across borders their education will not be dramatically disrupted, and they will experience a sense of belonging in two worlds. With suitable conditions to reach their personal and academic dreams, we envision many more students sharing Paloma's dream: "I want to go to college, this is my dream."

Notes

1. This perception is based on focus group with secondary teachers on March 21, 2018, Tijuana, Baja, CA.

References

Agirdag, O. (2014). The literal cost of language assimilation for the children of immigrants. In R. Callahan and P. Gándara (Eds.), *The bilingual advantage: Language, literacy and the U.S. labor market* (p. 178). Bristol, UK: Multilingual Matters.

Alfaro, C. (2008a). Global student teaching stories of significant experiences: A cultural and inter-cultural experience of difference. *Multicultural Education, 15*(4), 20–26.

Alfaro, C. (2008b). Preparing bilingual teachers: Developing culture and linguistic global competence. *Revista Colombiana de Educación Bilingüe. The Colombian Journal of Bilingual Education, 2*, 68–84.

Alfaro, C. (2018). The sociopolitical struggle and promise of bilingual teacher education: Past, present, and future. *Bilingual Research Journal, 41*(4), 413–427.

Alfaro, C., & Bartolomé, L. I. (2016). Preparing ideologically clear bilingual teachers: Honoring working-class, non-standard language use in the bilingual education classroom. Special Edition: Bilingual teacher education. *Issues in Teacher Education, 26*(2), 11–34.

Alfaro, C. & Quezada, R. (2010). International teacher professional development: Teacher reflections of authentic teaching and learning experiences. Special Edition: Internationalization of teacher education. *Teaching Education, 21*(1), 47–59.

Block, D. (2002). Destabilized identities and cosmopolitanism across language and cultural borders: Two case studies. *Hong Kong Journal of Applied Linguistics, 7*(2), 1–19.

Brabeck, K. M., Lykes, B. M., & Hunter, C. (2014). The psychological impact of detention and deportation on U. S. migrant children and families. *American Journal of Orthopsychiatry, 84*(5), 496–505.

Bunch, G. C. (2006). "Academic English" in the 7th grade: Broadening the lens, expanding access. *Journal of English for Academic Purposes, 5*, 284–301.

Bunch, G. C. (2013). Pedagogical language knowledge: Preparing mainstream teachers for English learners in the new standards era. *Review of Research in Education, 37*(1), 298–341.

CAASPP (California Assessment of Student Assessment and Progress). (2018). Retrieved from https://caaspp.cde.ca.gov/sb2018/default

Calderón, David (2015). Public policy for learning English in Mexico. Chapter 3 in Mexicanos Primero, "Sorry. Learning English in Mexico" (pp. 57–78). Mexico City: Mexicanos Primero.

Callahan, R., & Gándara, P. (Eds). (2014). *The Bilingual advantage: Language, literacy and the U.S. labor market*. Bristol, UK: Multilingual Matters.

Ceballos, C. B. (2012). Literacies at the border: transnationalism and the biliteracy practices of teachers across the US–Mexico border. *International Journal of Bilingual Education and Bilingualism, 15*(6), 687–703.

Cline, Z., & Necochea, J. (2006). Teacher dispositions for effective education in the borderlands. *The Educational Forum, 70*, 268–282.

Coady, M. R., Harper, C., & de Jong, E. J. (2016). Aiming for equity: Preparing mainstream teachers for inclusion or inclusive classrooms? *TESOL Quarterly, 50*(2), 340–368.

Cushner, K., & Brislin, R. (1996). *Intercultural interactions: A practical guide*. Thousand Oaks, CA: Sage Publications.

Darder, A. (2012). *Culture and power in the classroom: Educational foundations for the schooling of bicultural students*. New York: Paradigm Publishers.

Dataquest (2017). California Department of Education data system. Retrieved from https://dq.cde.ca.gov/dataquest/dqcensus/CohRate.aspx?cds=00&agglevel=state&year=2016-17&ro=y

de Jong, E. J., & Harper, C. A. (2005). Preparing mainstream teachers for English-language learners: Is being a good teacher good enough? *Teacher Education Quarterly, 32*(2), 101–124.

de Jong, E. J., Harper, C. A., & Coady, M. R. (2013). Enhanced knowledge and skills for elementary mainstream teachers of English language learners. *Theory Into Practice, 52*(2), 89–97. doi.org/10.1080/00405841.2013.770326

de la Luz Reyes, M., & Garza, E. (2005). Teachers on the border: In their own words. *Journal of Latinos and Education, 4*(3), 153–170.

de la Piedra, M. T., & Araujo, B. (2012). Transfronterizo literacies and content in a dual language classroom. *International Journal of Bilingual Education and Bilingualism, 15*, 705–707.

Ee, J., & Gándara, P. (2019). The impact of immigration enforcement on the nation's schools. *American Educational Research Journal*. doi.org/10.3102/0002831219862998

Ee, J., & Gándara, P. (2020). Under siege: The disturbing impact of immigration enforcement on the nation's schools. Cambridge: Immigration Initiative at Harvard. Policy Brief 2. Vol. 1, No. 2.

Faltis, C., & Valdés, G. (2016). Preparing teachers for advocacy and for teaching in linguistically diverse classrooms: A vade mecum for teacher educators. In D. Gitomer & C. Bell (Eds.), *Handbook on teaching* (5th ed., pp. 549–592). Washington, DC: AERA.

Feldman, S., & Flores Malagon, V. (2017). Unlocking learning: Science as a lever for English learner equity. Oakland: EdTrust West. Retrieved from https://west.edtrust.org/resource/unlocking-learning-science-lever-english-learner-equity/

Flores, N., & Rosa, J. (2015). Undoing appropriateness: Raciolinguistic ideologies and language diversity in education. *Harvard Educational Review, 85*(2), 149–171.

Gándara, P. C., & Contreras, F. (2009). *The Latino education crisis: The consequences of failed social policies.* Cambridge, MA: Harvard University Press.

Gándara, P., Maxwell-Jolly, J., & Driscoll, A. (2005). Listening to teachers of English language learners: A survey of California teachers' challenges, experiences, and professional development needs (pp. 1–32). Santa Cruz, CA: The Center for the Future of Teaching and Learning.

Gibson, M., Gándara, P., & Koyama, J. (2004). *School connections: U.S. Mexican youth, peers, and school achievement.* New York: Teachers College Press.

Hamann, E. T. (2008). Advice, cautions, and opportunities for the teachers of binational teachers: Learning from teacher training experiences of Georgia and Nebraska teachers in Mexico. In J. González & K. Singh (Eds.), *Second binational symposium resource book.* Tempe, AZ: Southwest Center for Education Equity and Language Diversity, Mary Lou Fulton College of Education, Arizona State University.

Hernández, A. M. (2015). Language status in dual immersion: The dynamics between English and Spanish in peer interaction. *Journal of Immersion and Content-Based Language Education, 3*(1), 102–126.

Hopkins, M. (2013). Building on our teaching assets: The unique pedagogical contributions of bilingual educators. *Bilingual Research Journal, 36*, 350–370.

Jacobo, M., & Jensen, B. (2018). Schooling for US-citizen students in Mexico. Los Angeles: Civil Rights Project, UCLA. Retrieved from https://tinyurl.com/ybvd683p

Jensen, B., Mejía Arauz, R., & Aguilar Zepeda, R. (2017). Equitable teaching for returnee children in Mexico. *Sinéctica, 48.*

Jacobo-Suárez, M. (2017). De regreso a "casa" y sin apostilla: estudiantes mexicoamericanos en México. *Sinéctica, 48.*

Kasun, G. S., & Saavedra, C. M. (2016). Disrupting ell teacher candidates' identities: Indigenizing teacher education in one study abroad program. *TESOL Q, 50*(3), 684–707.

López, F., McEneaney, E., & Nieswandt, M. (2015). Language instruction educational programs and academic achievement of Latino English learners: Considerations for states with changing demographics. *American Journal of Education, 121,* 417–450.

Lucas, T., & Villegas, A. M. (2013). Preparing linguistically responsive teachers: Laying the foundation in preservice teacher education. *Theory into Practice, 52*(2), 98–109.

Lucas, T., Villegas, A. M., & Freedson-Gonzalez, M. (2008). Linguistically responsive teacher education: Preparing classroom teachers to teach English language learners. *Journal of Teacher Education, 59,* 361–373.

Menken, K., & Antunez, B. (2001). An overview of the preparation and certification of teachers working with limited English proficient (LEP) students (p. 79). Washington, DC: National Clearinghouse for Bilingual Education; ERIC Clearinghouse on Teaching and Teacher Education.

Mexicanos Primero (2015). Sorry. Learning English in Mexico. Mexico City: Mexicanos Primero. Retrieved from http://www.mexicanosprimero.org

Mordechay, K., & Alfaro, C. (2019). The binational context of the students we share: What do educators on both sides of the border need to know? *Kappa Delta Pi Record, 55*(1), 30–35. doi:10.1080/00228958.2019.1549438

OECD (2017). Mexico. Overview of the education system. Retrieved from http://gpseducation.oecd.org/CountryProfile?primaryCountry=MEX&treshold=10&topic=EO

Olmedo, I. (2004). Raising transnational issues in a multicultural curriculum project. *Urban Education, 39,* 241–265.

Osterman, K. F. (2000). Students' need for belonging in the school community. *Review of Educational Research, 70,* 323–367.

Piña, M. (2018). Director, Curriculum, Ministry of Education, Baja California. Personal communication, August 16, 2018.

Ramirez, M., Castaneda, A., & Herold, P. (1974). The relationship of acculturation to cognitive style among Mexican Americans. *Journal of Cross-Cultural Psychology, 5*(4), 424–433.

Reyes, K. (2017). Quedan 12 mil fuera de "prepa" pública en BC, Frontera. Info. Online, July 26. Retrieved from https://www.frontera.info/EdicionEnlinea/Notas/Noticias/26072017/1240285-Quedan-12-mil-fuera-de-prepa-publica-en-BC.html

Romo, J. J., & Chavez, C. (2006). Border pedagogy: A study of preservice teacher transformation. *The Educational Forum, 70*(2), 142–153.

Ruiz, N. T., Baird, P. J., & Hernandez, P. T. (2016). Field practice in la Mixteca: Transnational teacher education in the service of Mexican indigenous students in U.S. schools. *Journal of Latinos and Education, 15*(2), 97–112.

Sánchez García, J., Hamann, E. T., & Zuñiga, V. (2012). What the youngest transnational students have to say about their transition from U.S. schools to Mexican ones. *Diaspora, Indigenous, and Minority Education, 6*(3), 157–171.

Santamaría, L. J., Santamaría, C. C., & Fletcher, T. V. (2009). Journeys in cultural competency: Pre-service U.S. teachers in Mexico study-abroad programs. *Diaspora, Indigenous, and Minority Education, 3,* 32–51.

Santibañez, L., & Gándara, P. (2017). Teachers of English language learners in secondary schools: Gaps in preparation and support. Los Angeles: Civil Rights Project, UCLA.

Santibañez, L., & Snyder, C. (2018). Teaching English learners in California. Getting down to facts II. Stanford, CA: Stanford University and Policy Analysis for California Education (PACE). Retrieved from https://www.gettingdown tofacts.com/sites/default/files/2018-09/GDTFII_Report_Santibanez.pdf

Santos, M., Darling-Hammond, L., & Cheuk, T. (2012). *Teacher development to support English learners in the context of common core standards.* Understanding Language. Stanford University.

Sawyer, A. (2014). Professional development across borders: the promise of U.S.-Mexico binational teacher exchanges. *Teacher Education Quarterly, 41*(4), 3–27.

Serna-Gutierrez, J. I. O., & Mora-Pablo, I. (2018). Critical incidents of transnational student-teachers in Central Mexico. *Profile: Issues in Teacher Professional Development, 20*(1), 137–150.

Steele, J., Slater, R., Zamarro, G., et al. (2017). Effects of dual-language immersion programs on student achievement: Evidence from lottery data. *American Educational Research Journal, 54*, 289s–306s.

Suarez-Orozco, M. M. (2001). Globalization, immigration, and education: The research agenda. *Harvard Educational Review, 71*, 345–365.

Umansky, I., & Reardon. S. (2014). Reclassification patterns among Latino English Learner students in bilingual, dual immersion, and English immersion classrooms. *American Educational Research Journal, 51*, 871–912.

Valentino, R., & Reardon, S. (2015). Effectiveness of four instructional programs designed to serve English learners: Variation by ethnicity and initial English proficiency. *Educational Evaluation and Policy Analysis, 37*, 612–637.

Yosso, T. J. (2005). Whose culture has capital? A critical race theory discussion of community cultural wealth. *Race, Ethnicity, and Education, 8*, 69–91.

Zúñiga, V., & Vivas, M. (2014). *Divided families, fractured schooling, in Mexico: Educational consequences of children exposition to international migration.* Mexico City: Centro de Estudios Mexicano y Centroamericanos.

Chapter 3

Normalista Perspectives on Preparing Mexican Teachers for American Mexican Students

Eric Ruiz Bybee, Bryant Jensen, and Kevin Johnstun

The most dramatic shift in Mexican-U.S. immigration over the past decade has been the increase in return flows to Mexico. Triggered by the Great Recession, there have been more Mexican immigrants returning to than leaving Mexico since 2009. In a report by the Pew Research Center, González-Barrera (2015) reports that most return voluntarily, although current immigration policy has made life so difficult for many that "voluntary" may not be wholly accurate. For the children of returning migrants, however, who undergo the experience of moving to a country they do not necessarily know and attending school in a language they do not necessarily speak, the transition can be challenging (Jensen & Jacobo, 2019).

In this chapter, we address the preparation of teachers to meet the educational, cultural, and linguistic needs of American Mexican[1] students in Mexican schools. We focus, in particular, on the curriculum of *escuelas normales* (normal schools) and share findings from a recent study conducted in two normal schools in communities in Central Mexico with relatively high rates of return migration. We couch our analysis in the historical context of Mexican normal schools, which began after the Mexican Revolution as rural middle-school programs in 1925 and evolved into four-year college programs by 1984 (INEE, 2017). Examining the perspectives of normal school educators and students (both of whom we refer to as *normalistas*), we find that both the formal and "imagined" curricula on diversity in these preparation programs focus primarily on disabled and indigenous students, not necessarily the complexities faced by transnationals like American Mexicans.

Currently more than 3% of all PK-12 students in Mexico—more than 600,000 students in all—were born in the United States (Jensen, Mejía Arauz, & Aguilar Zepeda, 2017). These "returnees" tend to be clustered in particular receiving communities like Baja California (which has reported 53,000 of these students in their schools—see Chapter 2) as well as in Central Mexican communities like those highlighted in our study. American Mexican students report feeling that they do not belong at school in Mexico (Bybee et al., 2020) and that their experiences and associated knowledge and skills from the United States are "invisible" to elementary and secondary educators in Mexico (Zúñiga, Hamann, & Sánchez García, 2008). They report difficulties speaking and comprehending Spanish at school and express uncertainty about their futures, which likely will be transnational (Hamann, Zúñiga, & Sánchez García, 2010). Mexican educators, by and large, do not speak English and are unfamiliar with U.S. schools or curricula (Zúñiga, Hamann, & Sánchez García, 2008), leading to higher rates of grade retention for American Mexican students (Hamann, Zúñiga, & Sánchez García, 2010).

Following our analysis of normal school curricula in Central Mexico, we conclude with some recommendations for Mexican and U.S. educators alike. We address the need for stronger binational initiatives in pre-service teacher education programs to integrate the complex realities and to meet the pressing needs of transnational students. Our recommendations address research, policy, and practice in teacher education.

La Escuela Normal in Mexico: Current Context

Mexico's public normal schools are responsible for preparing the majority of preschool to ninth grade teachers and have historically played a central role in the national education system. A recent report by Mexico's *Instituto Nacional para la Evaluación de la Educación* (INEE, 2017) provides demographics and a comprehensive overview of *escuelas normales*. In 2015–16, Mexico's normal schools enrolled 108,555 pre-service teachers. As in the United States, most *normalista* students are female (72%). However, unlike in the United States, the gender ratio is equal on some normal school campuses, and many rural campuses are single-sex boarding institutions.

Like other countries, Mexico currently faces a teacher shortage. Applications to *escuelas normales* fell from 88,994 in 2000 to 49,859 in 2015. Typically, normal schools accept about 50% of applicants, but acceptance rates are rising because of declining applications. This has impacted some disciplines more than others. *Escuelas normales*, for example, have particular difficulty meeting demand for STEM and arts teachers, especially in rural and indigenous communities (Arnaut, 2004).

Because they control the *planes de estudio* (curriculum mandates) for all normal schools, the federal government substantially influences the ways teachers are prepared. Federal reforms since 1996 have emphasized the need to transition *escuelas normales* from acting solely as teacher preparation institutions to research institutions of higher education. In response, Mexico's normal schools have developed 33 undergraduate majors. In addition to early and elementary education, *escuelas normales* offer teaching degrees in physics, chemistry, mathematics, special education, bilingual education, physical education, and others. *Normalista* faculty in this new orientation are encouraged to forge partnerships (called *cuerpos académicos*) with research colleagues from other institutions of higher education. These *cuerpos* are intended to increase research activity to improve education practices in Mexico. Some *normalista* faculty have entered into *cuerpo* partnerships with scholars in other countries, such as the United States.

La Escuela Normal in Mexico: Historical Context

Throughout Mexico's history, *escuelas normales* have had an institutional mandate to prepare teachers to meet the demands of educating all of Mexico's children, especially the working class. Over the years, this mission transitioned from preparing for agrarian, rural teaching to research and teacher preparation in urban schools and across Mexico (INEE, 2017).

Whereas normal schools began to grow rapidly in the post-revolution era after the 1920s, Watty (2004) traces their origins further to Scottish Freemason academies (*La compañia Lancasteriana*) that were set up to prepare Mexican teachers in 1822. During this time, the Mexican government moved away from relying on Catholic missions to organize the education of its citizens. Support of public education progressed under the liberal ideologies of dictator Porfirio Díaz, who seized power in 1876 and ruled Mexico with a group of allied technocrats knows as *los científicos*. During this 35-year period (known as the "Porfiriato"), *escuelas normales* became a system that allowed educators to be break ties with "colonial thought and establish a set of values like unity, piece, pragmatism, and secularity" (Watty, 2004, p. 39).

Once Mexico's normal schools were more formally established after the Revolution in 1925, they functioned as middle-school programs to enhance elementary school access for rural communities. By 1978, normal schools functioned nationwide as high school (*preparatoria*) programs, and in 1984 a significant federal reform made *escuelas normales* institutions of higher education with four-year bachelor degree programs (*licenciatura*) (INEE, 2017). In this progression from middle schools to prepare teachers to work in rural, agrarian communities to institutions of higher education, *escuelas normales* have had to navigate shifting academic and social goals (Figueroa Millán, 2000). The essential tension has been between activism (i.e., preparing large numbers of educators to expand school access to underserved communities) and quality (i.e., identifying and maintaining teacher preparation standards). With roots in the Mexican revolution during the 1910s, normal schools grew alongside collectivist values in Mexican society, which continue to orient *normalista* education. The belief in a free education for all continues to anchor the approach of Mexican normal schools (Navarrete-Cazales, 2015).

A *normalista* education socializes educators to be activists—to take on leadership roles in the school and community. Stories of *normalistas* who led revolutions in rural communities form part of their societal image. For example, Díaz González (2017) documents collective action taken by *normalistas* in 1976 to overtake the municipal government that ruled in an indigenous community. Santos (2017) describes the actions by a group of educators during the student revolts of 1968. More recently, *normalista* activism in 2014 formed the basis for the disappearance of 43 students from the all-male *Escuela Normal Rural de Ayotzinapa*—a crime that drew international condemnation and cries for the return of *los 43 desaparecidos* (Villegas, 2018). After commandeering several buses to travel to Mexico City to commemorate the 1968 massacre at Tlateloco, these *normalista* students were kidnapped and presumed murdered by corrupt public officials working with organized crime outside Iguala, Guerrero.

Notwithstanding the strong social values and traditions of Mexico's normal schools, some scholars argue that *escuelas normales* have come to rely too much on foreign models of teacher preparation that emphasize empirical research and dismiss local community knowledge (Marín & Delgado, 2001). These arguments and the tensions between evidence-based practice and local customs and tradition have existed for decades (Figueroa Millán, 2000) and continue to evolve.

Recent Curricular Reforms and Approach to Diversity

Over the years, the Federal Education Ministry (*Secretaría de Educación Pública* [SEP]) has launched several policy and curricular reforms concerning *escuelas normales* that have often been met with local resistance. In 2012, for example, the *Plan de Estudio* changed guidelines for capstone projects from the 1997 law. It revised the capstone requirement from an assignment that had students write about a problem in teaching, in terms of theory and practice, to a choice among three options: (1) a portfolio and associated defense, (2) a practice report of an instructional intervention and an associated defense, or (3) a research project and associated defense. Though these capstone options were designed to be more rigorous to advance scholarly research in *normales*, many continue to follow the 1997 capstone guidelines (INEE, 2017).

The 2012 changes also introduced new courses designed to improve pre-service teachers' ability to work with culturally diverse students. These courses included *Adecuación Curricular* (Curricular Adaptation) in the third semester, *Atención a la Diversidad* (Addressing Diversity) in the fifth semester, and *Atención Educativa para la Inclusión* (Addressing Educational Inclusion) in the seventh semester. These changes have been the subject of some critique. Delgado and Reyes (2018), for example, assert that diversity curricula were written for a mainstream educator audience, positioning non-majority students as problems to fix. Curricular materials do not distinguish between students who are marginalized because of disabilities versus life circumstances or institutional inequity. This engenders a deficit framing of marginalized students in the minds of many *normalistas* and leaves them without a plan of action for engaging the abilities and relative assets of children from marginalized communities. Moreover, we discuss in the sections that follow how these three courses fail to address the educational needs of other diverse student groups in Mexico, particularly American Mexicans and other transnationals.

In 2018, a new curricular map, including revisions to standards and courses, was released by the SEP. For example, pre-service teachers in elementary education programs now take the *Educación Socioemocional* (Socioemotional Education) course in the place of *Adecuación Curricular* (Curricular Adaptation) during their third semester. During the fourth semester, *normalista* students take *Atención a la Diversidad* (Addressing Diversity), and during the fifth semester they now take *Educación Inclusiva* (Inclusive Education). Some course changes have been published on the SEP website (https://www.dgespe.sep.gob.mx), though at the time of data collection for this chapter, none of the 2018 diversity or inclusion courses were published online.

Approach to Data

We collaborated with two *cuerpos académicos* to gather information for our study in two different *escuelas normales*. Both were in Central Mexico, about a 90-minute drive between them. The first, which we call *Cívica* (pseudonym), was an urban normal school in the state's second-largest city. Historic migration levels, including recent rates of return migration, were moderate in this community compared to the national average. The school enrolled approximately 400 students, young men and women studying one of three licensure programs: preschool teaching, special education teaching, and elementary and middle-school teaching (*educación básica*). The student body at *Cívica*, like at most *normales*, was politically active. Student activists showed us their headquarters on campus, and classes were canceled for political protest more than once while we interviewed *Cívica* faculty and students. In interviews, students also told us about the traffic stops they organized to advocate for educational and other policy reforms.

The second normal school, *Amistad* (pseudonym), was a rural boarding campus. It enrolled women only, who came from all over the country, largely from rural communities themselves. Referred to as *internadas* (interns), *Amistad* students grew their own food and rotated responsibilities to maintain campus facilities. *Educación básica* was the only licensure program available at *Amistad*. Many of the students and some of the faculty at *Amistad* had personal experiences with U.S. migration. Elementary and middle schools served by *Amistad* were in rural communities that had strong historic levels of migration to and from the United States. Mexican Census data from 2015 show that 5% to 8% of children in communities served by *Amistad* were born in the United States, significantly higher than the national average (Jensen, Mejía Arauz, & Zepeda,

2017). In addition to the political activism and shared management of facilities, the collectivist orientation at *Cívica* and *Amistad* was evident in several large murals of heroes of the Mexican Revolution, leftist icons like Che Guevera, and *los 43 desparecidos* from *Ayotzinapa* (see Figure 3.1). Indeed, the participants from all-female *Amistad* indicated that they were part of the same national network of 17 rural normal schools as the all-male Ayotizapa and that students from these campuses would travel regularly to gather for social events like dances.

Data collection with *normalistas*—i.e., students and teacher educators at *Amistad* and *Cívica*—was conducted within a broader study analyzing the transition of American Mexican children and youth to schooling and life in rural Mexico (Bybee et al., 2020). We held regular meetings with *Cívica* and *Amistad* faculty for more than a year to coordinate our visit and spent six weeks full-time as a team of seven researchers (two university faculty and five students) gathering data at both campuses. In exchange for discussing teacher education curricula with *normalistas*, five bilingual university students from the United States provided weekly, on-campus English classes for *Cívica* students. We conducted individual and group interviews with 22 *normalista* administrators, faculty, and students about the ways the federal curriculum prepared pre-service teachers to meet the needs of children from migrant families in general and those with U.S. experiences more specifically. This group included three individuals

Figure 3.1. Mural at *Amistad*.

Table 3.1. Research Participants at *Amistad* and *Cívica*

Cívica		*Amistad*	
Name	**Role**	**Name**	**Role**
Maria*	*Normalista* Educator, Special Education	Lucia	*Normalista* Administrator/Educator
Lucia	*Normalista* Administrator/Educator	Elena	*Normalista* Educator
Rogelio	*Normalista* Educator, Special Education	Victor**	*Normalista* Educator, English
Alejandra	*Normalista* Administrator/Educator	Mariela	*Normalista* Educator, Special Education
Aurelio	*Normalista* Educator	Claudio	*Normalista* Educator, History
Natalia	*Normalista* Educator, Early Childhood	Antonio	*Normalista* Educator
Carlos	*Normalista* Student	Rosana	*Normalista* Educator
Selena	*Normalista* Student	Cristina**	*Normalista* Student
Cristofer	*Normalista* Student	Dolores**	*Normalista* Student
Rosario	*Normalista* Student	Sara	*Normalista* Student
Noemi	*Normalista* Student	Gabriela	*Normalista* Student

*All names are pseudonyms.
**Normalistas* with U.S. Schooling Experience.

(Victor, Cristina, and Dolores) who had lived and attended school in the United States.

We met with *normalistas* to identify which of their courses (still using the 2012 curriculum) addressed the needs of diverse students like migrants, and they identified three courses: 1) *Adecuación Curricular* (Curricular Adaptations), 2) *Atención a la Diversidad* (Addressing Diversity), and 3) *Atención Educativa para la Inclusión* (Addressing Educational Inclusion). In addition to interviews, we analyzed these courses by coding official curricular materials, writing analytic memos, and using tools from linguistic software to identify themes and trends. This analysis, alongside conceptions of diversity and inclusion articulated by *normlistas*, provides insight into how Mexican teachers are prepared to meet the needs of diverse students in general and American Mexicans in particular.

The curriculum map for Mexican normal schools details seven semesters of coursework with the final eighth semester reserved for a certification course and student teaching. Our initial analysis of the curricula revealed that none of the materials for the three diversity courses made specific reference to migration or transnationalism (see Table 3.2 below). Thus, in addition to examining diversity and inclusion in the formal curricular materials, we used interview data to understand how *normalista* administrators, faculty, and students "imagine"—or make informal sense of (Ginsberg & Clift, 1990)—migration and transnationalism.

Findings

To examine the frequency of terms used in the three *normalista* courses that address diversity and inclusion, we inputted the complete text of curricular materials into a linguistic analysis software. Table 3.2 provides key terms that were relevant to our analysis. Perhaps the most important insight concerns terms *not* included on this list—any reference to migration or

Table 3.2. Key Term Frequency across Three Curricula (Emphasis Added)

Rank	Frequency	Word	Rank	Frequency	Word
13	228	*educación*	41	66	*actividades*
16	164	*aprendizaje*	42	66	*situaciones*
19	**119**	**diversidad**	44	60	*docente*
24	94	*alumnos*	45	59	*barreras*
27	**87**	**inclusión**	46	59	*estrategias*
28	85	*situación*	47	58	*social*
29	83	*estudiantes*	**48**	**57**	**curricular**
30	81	*escuela*	50	56	*curso*
31	**80**	**discriminación**	52	55	*didácticas*
33	77	*unidad*	**55**	**52**	**género**
34	76	*caso*	56	50	*diferentes*
38	70	*educativa*	**58**	**48**	**discapacidad**
39	69	*atención*	**59**	**48**	**inclusiva**
40	67	*didáctica*	**145**	**23**	**indígenas**

transnational students. We analyzed notions like *diversidad* (diversity) and *inclusión* (inclusion) vis-à-vis the three diversity courses. *Discriminación* (discrimination) and *barreras* (barriers) were frequently mentioned, and the table also provides insight into social groups that are identified to experience discrimination and barriers—social differences related to 1) *género* (gender), 2) *discapacidad* (disability), and 3) *indigenismo* (indigeneity).

Interestingly, though gender was the social category referenced frequently in course materials, it did not surface much in our interviews with *normalista* students and faculty. By contrast, disability and indigeneity figured most prominently in the minds of our participants. In the next sections, we present an overview of both the formal curricula of each class, followed by the "imagined" curricula that emerged in interviews with our participants.

Adecuación Curricular

Formal curriculum. This course is where *normalistas* learn about adapting (or accommodating) curriculum and instruction to meet the learning needs of individual students, especially their cognitive processing needs. Course content introduces and describes the purposes of teacher-designed lesson plans and integrating diverse perspectives, strategies, and past experiences of students into these plans. Teachers are expected to incorporate students' cultural, social, and linguistic needs into class activities and interactions. Key elements of the course are group projects and presentations, technology use, group collaboration, teacher observation, joint analysis, and teacher responsibility to reproduce content through integrative means that are sensitive to students' cultural expression and how they perceive the value of learning.

The curriculum repeatedly references *La Reforma Integral de la Educación Básica* to establish its support of teaching practices to create more meaning with diverse students in the classroom (Ronzón, Treviño, & Vadillo, 2014). Teachers are instructed to consider students' academic and social proficiencies while developing lesson plans, and to accommodate plans as needed. Again, there was no mention of immigrant populations in materials for this course.

Though materials identify a range of potential student needs that should be considered and accommodated, they focus more on lesson preparation and curricular planning than on examples of specific student needs. They focus on creating effective learning environments, assessing students, communication with students, observation of peer teachers, and technology use to provide clear and relevant teaching. The course frames these features of planning and teaching in terms of current credentialing requirements to meet the needs of diverse students.

"**Imagined" approaches to curricular adaptation.** The notion of curricular accommodation came up multiple times in interviews with *normalista* administrators, educators, and students. When asked how *normalista* education addressed American Mexican students, some mentioned a formal obligation they had to adapt curricula to meet the needs of all students. For example, Carlos, a *normalista* studying special education at *Cívica* shared:

> *Yo lo que vi en algún momento de alguna materia, no me recuerdo, me imagino que habría sido en propósitos y contenido de la educación básica en la primaria . . . eh . . . que una obligación que tenía el maestro de educación básica regular que nosotros teníamos que aprender ese currículo, o ese programa, era que nosotros teníamos que adaptar a ellos . . . a su contexto . . . a su idioma, a su religión, necesidades, [. . .] es algo que nosotros tenemos como obligación a hacer, de que sí yo estoy viendo que un alumno obviamente no tiene el mismo lenguaje que yo tengo, tengo que hacer adecuaciones, más yo como educador especial, en la educación especial se hacen adecuaciones . . . entonces esas adecuaciones son las que van a ayudar a ese niño . . .*

> [What I saw [about American Mexican students] in one particular moment in a subject, I don't remember which, I imagine that it would have been in purposes and content of basic elementary education . . . eh . . . was an obligation that the regular basic elementary teacher had that we had to learn that curriculum, or that program; it was that we had to adapt to them . . . to their context, to their language, to their religion, their needs, [. . .] it's something that we are obligated to do, if I see a student who obviously doesn't speak the same language that I do, I need to make adjustments, yet me, as a special educator, in special education, many adjustments are made . . . and so these adjustments are those that are going to help this student . . .] (Carlos Interview, 5/17/17)

Carlos searches to identify how his preservice experiences prepared him to address the needs of American Mexican students, saying things like "one particular moment in subject . . . I don't remember which." In searching for the connection, he ultimately settles on the notion of *adecuaciones* that he could make for students who are part of a linguistic or religious minority, or the population that he works with as a special educator. Though reflecting on his preparation to meet the needs of various populations is commendable, the lack of specificity about the actual needs of transnational students is concerning.

The same limitation was demonstrated in a conversation with Maestra Elena, a *normalista* literacy educator from *Amistad*. When asked about the needs of American Mexicans, she shared about the practicum work of the *normalista* students she supervised:

> *las alumnas se integran al inicio del año escolar, y están observando, escuchan los problemas,* **ven como se detectan, se diagnostican,** *se hace un proyecto de mejora, y entonces ellos le dicen de ruta, este . . . de ruta escolar,* **entonces ellos hacen un proyecto en donde atienden las necesidades** *que son apremiantes, entonces eso las estudiantes participan ahí, también* **se incorporan ahora sí que a las actividades docentes,** *y participan y* **le dan seguimiento** *a todos los casos, no? Por ejemplo, le decía* **lo de la lectoescritura.** *Por ejemplo ahí, hacen* **estrategias de dictado** *de lectura diaria al inicio de la sesión de trabajo, van haciendo que los niños lean, que les guste la lectura, y ellas participan en esas estrategias que propone la escuela, no? Pero sí, ahí donde yo vería, es que las mismas escuelas primarias,* **ellos sí les podrían ayudar con este seguimiento de casos ya detectados** *[. . .] cuáles son las estrategias que han utilizado para adaptar o incluir a los niños a la escuela, no?*

> [**The [normalista] students are integrated at the beginning of the academic school year**, and they are observing, **they listen to the problems, see how they [American Mexican students] stand out**, how they are **diagnosed**, they plan an **improvement project**, and then they tell them from a **scholarly standpoint,** and so they do a project where they attend to pressing needs, and so the students participate there, as well as incorporate themselves in these **teacher activities**, and participate and they give follow up on all the cases, no? For example, I was

telling you about **literacy**. In that case for example, they come up with **teaching strategies for daily reading dictation** at the beginning of the work session, and have their students read, that they like the **reading assignment,** and the **students participate in these strategies** that the school suggests, right? [. . .] **which strategies that they have used to adapt or include the school's children,** no?] (Elena Interview, 5/23/17—emphasis added)

Like Carlos, Maestra Elena's comment frames the needs of American Mexican students abstractly, with academic needs that would be met through existing classroom tools and accommodations. Their idea is that these students will simply "stand out" when administering common assessments, after which teachers would formulate a plan to address their needs. Whereas Maestra Elena's assumptions are understandable, they do not reflect the experiences of American Mexican students, many of whom report feeling "invisible" to their elementary and secondary teachers (Zúñiga, Hamann, & Sánchez García, 2008). Like Carlos, Elena draws from her content area expertise (literacy) to imagine *adecuaciones* and strategies that American Mexican students will need with regard to daily reading and literacy activities. Though some evidence suggests that American Mexican students struggle with *el dictado* (see Chapter 5), this intervention is based on assumptions about the visibility of students and their needs for intervention.

Atención a la Diversidad

Formal curriculum. In this course, *normalistas* discuss issues of cultural difference, analogous to courses like "multicultural education" in the United States. With four units and a total of 53 pages, *Atención a la Diversidad* was the most extensive of the course curricula that we analyzed (*Adecuación Curricular* is 23 pages, and *Atención Educativa para la Inclusion* is 16 pages). The first unit addresses the term "different" and how schools either accept or reject "different" kinds of students. It analyzes the accessibility and function of school support services for minority students. The second stimulates introspection about the teacher responses to discrimination and encourages them to combine personal experience with case study examples in order to understand how discrimination affects day-to-day life. Institutionalization, invisibility, and naturalization were three "mechanisms" of discrimination identified in this unit. The third unit requires that teachers design intercultural teaching methods that purposefully communicate appreciation for cultural diversity. It encourages teachers to capitalize on learning opportunities and activities that strengthen the "coexistence of multiple cultures in the scholastic community" (p. 40). This unit also establishes a scale of reaction to diversity that moves from outright discrimination to tolerance, respect, valorization, and, finally, appreciation. Teachers are required to identify these reactions and be aware that others in and outside school may react to diversity or intellectual disability in any of the above ways. The fourth unit has teachers develop their own methods for fostering inclusive learning in classrooms. Each unit builds on the previous one to create paradigm-shifting experiences about discrimination, using written examples to illustrate real-time situations where intercultural teaching should occur.

Course materials suggest that classrooms are critical settings to understand social inequality. They assert that the meaning students make and the values they espouse are established through social and cultural factors—through their daily experiences in and out of school. *Normalista* students are expected to develop teaching habits that transcend social discrimination that may be commonplace at school. They are instructed to consider how global forces influence students' personal lives, which could include factors like international family migration. In one unit, a simulation of a shipwrecked cultural group obtaining new linguistic meanings meets the rest of the class, which was unaware of such changes. The role-play is a hands-on teaching activity about how discrimination functions and the social roles of different types of individuals, "rejectors," "overprotectors," or supporters.

Pages 12 to 55 of the curriculum provide cases of children experiencing various injustices at school related to gender, race, language, or disability. *Normalista* students are expected to develop classroom activities and teaching strategies to overcome this discrimination. In these examples, distinctions are made between responding to students with disabilities and responding to students experiencing racial, ethnic, or gender discrimination. Examples of racial diversity are limited to indigenous students, typified in a lesson on *El caso de Juan, el niño triqui* [The case of Juan, the Trique child]. In these lessons, *normalista* students are directed to a website where they learn about Juan and his family's language and customs as part of the Trique indigenous people in Oaxaca (see Figure 3.2 below). While case studies open up general discussion of different linguistic and cultural identities, once again, transnational children like American Mexicans are not mentioned.

Figure 3.2. Website Screenshot, "El Caso de Juan, el Niño Triqui."

"Imagined" approaches to diversity. When asked about how *normalistas* were prepared to address issues of *diversidad* in their classrooms or about their own conceptions of diversity, *normalista* educators and students often made connections to factors like disability and especially to indigeneity. For example, when asked, "*. . . como se relaciona la diversidad a la educación?*" [". . . how is diversity related to education?"], Carlos, a *Cívica* student, shared that Mexican educators were more likely to focus on disability than on other factors:

> *Yo digo que la gente . . .* **se va más por la discapacidad,** *no? La inclusión . . . pero no toma en cuenta eso . . .* **la etnia y todo** *. . . Como que la gente no se imagina que también es eso una inclusión, sino que lo rechaza al contrario porque piensa que no pertenece a eso, o sea no lo ve desde ese punto de vista . . . y como lo dice usted . . .* **hay personas que vienen de . . . no sé . . . de otros países,** *y no saben cómo darle una clase a ese niño y solamente lo tienen, no sé . . . Dibujos o algo así . . . por que? Porque* **no hay tanta gente este . . . capacitada no se . . . para hablar nahuatl, inglés, y todo eso** *. . .*

> [I think people **generally lean toward disability**, no? Inclusion . . . but it **doesn't take that into account . . . ethnicity and all** . . . Like people don't imagine that there is a need for inclusion in that regard as well, but rather they reject that because they think that it doesn't have to do with disability, or rather they don't see it in that way . . . and like you said . . . **there are people who come from** . . . I don't know . . . from **other countries**, and [teachers] **don't know how to teach a class to that kind of child** and they only have him, I don't know . . . do drawings or something like that . . . why? Because **there's not enough people** like him . . . **capable of, I don't know . . . of speaking Nahuatl, English,** and all that . . .] (Carlos Interview, 5/17/17—emphasis added)

Here, Carlos is referencing the prevalence of discourse on disability, even when students speak other languages like Nahuatl or English. Although his inclusion of English can be interpreted as perhaps an implicit reference to American Mexican students who struggle to learn Spanish (Hamann, Zúñiga, & Sánchez García, 2010), Carlos does not explicitly reference this population.

Other normal school students and educators made more reference to indigenous students and the contextual and linguistic challenges they face. Selena, also a student at *Cívica*, shared the following to characterize the role of diversity in her future practice as a teacher:

> *Bueno, yo creo que este una vez entrando en la primaria tenemos que ver en qué contexto nos encontramos, no? Por ejemplo, **si la comunidad tiene una lengua que habla nahuatl u otra lengua**, pues este . . . tenemos que quizás investigar entre, con nosotras, buscar una manera de comunicarnos con los niños porque a veces llegamos a comunidades que hablan otro dialecto y nosotros no.*

> [Well, I believe that once you enter to the elementary school, we have to see the contexts in which we are, right? For example, **if the community has a Nahuatl language or another language**, well . . . maybe we have to find out among ourselves, look for a way to communicate with the children because sometimes we go to communities that **speak with other dialects** and we don't.] (Selena Interview, 5/17/17—emphasis added)

Selena's comment reflects an awareness of Mexico's linguistic diversity (including 68 officially recognized indigenous languages) and how these languages vary by community, and the importance of teacher sensitivity to these issues. In like manner, Víctor, a *normalista* English educator at *Amistad*, provides a definition of diversity that explicitly references Mexicans who speak (indigenous) languages other than Spanish.

> *A la diversidad, yo me refiero a alumnas que vienen de contextos diferentes, bueno aquí . . . es una zona rural . . . y las alumnas vienen de lugares muy remotos . . . de Oaxaca, del estado México, de Guerrero . . . donde . . . hay veces que hasta hablan muy poco español . . .*
>
> [Diversity . . . I am referring to the students that come from different contexts. Well . . . this is a rural zone, and the students come from remote places . . . from Oaxaca, the state of México, from Guerrero . . . where sometimes Spanish is spoken very little]—(Victor, 5/30/17)

Víctor's failure to acknowledge diversity or discrimination in terms of transnationalism in our interview was surprising given that he, though born in Mexico, had U.S. schooling experiences himself, and the language skills he acquired while attending middle and high school in Texas formed the basis for his career as an English teacher educator. Víctor's personal experiences as a transnational did not translate to considering the diverse needs or discrimination of students with migrant pasts. Indeed, comments by Carlos, Selena, and Víctor all signal their imagined discursive connections between the notion of "diversity," disability, and especially indigenous students. This focus is likely a reflection of the focus of the *Atención a la Diversidad* curriculum.

Atención Inclusiva para la Educación

Formal curriculum. This course is comparable to "Inclusive Education" courses in the United States and represents attempt to calibrate *escuelas normales* with Mexico's movement toward all-inclusive education. It addresses interregional and international legal foundations to guide the development of practices and attitudes in schools to meet the needs of all students. It is designed to prepare teachers in their final semester of coursework to integrate content from previous courses. Recurring words in course materials include "barriers" and "obstacles" to learning. The course overview articulates current or recent education policies, programs, and movements that seek to change school norms about students with disabilities, indigenous minorities, social models of learning, and other aspects regarding the inclusion of diverse students. Acronyms used throughout course materials are NEE (*necesidades educativas especiales* (special education needs]) and BAP (*barreras para la aprendizaje y la participación* [barriers to learning and participation]).

The course prepares teachers to identify forms of student diversity and disability in their future classrooms—to eliminate or minimize BAPs by creating meaningful experiences that incorporate the knowledge of students from marginalized communities. A common phrase used in course materials, *educación para todos* (education for everyone), can be interpreted to include transnational students, but we did not find any reference to migrants in course curriculum. We did, however, find a focus on gender—e.g., *los que sufren inequidad de género* (those who suffer gender inequities).

The course provides a historical overview of how changes in policies for educational inclusion have developed in Mexico, especially during the early 1990s with the *Acuerdo Nacional para la Modernización de la Educación Básica* (1992) and the *Reforma Integral para la Educación Básica* (1993). The three contexts identified as sources of student diversity are schools, classrooms, and families. Each one, the course posits, affects children's development and should direct how curriculum, lesson plans, and instructional activities are designed. Navigating current policies about inclusion, the course instructs, should help educators enhance learning and development for diverse and disabled students.

Learning unit diagrams on pages 9 to 16 of the *Atención Inclusiva para la Educación* curriculum guide *normalista* students to collaborate to analyze scenarios and to make decisions about inclusion. They use these diagrams to identify NEEs and BAPs in teaching scenarios that they read about and to gather qualitative observations to determine the extent to which their own and others' teaching practices are inclusive. Each *normalista* student is evaluated for how well s/he 1) understands the evolution of inclusion in educational policy and practice, and 2) applies inclusive practices in her/his own teaching.

Imagined approaches to inclusion. In our interviews, *normalista* educators and students framed notions of inclusion primarily in terms of processes to integrate special education students. Maestra Elena typified this view:

> *Cuando hablamos de la asignatura de **inclusión educativa**, estamos hablando de que **se detectan las necesidades educativas especiales concretamente**, de que se detectan aquellos niños que presentan alguna discapacidad y entonces ese tipo de alumnos que requieren de un apoyo, de parte del docente, este. . . . Pues se **diagnostican** al principio, se hace un **diagnóstico** de esa necesidad de la que refieren alumnos, posteriormente las alumnas una vez que ya diagnosticaron ellas hacen una **adecuación curricular**, en torno a **los contenidos que se trabajan** dentro de lo que sería el plan de estudios [. . .] pero en sí, los niños que tienen problemas de . . . o sea . . . **que son inmigrantes, o que algunos que regresa verdad, regresan del extranjero** para incluirse a sus lugares de origen, no tenemos esa información tal cual porque no hemos tenido todavía, eh . . . no nos han informado. Lo que nosotros sí **tenemos es problemas de** este . . . escritura, problemas de **desintegración familiar, problemas de hiperactividad, problemas de síndrome de Down***

[When we talk about the subject of **inclusive education**, we are talking **about detecting the special education needs particularly** . . . **detecting those children that present some disability and then this type of students that require help from the teache**r . . . These kids are identified at the beginning, you make a **diagnosis** of the needs of the children. Then, the students, once they made a diagnosis, they do **curricular adaptations** on regards of the topics that are worked in the curriculum [. . .] **However, children that** have problems of . . . I mean **that are immigrants, or that some return**, right? They **return from the US** to their places of origin . . . **We don't have that information** because we haven't had yet . . . We haven't been informed . . . **What we do have is problems of writing, family disintegration problems, hyperactivity problems, Down syndrome problem**s . . .] (Elena Interview, 5/23/17—emphasis added)

With her comment, Maestra Elena frames the notion of inclusive education in relation to the process of identifying special education students. She speaks of the process of "detecting" and making a "diagnosis" of students with disabilities to make curricular accommodations. These connections are understandable given the provenance of inclusion in disability rights and special education contexts, even as some scholars have used the term in more expanded ways to mean addressing "the specific needs of every child of school age regardless of gender, race, ethnicity, language, culture, economic status, or disability" (McLaughlin, 2006, p. 928). Because of our prompting in the interview, Maestra Elena briefly considers American Mexican students, though she says that she does not "have information" about them. Instead, she reframes the inclusion concern in terms of "problems of writing, family disintegration problems, hyperactivity problems, Down syndrome problems." Inclusion, for her, is about disability.

Another example of this emerged in our interview with Dolores, an American Mexican *normalista* student from *Amistad*:

> *Incluir a todos nuestros alumnos por ejemplo también sabemos que no nada más cabe la posibilidad de que existan niños este . . . que lleguen de Estados Unidos, sino también que exista algún niño con discapacidad, entonces la integración se refiere a que trabajemos de la misma manera con los niños, o no de la misma manera, pero sí que los niños con alguna discapacidad o los niños migrantes lleguen y se integren al grupo . . .*
>
> [To include all our students, for example, we also know that we don't just have the possibility of students who . . . who arrive from the United States, but also those children with disabilities, and so integration suggests that we work in the same way with the children, or not in the same way, but making sure that the kids with any kind of disability or migrant children come and are integrated into the group]. (Dolores Interview, 6/1/17)

In speaking of including all students, Dolores draws a connection between "students who arrive from the United States" and "children with disabilities." Later in her comment, she reiterates this connection by stating that "kids with any kind of disability or migrant children" must be "integrated into the group," even though the needs of the two groups are vastly different.

Cristina was another American Mexican *normalista* student who described a much more difficult transition to Mexican schools than Dolores because of her limited Spanish. Cristina referred to this in describing her own conceptions of inclusion:

> *Cuando hablan de inclusión, por decir, en la materia de inclusión, salía el maestro, ¿no? Pregunta abierta: "Que creen ustedes que es inclusión?" o "Cual sería una buena forma de incluir a los niños?" y ahí voy yo como siempre . . . "no pues, no solo se trata de los niños con discapacidad, sino de también otros niños que tienen decadencias en ciertas materias. No porque necesariamente se fueron y regresaron, sino que simplemente son . . . mmm . . . cosas que van de un maestro a otro que no lo abarca así que el niño llega con decadencias al siguiente maestro. Y hay muchas otras veces que . . . mmm . . . me mencionan . . .—"no pues, como incluirían a Cristina dentro de su salón de clase, si ha ido a Estados Unidos, y no sabe nada."*

[When they speak of inclusion, for example. The teacher was brought up in the subject of inclusion, no? Open question: "What do you all think inclusion is?" or "What would be an effective way to include all the children?" and there I go, like always, "No, it's not just about addressing children with disabilities, but also other children who have challenges in certain subjects. Not necessarily because they left and came back [from the United States], but simply because . . . mmm . . . things that go from one teacher to another that the student hasn't covered means that he arrives with challenges in that area when he gets to the next teacher. And there are many times when . . . they mention to me . . ."—"No well, like how they would include Cristina in the classroom, if she has gone to the United States, and doesn't know anything."] (Cristina Interview, 5/23/17)

Like Maestra Elena and Dolores, Cristina references the implicit association between children with disabilities and transnational students. Specifically, in responses to questions about inclusion in her *normal* classes, she states that inclusion is "not just about addressing children with disabilities, but also other children who have challenges," including those who "left and came back [from the United States]." Her comment seems to reflect frustration at the dominant idea that inclusion solely applied to students with disabilities when students like her also struggle to feel included at school. Although her speaking up opens up space for her teachers and classmates to discuss "how they would include [a student like] Cristina in the classroom, if she has gone to the United States," the description that such a student "doesn't know anything" reflects a lack of understanding the educational assets and experiences of American Mexican students. In the absence of focused content about the schooling and inclusion of transnational students, teacher educators like Elena and students like Dolores and Cristina were left to make sense on their own of the needs of migrants, which most had not considered in any systematic way. Though Dolores and Cristina's personal experiences gave them tools to broaden the conversation to include American Mexican students like themselves, their statements reflect the same conflating of migrant experiences with disability that we encountered with other participants.

Discussion and Conclusion

We found little evidence in our analysis that *normalista* education addresses the needs of American Mexican students whom educators will likely teach. In materials for the three courses designed to address student diversity and inclusion, there is no specific mention of migration, transnationalism, or the children and youth whose lives are affected on a daily basis by these phenomena. This is alarming given that among all 9 million "students we share" between the United States and Mexico, American Mexicans in Mexico are the fastest growing, currently estimated at more than 600,000 from preschool to high school, more than 3% of the total student population in Mexico.

Thus, though *escuelas normales* in Mexico have evolved over time to become more responsive to the needs of all students, current curricula reveal significant gaps in meeting the needs of transnational students. In interviews, prospective teachers and teacher educators associated migration experiences with disability in the types of accommodations they consider and in how they described inclusion in classrooms. A similar connection between disabled and American Mexican students was reflected when we asked about the concept of diversity, though in this case *normalistas* drew more on connections with needs of indigenous students. This association between disability and immigrant second language and disability has been well documented in U.S. classrooms, especially in newer migration destinations where special education classrooms are perceived to be the place where teachers are sensitive to learning differences (Artiles et al., 2010). Our findings are also consistent with Delgado and Reyes (2018), who assert that Mexican normal school curricula reflect a deficit framing of marginalized students and do not clearly distinguish between students who are "at risk" because of disability versus life circumstances or institutional inequities. This lack of clarity leaves Mexican educators without a clear or coherent approach to understanding or addressing the needs of marginalized American Mexican students who face significant challenges in Mexican schools.

We provide four recommendations to improve *normalista* preparation to meet the needs of transnationals and other underserved students in Mexico. The first underscores the latter three: move from an equality to an equity orientation. A well-documented ethic in Mexican schooling, from *primarias* to *normales*, is that "we are all equal"—the notion that all students deserve the opportunity to succeed and that group identity and solidarity trump individual differences (Levinson, 2001). Historically significant in Mexico—captured in the ubiquitous sentiment *somos una raza*—the equality ethic can erase important differences in students' backgrounds and identities that need to be better understood, respected, appreciated, and integrated into classroom life in order for marginalized students to succeed. This includes American Mexicans. Acknowledging and discussing their differences—e.g., knowledge of U.S. society, bilingualism, national identity—should be a source to enhance rather than weaken solidarity in Mexican classrooms. Promoting equity in classrooms requires an intentional, concerted effort to shift values a bit—to see student differences, including transnationalism, as strengths to be incorporated rather than problems or threats to group cohesion.

Second, materials for the three diversity courses that we examined should be updated to address the experiences of a broader range of social/cultural groups, especially migrants and their children. These revisions would not be difficult to make, given that current course materials are well designed and thoughtful about issues of student diversity and inclusion. Revisions could add case studies that address the nuanced experiences of transnational students and their families. Normal school curricula would benefit from bringing the sensitivity and specificity reflected in *El caso de Juan el niño triqui* [The case of Juan, the Trique child] to the experiences of transnational students. They need to know as much about transnationals as they do about the experiences and needs of disabled and indigenous students, addressed so thoroughly across existing course materials and in interviews with *normalista* faculty and students.

Third, perhaps more significantly, the imagined curriculum needs to be more responsive to the experiences, assets, and needs of American Mexican students. We were struck that even normalistas with personal experiences in the United States, themselves transnationals, could not shake deficit orientations about students with migrant pasts. In other work, we have documented the cultural stigma of being a return migrant in public schools in rural communities in Central Mexico (Bybee et al., 2020). We saw little in the imagined curriculum with *normalistas* that would change this insidious perception, which is why the transnational experiences of so many American Mexicans remain invisible to their teachers and school administrators (Zúñiga, Hamann, & Sánchez García, 2008). We have found that transnational children and their family members often hide their migrant pasts in order to feel included. This needs to change. Talking openly and respectfully about what children and families lost and gained from their migrant experiences, especially in normal school settings, will certainly help with this.

Last, U.S. educators and researchers should collaborate more with *normalistas* to study and design teacher education improvements to prepare for the students we share. We learned a lot from our *normalista* colleagues (e.g., an ongoing tradition of activism and public service) and were often amazed by their generosity and openness with us. We found them eager to learn from research and to conduct research themselves. Chapter 2 describes a collaboration among U.S. educators, *normalistas*, and the UPN to create a curriculum that focuses specifically on the needs and assets of transnational students we share in Baja California. Hopefully this project will prove to be a model for others throughout Mexico. Newly formed *cuerpos académicos* provide a wonderful incentive for us to engage in collaborative scholarship. We continue our work with *normalistas* and hope other binational *cuerpos* will do the same. No serious venture to improve teaching or teacher education in Mexico can avoid direct engagement with *normalista* partners.

Note

1. Following Zúñiga and Hamann (2013), we use "American Mexican" to designate the national and ethnic origin of these students. We prefer this term to "returnees" because most of these students are moving to Mexico for the first time.

References

Arnaut, A. (2004). El sistema de formación de maestros en México. Continuidad, reforma y cambio. *Cuadernos de Discusión, 17*.

Artiles, A., Klinger, A., Sullivan, A., & Fierros, E. (2010). Shifting landscapes of professional practices: English learner special education placement in English-only states. In P. Gándara M. & Hopkins (Eds.), *Forbidden language: English learners and restrictive language policies*. New York: Teachers College Press.

Bybee, E. R., Whiting, E., Jensen, B., Savage, V., Baker, A., & Holdaway, E. (2020). "Estamos aquí pero no soy de aquí": American Mexican youth, belonging and schooling in rural, central Mexico. *Anthropology and Education Quarterly, 51*(2), 123–145.

Delgado, C. C., & Reyes, M. M. (2018). Formación docente para la inclusión y la diversidad: Retos y agenda pendiente en México. *Atenas, 3*(43), 69–85.

Figueroa Millán, L. M. (2000). La formación de docentes en las escuelas normales: entre las exigencias de la modernidad y las influencias de la tradición. *Revista Latinoamericana de Estudios Educativos, 30*(1).

González, G. D. (2017). Normalismo rural y acción colectiva en la Sierra de Zongolica, México. *Revista Convergência Crítica, 1*(10).

Ginsberg, M. B., & Clift, R. T. (1990). The hidden curriculum of preservice teacher education. In W. R. Houston (Ed.), *Handbook of Research on Teacher Education* (pp. 450–465). New York: Macmillan.

González-Barrera, A. (2015). *More Mexicans leaving than coming to the U.S.* Washington, DC: Pew Research Center.

Hamann, E. T., Zúñiga, V., & Sánchez García, J. (2010). Transnational students' perspectives on schooling in the United States and Mexico: The salience of school experience and country of birth. In M. O. Ensor & E. M. Gozdziak (Eds.), *Children and migration: At the crossroads of resiliency and vulnerability*. New York: Palgrave Macmillan.

Instituto Nacional para la Evaluación de la Educación (2017). *La escuela normal en Mexico: Elementos para su análisis*. México, DF: INEE.

Jensen, B., & Jacobo, M. (2019). Integrating American-Mexican students in Mexican classrooms. *Kappa Delta Pi Record, 55*(1), 36–41.

Jensen, B., Mejía Arauz, R., & Aguilar Zepeda, R. (2017). Equitable teaching for returnee children in Mexico. *Sinéctica, 48*, 1–20.

Levinson, B. U. (2001). *We are all equal: Student culture and identity at a Mexican secondary school*. Durham, NC: Duke University Press.

Marín, S. E., & Delgado, M. E. (2001). Repensar el normalismo. Una nota sociohistórica sobre expectativas y demandas de la formación docente. *Caleidoscopio-Revista Semestral de Ciencias Sociales y Humanidades, 5*(10), 153–174.

McLaughlin, M. J. (2006). Inclusive education. In G. L. Albrecht (Ed.), *Encyclopedia of disability* (Vol. 2, pp. 928–930). Thousand Oaks, CA: SAGE Reference.

Navarrete-Cazales, Z. (2015). Formación de profesores en las Escuelas Normales de México. Siglo XX. *Revista historia de la educación latinoamericana, 17*(25), 17–34.

Ronzón, E. T., & Vadillo, R. C. (2014). La reforma integral de la educación básica en el discurso docente: Análisis desde el ángulo de la significación. *Perfiles educativos, 36*(144), 50–68.

Santos, M. H. (2017). El movimiento estudiantil mexicano de 1968 en las Escuelas Normales Rurales/The 1968 Mexican student movement at rural normales school. *Revista Latinoamericana de Políticas y Administración de la Educación*, (7), 70–80.

Secretaría de Educación Pública. (2018). Planes de Estudio 2012. Retrieved from https://www.cevie-dgespe.com/index.php/planes-de-estudios-2018/

Watty, P. D. (2004). Origen de la escuela normal superior de México. *Revista Historia de la Educación Latinoamericana*, (6), 39–56.

Villegas, P. (2018, September 3). An old score for Mexico's next president: The 43 missing students. *New York Times*.

Zúñiga, V., & Hamann, E. T. (2013). Understanding American Mexican children. In B. Jensen & A. Sawyer (Eds.), *Regarding educación* (pp. 172–188). New York: Teachers College.

Zúñiga, V., Hamann, E. T., & Sánchez García, J. (2008). *Alumnos transfronterizos: Las escuelas mexicanas frente a la globalización*. México, DF: Secretaría de Educación Pública.

Part II
Transnational Teaching

Chapter 4

What Educators in Mexico and in the U.S. Need to Know and Acknowledge to Attend to the Educational Needs of Transnational Students

Edmund T. Hamann and Victor Zúñiga

As noted in this volume's introduction, "A critical challenge in both countries is to prepare teachers (as well as school administrators and para-educators) to meet the teaching needs of transnational students in ways that respond rather than add to their already-long list of demands, and to do so equitably" (Jensen & Gándara, 2021, p. 6). The purpose of this chapter is to make a deep conceptual dive at what "educators bridging borders" means, responding to the following questions: What knowledge is necessary for bridging borders? What commitments are necessary? What future world are "bridged" educators helping children prepare for? What is the problem that bridging borders is trying to resolve? We acknowledge that the very term "bridging" is a potent metonymy. Bridges connect places. They often offer sturdy passage over what otherwise would be hazardous or difficult terrain to cross (like a river or canyon), but they also require design and maintenance.

The first step of bridging borders is to know the educational needs students have. Defining educational needs—what teachers need to know and what students need to learn—may seem like a straightforward task. In terms of knowledge that all students should learn, Mexico's *Secretaria de Educación Pública* (the national education ministry) delineates a national curriculum with content standards by subject area and grade level (from preschool to ninth grade).[1] In this sense, the mandatory schooling in

Mexico is a centralized organization with homogeneous purposes, even if regional differences and disparities in resource distribution make for heterogeneous implementation.

While what needs to be learned gets a little fuzzier in an American context, because defining the curriculum (historically a task of local school districts and in more recent decades a state-level task as part of the Standards Movement) is a multi-entity rather than single national task, 46 of the 50 U.S. states endorsed a Common Core of curriculum in the past decade.[2] Perhaps more importantly, even in states that are not part of the Common Core (e.g., Nebraska, Virginia, and Texas), the skills and content that students are expected to master look quite similar to those in the Common Core. Indeed, Thomas Jefferson's long-standing "3 R's—Reading, wRiting, and 'Rithmetic"—with a more recent addition of science, still summarizes well the centerpieces of what American schools are expected to teach (with topics like health and physical education also common, but not prominent) (Proefriedt, 2008).

With the key distinction that Mexican schools teach overwhelmingly in Spanish and U.S. schools overwhelmingly in English and that the particular content of national history and civic traditions varies, there is a substantial overlap in what students are expected to learn in primary and secondary education in both countries. However, this apparent, significant overlap in what children are officially supposed to learn and related implications for what teachers should teach does not fully encapsulate what educators in Mexico and the United States need to know as both countries' school systems continue to become more intertwined, nor does it encompass much of what transnational students need to learn.

One key limitation is that, despite broad dissemination of nearly uniform curricula, there are important debates in play in both countries regarding whether what is currently being taught is what today's youngsters most need to learn. As Allan Collins (2017) and others (e.g., Hank Rubin [2008]) who study technology and education have noted, in this digital age, with its concurrent explosion of quickly accessed facts and new imperative on differentiating the salient and accurate from the unimportant and misleading, learning the core concepts of the various disciplines is, at best, an incomplete exercise. Students may well need to know something very different from what they have long been taught, and teachers may well need to conduct classrooms in very different ways than in the past. Kalman and Rendón (2014), in their article "Use before know-how," concluded that teachers in public junior high schools in urban Mexico who "do not use the computer themselves in their everyday life or navigate the Internet on a regular basis are faced with not only learning how to teach with these tools, but first learning how to use them" (p. 992).

But the challenges of fast-changing technologies and near-instant access through the internet to whole libraries of unmediated information are not the only dynamics that raise questions about what current and future students need to know and what teachers need to teach. The demographic facts that are the consistent focus across the chapters of this book—the facts that there are hundreds of thousands of children with prior experience in U.S. schools now in Mexico (Masferrer et al., 2019; Zúñiga & Hamann, 2015) and millions in U.S. schools with direct ties to Mexico—also point to reasons why U.S. and Mexican educators need to know and do different things than have sufficed for their previous practice.

As we have long argued (e.g., Hamann, Zúñiga, & Sánchez García, 2006), the continued large-scale movement between the United States and Mexico, including by children traveling with or without their families, means there is a substantial population with enduring attachment to both sides of the border. This population needs to be skilled in English *and* Spanish, to know U.S. history and civic responsibilities *and* also the logics of citizen participation in Mexico, to be *of* two cultures and societies, rather than caught *between* them. To paraphrase Susan Meyers (2014), who studied youth and families moving between Villachuato Michoacán Mexico and Marshalltown Iowa, literacy is now transnational for these families and cannot be fully encapsulated with reference just to either side of this transnational movement. Thus the knowledge, understandings, and perspectives that these children need (and that, at least in rudimentary form, they bring to schools) cannot be understood in mononational terms. In the words of Regina Cortina's (2019, p. 471) recent presidential address to the Comparative and International Education Society, "National systems of public education in Latin America are outdated in their focus on steering diverse populations to a single language and one nation."

The remainder of this chapter is structured in four sections. The first section summarizes our empirical findings, collected since 1997, from our studies in Georgia and then in Nuevo León, Zacatecas, Puebla, Jalisco, and Morelos. It also notes the recent and current context of children's migration between Mexico and the United States to set up informed conjecture about what teachers need to know. In the second section, our purpose is to highlight dimensions of the transnational children and youths' experiences that pertain to their negotiation of classrooms and what, in turn,

American and Mexican teachers need to know for best serving children circulating between both school systems. The third section addresses conceptual concerns related to the "students we share."

Finally, we acknowledge two policy issues: (a) While it is easy in these dystopian times (with rhetoric of walls, resurgent xenophobia, and persistent drug trade violence) to lament the challenges that complicate the American-Mexican relationship and the teachers who must negotiate it, it is worth remembering that never before have there been so many children and parents in both countries with experience in the other country. This greater interconnectedness than ever before can be conceptualized as challenging, but just as readily it can be seen as an opportunity if teachers are supported in helping to make it so; (b) While people may be questioning globalization more noisily now than at any time in the past 30 years, the persistent and heightened interconnectedness of American Mexican/Mexican American families across political borders creates both a need and an opportunity to think more expansively and inclusively about what Mexican and U.S. teachers "need to know and acknowledge" to best serve the children in their charge. The educational task is no longer just to prepare Mexican children for Mexican futures (or American children for American futures), but rather to prepare bicultural/bilingual children for North American futures.

International Migrant Children Negotiating Two Systems

When we first began this work in 1997, there was scant research on students in Mexican schools with prior experience in the United States, and the bulk of the research on newcomers from Mexico to U.S. schools conceptualized these students in two related categories—English learners and immigrant students. Indeed, our first foray (Hamann, 2001) at studying students in Mexican schools with U.S. school experience started with the word "theorizing" and presumed that there might be some students with this biography based on the fact that roughly a quarter of Mexican newcomer parents interviewed in Georgia (United States) forecast that they and their families would not still be in Georgia three years later (Hernández-León & Zúñiga, 2000). We wondered, or theorized, about where they might go, but there was little published research at that time describing students in Mexican schools with prior experience in the United States.

When we first began collaborating, the dominant dynamic for "the students we share" was students moving from Mexico to the United States.

Indeed, that is why we met. We were both involved in the Georgia Project (Hamann, 2003)—a binational collaboration that brought Mexican educators and scholars to Dalton, Georgia, to help local school districts respond to the needs of rapidly growing and unprecedented Latinx enrollments. One of us, Víctor, was the sociologist who led Mexico's side of the effort, while the other, Edmund, gained access to his dissertation research site by writing a $500,000 Title VII Systemwide Bilingual Education Grant for one of the principal school districts. (See further discussion in Hamann and Zúñiga [2011].) At that time, 49% of the Latinx children enrolled in Dalton Public Schools were foreign born, with practically all of those born in Mexico. (That tally by the school district also identified a few children born in Guatemala, which raises a theme—Central American children and youth in the United States and Mexico—that we briefly return to later.) As we noted then and as our work in Georgia illustrated, in addition to Mexican migration into traditional U.S. receiving regions (i.e., California, Arizona, Texas, Chicago), this turn-of-the-century migration also created a "New Latino Diaspora" (Hamann & Harklau, 2010; Wortham, Murillo, & Hamann, 2002) with newcomer populations moving to regions that had not previously hosted significant numbers of Latin American–origin newcomers. This matters later, as the geographic complexity of Mexican migration north into the United States also means that the migration from the United States to Mexico includes a range of U.S. sending communities (like Omaha and Atlanta, in addition to locales like Los Angeles and Houston, as well as smaller cities and towns like Garden City, Kansas; and Dalton).

Since the turn of the century, the migration from Mexico to the United States subsequently has dramatically slowed (Passel, Cohn, & González-Barrera, 2012). Indeed, since 2005, and more clearly since the U.S. recession in 2009, the flow from the United States to Mexico has slightly exceeded the flow from Mexico to the United States in what we (e.g., Hernández-León and Zúñiga, 2016; Zúñiga & Hamann, 2019) and others (e.g., Boehm, 2016) have called the "Great Expulsion." But our initial work in Mexico using stratified random samples to survey thousands of children looking for students with prior experience in the United States precedes this larger demographic reversal. Indeed, when we first gained funding from CONACYT (Mexico's federal *Consejo Nacional de Ciencia y Tecnologia*, or its National Science Foundation equivalent) to look for the students we share in Nuevo León in 2004–05 and Zacatecas in 2005–06, the flow was still primarily South to North, although it was also circular, and 1.8 percent of the students in Nuevo León and 3.0 percent of the students in Zacatecas (in *educación básica*, or grades 1–9) described prior experience in the United States (Hamann, Zúñiga, & Sánchez García, 2010; Zúñiga, Hamann, & Sánchez García, 2008). To illuminate the scale of this demographic reversal, we compare the number of minors who moved from the United States to Mexico in 1990 with those who did it in 2010. According to the Mexican Populations Censuses of those years, 147,920 minors moved to Mexico in 1990. This figure more than quadrupled 20 years later to 633,124 (the vast majority of minors moving to Mexico come from the United States; Zúñiga & Giorguli, 2018).

There are two key implications of this work worth emphasizing before we move on. First, irrespective of the direction in which the larger migration needle points (i.e., more movement North or more movement South), there is counter-flow migration that goes in the other direction that places children in schools in a new country. Second, we have long known that the reasons for transnational students' presence in Mexican schools are plural. In a more recent article that looked at student interviews carried out between 2004 and 2013 (Zúñiga & Hamann, 2015), we chronicled several explanations for relocation, from long-standing circular migration to engage in agricultural harvests, to parents' need to return to care for their for children's grandparents, to parents staying in the United States but sending their children to live in Mexico with extended family, to relocation because of deportation and family reunification in Mexico, although even that list was not exhaustive.

Our successful early work with CONACYT support led to interest from Mexico's *Secretaria de Educación Pública*, which supported the publication and free dissemination of *Alumnos Transnacionales: Escuelas Mexicanas Frente a la Globalización* (Zúñiga, Hamann, & Sánchez García, 2008) and related "train the trainer" workshops to initiate in-service efforts to raise Mexican teachers' awareness of the presence of the students we share. Additionally, it supported more study of transnational students in Mexico, this time in the states of Puebla (2009–10) and Jalisco (2010–11). It also precipitated our links with educational leaders in Morelos, where our study of transnational students and teacher needs is ongoing.

Before we more directly focus on the students we share, we have two last points. First, our knowledge on this topic is a product of two decades of comprehensive, multi-site work in both the United States and Mexico that spans changes in larger migration dynamics. That work involves surveying more than 55,000 students, identifying more than 1,200 with transnational experience, conducting hundreds of interviews with such students, and dozens with their parents and teachers. It is worth positioning readers to know from whence we speak. Second, we want to emphasize that the "students we share" are *international* migrant children and adolescents because they move from one country to another, which also means they move from one school system to another. We emphasize *international* to raise the thesis that thinking of these students as "Mexican" or "American" is intrinsically incomplete, and thinking that their schooling should only be a concern of one country or the other ignores the realities of their pluri-national lives. At this stage of our research, we have found that the first step in the process of training teachers who serve the students moving between Mexico and the United States is to invite them to know and acknowledge the most preeminent trait that defines them: they are international migrants and transnational students. Once teachers recognize these essential elements of the children/student ontology, they might attend more to their trajectories and value more their competencies.

Conceptualizing the Students We Share

There are still children and youth moving from Mexico to the United States, albeit in smaller numbers than in years past, and their experiences and backgrounds, scholastic and otherwise, vary significantly. While there is an intriguing dynamic along the border of children literally attending U.S. schools during the day and sleeping in Mexico at night (Brown, 2012), U.S. schools well away from the physical border also enroll students with previous experience in Mexico. These students are more commonly from rural areas than a random distribution of the population would predict, as rural areas of Mexico have higher participation rates in international migration than do more urban and economically prosperous ones (Terán, Giorguli, & Sánchez, 2015). In turn, the relative limitations of schooling in rural parts of Mexico (where *telesecundarias* are common—school grades 7–9, where the expected paucity of teacher content area expertise means curriculum is often shared using videotapes or DVDs and television monitors) can mean that children arrive with weak academic preparation. Yet there are also strong schools in rural Mexico, and it is worth remembering that even if the transnational population flowing north is more rural than Mexico writ large, the flow is still predominantly from more thickly settled areas, as nearly four-fifths of Mexico's population now reside in urban municipalities (CONAPO, 2012).

As a second point, it is worth noting that some of the population flowing North comes from indigenous backgrounds. Indigenous in Mexico does not principally reference genetic heritage—most Mexicans have some ancestry with the population that predated European arrival in 1519. Rather, indigenous better references those parts of the country where languages other than Spanish still persist and incorporation into the national identity has lagged. While there continue to be indigenous populations in most states in Mexico (partially because of internal migration dynamics like those that have made the populations of Monterrey, Guadalajara, and Mexico City grow so much in the last 100 years) (Olvera, Doncel, & Muñiz, 2014), some Mexican states have substantial indigenous populations, notably southern states like Oaxaca, Guerrero, and Chiapas, plus those on the Yucatán peninsula, as well as states like Michoacán and Veracruz.

Leco Tomás (2015) has looked at educational implications of Purépecha moving between Michoacán and North Carolina, and there is a significant literature on "Oaxacalifornia"—the migration between Oaxaca and California that includes speakers of various versions of Mixtec and Zapotec, as well as less common languages (e.g., Kearney, 2005; Perez, Vasquez, & Burie, 2016). On this theme, we have written about a high school student in rural Nebraska who was bilingual in English and Spanish, whose mother was bilingual in Spanish and Chinanteco (an indigenous language in Oaxaca), and whose grandmother was monolingual in Chinanteco. All three women lived in the same U.S. home (Hamann, Vandeyar, & Eckerson, 2012). While most students coming from Mexico to the U.S. speak Spanish as their first language, it is important to not presume that this is the case for all newcomer students and parents from Mexico.

More generally, if one key point is that students coming from Mexico to the United States vary significantly, it is important to also note that as South-North migration ebbs, it is increasingly common for Mexico to be biographically relevant as the birthplace of the parents of U.S. schoolchildren rather than of those children themselves. That means these parents' expectations of how school works, expectations of their own role vis-à-vis school, and the role of teachers may better reflect their Mexican socialization than what their children are encountering or their children's American teachers are anticipating. While the paternalism of parent education programs for Mexican newcomer parents has been powerfully and appropriately called out (e.g., Villenas, 2002), it is useful to note both (a) that it can be helpful to position newcomer parents to consider the different assumptions of the different systems (Gallo,

Wortham, & Bennet, 2015) and (b) that parents can even co-opt the ostensible purpose of parent-targeting English and family literacy classes. Stacy (2016) identified Mexican parents who explained that they knew their participation in family literacy classes helped story their children as coming from families that cared, interrupting possibly more pejorative assumptions. The newcomer parents' rationale for attending differed from the system's reason for offering such classes.

Ultimately, the U.S.-based educators of the students we share need to remember that the labels "Mexican student" or "Mexican parent" can obscure the diversity of the arriving or second-generation population. While teachers cannot be expected to know all of the ways rural Mexican versus urban Mexican points of origin might matter, it is important that they know this is a possible source of difference. Similarly, U.S. teachers may not know much about the 60 or more still-extant indigenous languages in Mexico, but they should know that there is a chance that some Mexican origin students and parents speak and/or identify with them. (Leco Thomas [2015, p. 94] cited *Secretaría del Migrante de Michoacán* figures from 2011 that counted 120,000 Purépecha in the United States, approximately 20% of whom were school age.) Furthermore, U.S. teachers need to know that, like in their own country, the quality and resource base of Mexican schools vary. There are children and parents arriving from Mexico who have had world-class educations and others who have negotiated resource-poor, difficult-to-staff schools where instructional quality was very low.

As noted, transnational movement can also be from North to South, which has implications not just for "receiving" schools in Mexico, but also for the teachers in "sending" U.S. schools as well. We have been part of some nascent efforts to get U.S. teachers to think about how the prospect that some of their students might continue their education in Mexico, temporarily or more permanently, has implications for what their teaching should accomplish (e.g., Hamann & Mitchell-McCollough, 2019; Hamann, Perez, et al., 2017). The reasons and circumstances for moving to Mexico vary widely. We have chronicled students returning with parents so parents can care for elderly and ailing grandparents, to live in homes that they have built slowly over time with earnings from U.S. income, and/or because parents are tired of the "rat race" that can characterize immigrant efforts to make it in the United States (Zúñiga & Hamann, 2015). We have chronicled single parents returning with children after a divorce in the States or family trouble in the States with marriages actually breaking up after the return to Mexico. In these scenarios, sometimes the parent expects to stay in Mexico (with children now part of extended-family households). Other times they are there to help their child settle in to living with grandparents before the parent then returns to the United States with the intent of sending earnings back as remittances (Sánchez García, Hamann, & Zúñiga, 2012). (This is a dynamic Dreby [2010] notes as well.) We have had parents temporarily bring their children to Mexico so that, per parent explanations, children can know that side of their heritage (Hamann et al., 2018).

Although this was rare when we first began studying transnational students in Mexican schools, increasingly children move to Mexico because of a deportation. The children are not necessarily the ones being deported—the 1982 *Plyler v. Doe* U.S. Supreme Court decision prohibits U.S. schools from being sites of immigration enforcement, and children, if they are U.S. born, have U.S. citizenship by birthplace (Sugarman, this volume). Rather, deportation can send children to Mexico as part of parent decision making to keep the nuclear family together. But the children do not necessarily fare well in unfamiliar Mexican schools, and we have had parents ask us whether we advise having their children return to the United States to go to school there while living with relatives or older siblings (Hamann, et al., 2018).

Research in the United States related to Spanish as heritage language education programs—essentially Spanish taught as a world language to students who come to the classroom with some community and/or household familiarity with Spanish—highlights that the students entering such programs vary widely in terms of adeptness with Spanish (Beaudrie & Fairclaugh, 2012; Draper & Hicks, 2000; Eckerson, 2015). It follows that students moving/returning to Mexico also vary in terms of their familiarity and adeptness with Spanish (which has usually not been much developed in U.S. schools, except in rare dual-language immersion, or strong bilingual, programs). Yet, because students often "look" or "seem" Mexican, limitations in and little experience with academic Spanish can be misinterpreted by Mexican teachers as just a facet of a child being naturally quiet (Zúñiga & Giorguli, 2018).

Students' move to Mexico is not always their first move. In many instances in our data set children were born in Mexico, moved to the United States, and then returned to Mexico. But in between these international moves, they lived in more than one U.S. state or school district. We even have more complicated cases of students born in the United States who moved to Mexico, returned to the United States, and then moved again to Mexico. Often transnational children are part of mixed-status families (with varying "rights" to be in the United States temporarily or permanently). In sum, transnational students, especially those who are U.S. born, are creating a new form of international circulation, as the recent ethnographic works of Román and Carrillo (2017) showed. Per a logic of "transnationalism from below" (Smith & Guarnizo, 1998) that we have previously discussed extensively (e.g., Hamann, Zúñiga, & Sánchez García, 2006), wherein extended families strategize about ways to reduce their economic vulnerability, the prospect of legal return to the United States (as a young adult) is regularly noted.

All of this means that students who move from South to North and North to South vary along a number of dimensions. Like other contributors to this volume, we think the shared status of having crossed an international border and having experience in two countries as part of one's coming of age matters. But how it should matter in terms of teacher praxis is not always the same.

Educator Narratives and Possible Narratives

Part of the task of bridging borders for teachers involves the very acknowledgment that bridging is needed. Per the noted metonymy, teachers can help students link otherwise disparate worlds. They can help with sturdy passage "across the bridge" by supporting transnational students in their pedagogical, linguistic, and cultural transitions. And they can acknowledge that students and their families are using both sides of the border to limit vulnerability and create opportunity. Failing to do so, however, can leave a student vulnerable and disadvantaged.

While migration is almost intrinsically disruptive (pulling individuals largely out of one social network and political ecology and placing them in another) (Boehm et al., 2011), that disruption is not necessarily bad or avoidable. In a study of schooling in Michoacán, Mexico, in a community with significant links to Iowa, Susan Meyers (2014, pp. 4–5) noted,

> [T]eachers in Mexico seem to be saying . . . [that] students don't care sufficiently about school. In particular, the majority of the teachers and administrators whom I interviewed in rural Mexico voiced concern that their students would choose

migration over education. Students often make the wrong choices, their teachers contend; they hold the wrong priorities. But how is a fifteen-year-old in rural Mexico going to pursue a high school education if bus fare is two dollars a day, and her father only earns ten dollars a day to feed a family of six? Despite these teachers' critiques, more students in rural Mexico access post-middle school education by virtue of remittances sent down by family members in the United States than through the transportation and supplies scholarships that some Mexican states offer. Therefore, in absolute economic terms, international migration facilitates formal education—at least for certain family members. Even so, rhetoric on both sides of the border continues to downplay migration, positing it as a life choice that is antithetical to education.

While Meyer's example registers Mexican teachers' skepticism of migration, our work in the United States has verified the commonality on the North side of the border too of teachers lamenting/disliking migration. Complaints of families being gone for vacations during school periods or students "disappearing" (i.e., moving to Mexico) are frequent from the United States side too. A first element of bridging teachers in support of the students we share is to stop seeing migration as bad. It may complicate schooling as traditionally constructed, but it is not antithetical to education.

Moreover, students in Mexico with prior experience in the United States told us regularly that they continue to communicate with family members and friends in the United States using social media. With WiFi ubiquitous and social media, like WhatsApp, allowing free video-calling, the students we share are modeling ways to link life on one side of the border with life on the other. Why can't teachers act similarly? That is, why can't teachers use the wondrous technologies of the current era to help transnational students' academic work bridge the two worlds that they know and the two worlds they likely will continue to negotiate in adulthood? Of course, this presumes some time and discretion on teachers' part (as well as more direct support) to be able to make such connections. But given that there are children in the balance, why shouldn't teachers have that time, discretion, and support? Of course, the 2020–21 pandemic accelerated most U.S. teachers' familiarity with distance education, which may make these connections more possible and likely into the future.

Our understanding of "what could be" has long been grounded by constructivist learning theory and, more particularly, Erickson's (1987) use of Vygotsky to remind us that (a) learners use the familiar to make sense of the unfamiliar and (b) that learning environments need to feel safe and trustworthy if students are to fully engage in them. It follows that teachers on either side of the border need to better understand what students know from "*el otro lado*" (the other side), and they need to consider what makes their classroom feel safe instead of uncomfortable for a newly arriving student. We visited a *secundaria* (junior high school) in Tijuana with such a high *transfronterizo* population that it had routinized matching newly arriving students from the United States with peers who had moved/returned from the United States earlier. Veteran *transfronterizos* helped welcome and orient new ones. While that would not work at every school—it would be hard in schools with very low *transfronterizo* populations—it certainly could become much more commonplace.

One striking theme we have noticed in both the United States and Mexico is how common it is for teachers to be monolingual—monolingual Spanish speakers in Mexico and English speakers in the United States. In a few instances, we have seen teachers on both sides welcome transnational students' facility with a second language, but much more commonly we have witnessed transnational students' multilingual capacity as something to be feared or ignored.

Speaking autobiographically and noting that our first languages differ, we have been able to forge a 20-year, multifaceted collaboration by alternating our use of our weaker second languages and combining that with patience and what some linguists call a "willingness to repair" (Singh, Lele, & Martohardjano, 1988). Bi/multilingualism has a long list of favorable benefits associated with it, but two of them are that it could help teachers communicate with students and it could help teachers communicate with teachers from *el otro lado*. Not developing teachers' multilingualism means not fully attending to what some students could greatly gain from it.

Developing bilingualism among U.S. and Mexican teachers requires not only learning a second language. Opting for bilingualism also means accepting a cultural transformation. Teachers have learned on both sides of the border that languages are essential components of the nation, an almost sacred element of nationalism. In Mexican schools during several decades of the 20th century, Spanish was known as the national language (*lengua nacional*). Even if that's no longer the dominant terminology, teacher monolingualism remains both common and untroubled. Thus, teachers' recognition of the significant value of other languages would represent a still-very-incomplete cultural revolution in ideas of nation and identity.

Challenge and/or Opportunity

Bridging educators is a daunting task and perhaps feels more daunting in the current political climate with angry calls for walls and the tragic division of parents from their children. Still, it is worth remembering that never have there been so many children and parents in both countries with experience in the other country. Never has there been so much at least incipient bilingualism and biculturalism. And never have academically pertinent habits identified more with one culture than the other (e.g., reading to children before bed or drawing children's attention to their comportment) so readily crossed borders. This greater interconnectedness than ever before can be understood as an opportunity if teachers are supported in helping to make it so.

Generally, educators in both systems ignore each other. That stance has to change given the circulation of so many students across borders. The educational task is no longer just to prepare Mexican children for Mexican futures (or American children for American futures), but rather to prepare bicultural/bilingual children for North American futures. Students/children are circulating in both directions. Through that circulation, they are gaining linguistic, historic, geographic, and political knowledge that both sides need if they want to better understand and better cooperate with those on the other side. We can recognize that reality and convert these migratory experiences into assets. Or we can ignore or decry them and then be complicit with students' relative diminished capacity, diminished opportunity, and diminished success.

Migrant children move. They move from one region to another one, they move from a city to another city, or they move from one country to another one. Their mobility—dislocation—is an essential trait of their ontology. They move while schools do not move. Schools are the archetypical institution that has roots in one, and only one, community, neighborhood, town or city. So when transnational children have to go to the school, they have to do so in a particular place, usually a place that did not expect them and did not plan for their arrival.

As a consequence of this contradiction, we have mobile students (children and adolescents) attending immobile institutions (Zúñiga & Hamann, 2008). The pedagogical relation that results from this contradiction is that the migratory experiences of students are not incorporated into the learning process. However, we have now a historical opportunity for U.S. and Mexican schools to welcome the richness of the migratory experiences of these binational, bilingual, and bicultural children and youth moving in both countries. Schools, teachers, principals, and administrators who serve international migrant students need to build institutions welcoming children's migratory experiences. To do so, school actors need to understand what migration is and to value the competencies that migrant students develop because of their migration experience. This chapter has traced that need, but we would be remiss if we did not mention that we can help educators better address this need. The film *Una Vida Dos Paises* (2016) with accompanying Teacher's Guide (Kleyn, 2015) and the *Mientras Llego a Mi Escuela* student workbook (Romero García & Morfín Stoopen (2009) are both brilliant examples of resources with prospective applications. Teachers can learn from them and use them as resources with students. Of course, there is always a need to create more. Moreover, teachers' increased familiarity with distance learning, wrought by the pandemic, may provide new possibilities for "bridging" students who move back and forth across borders.

Notes

1. See, for example, the *Nuevo Modelo Educativo* articulated by the subsecretariat for *educación básica*, retrieved from http://basica.sep.gob.mx/publications/pub/739/Nuevo+Modelo+Educativo#

2. Although four of those states—Alabama, Arizona, Indiana, and Tennessee—have since rescinded their participation in the Common Core.

References

Beaudrie, S., & Fairclough, M. (Eds.). *Spanish as a heritage language in the United States: State of the field*. Washington, DC: Georgetown University Press.

Boehm, D. (2016). *Returned: Going and coming in the age of deportation*. Berkeley: University of California Press.

Boehm, D. A., Hess, J. M., Coe, C., Rae-Espinoza, H., & Reynolds, R. R. (2011). Introduction: Children, youth, and the everyday ruptures of migration. In C. Coe, R. R. Reynolds, D. A. Boehm, J. M. Hess, & H. Rae-Espinoza (Eds.), *Everyday ruptures: Children, youth and migration in global perspective* (pp. 1–19). Nashville: Vanderbilt University Press.

Brown, P. L. (2012). Young U.S. citizens in Mexico brave risks for American schools. *New York Times* (January 16). Retrieved from https://www.nytimes.com/2012/01/17/us/young-us-citizens-in-mexico-up-early-to-learn-in-the-us.html

Collins, A. (2017). *What's worth teaching? Rethinking curriculum in the age of technology*. New York: Teachers College Press.

CONAPO (2012). *Sistema urbano nacional 2012*. Mexico: Consejo Nacional de Población.

Cortina, R. (2019). "The passion for what is possible" in comparative and international education. *Comparative Education Review, 63*(4). Retrieved from https://www.journals.uchicago.edu/doi/pdfplus/10.1086/705411

Draper, J., & Hicks, J. (2000). Where we've been, what we've learned. In J. Webb & B. Miller (Eds.), *Teaching heritage language learners: Voices from the classroom* (pp. 15–35). Yonkers, NY: ACTFL.

Dreby, J. (2010). *Divided by borders: Mexican migrants and their children*. Berkeley: University of California Press.

Eckerson, J. (2015). Teacher perspectives on professional development needs for better serving Nebraska's Spanish heritage language learners. PhD diss., University of Nebraska-Lincoln. Lincoln, NE. Retrieved from http://digitalcommons.unl.edu/teachlearnstudent/62/

Erickson, F. (1987). Transformation and school success: The politics and culture of educational achievement. *Anthropology & Education Quarterly, 18*(4), 335–356.

Gallo, S., Wortham, S., & Bennet, I. (2015). Increasing "parent involvement" in the New Latino diaspora. In E. T. Hamann, S. Wortham, & E. G. Murillo (Eds.), *Revisiting education in the New Latino diaspora* (pp. 263–281). Charlotte, NC: Information Age Press.

Hamann, E. T. (2003). *The educational welcome of Latinos in the New South*. Westport, CT: Praeger.

Hamann, E. T., & Harklau, L. (2010). Education in the New Latino diaspora. In E. G. Murillo (Ed.), *Handbook of Latinos and education* (pp. 157–169). New York: Routledge.

Hamann, E. T., & Mitchell-McCollough, J. (2019). The paradoxical implications of deported American students. In E. Crawford, L. Dorner, & E. Bonney (Eds.), *Educational leadership of immigrants: Case studies in times of change* (pp. 88–95). New York: Routledge.

Hamann, E. T., Perez, W., Gallo, S., & Zúñiga, V. (2017). *Equity by design: The students we share: US teachers' responsibilities given that some of their students will later go to school in Mexico*. Indianapolis, IN: Midwest and Plains Equity Assistance Center. Retrieved from https://greatlakesequity.org/resource/students-we-share-us-teachers-responsibilities-given-some-their-students-will-later-go

Hamann, E. T., Vandeyar, S., & Eckerson, J. (2012). Rural Latino high school students considering identity and belonging through comparative study of newcomer youth in South Africa. *Encyclopaideia: Journal of Phenomenology and Education, XVI* (34), 73–92.

Hamann, E. T., & Zúñiga, V. (2011). Schooling and the everyday ruptures transnational children encounter in the United States and Mexico. In C. Coe,

R. Reynolds, D. Boehm, J. M. Hess, & H. Rae-Espinoza (Eds.), *Everyday ruptures: Children and migration in global perspective* (pp. 141–160). Nashville, TN: Vanderbilt University Press.

Hamann, E. T., Zúñiga, V., & Sánchez García, J. (2006). Pensando en Cynthia y su hermana: Educational implications of U.S./Mexico transnationalism for children. *Journal of Latinos and Education, 5*(4), 253–274. Retrieved from http://digitalcommons.unl.edu/teachlearnfacpub/60/

Hamann, E. T., Zúñiga, V., & Sánchez García, J. (2010). Transnational students' perspectives on schooling in the United States and Mexico: The salience of school experience and country of birth. In M. Ensor & E. Gozdziak (Eds.), *Children and migration: At the crossroads of resiliency and vulnerability* (pp. 230–252). New York: Palgrave Macmillan.

Hamann, E. T., Zúñiga, V., & Sánchez García, J. (2018). Where should my child go to school? Parent and child considerations in binational families. In M. T. de Guzman, J. Brown, & C. Edwards (Eds.), *Parenting from afar: The reconfiguration of the family across distance* (pp. 339–350). New York: Oxford University Press.

Hernandez-Leon, R., & Zuñiga, V. (2000). "Making carpet by the mile": The emergence of a Mexican immigrant community in an industrial region of the U.S. historic South. *Social Science Quarterly 81*(1), 49–66.

Hernández-León, R., & Zúñiga, V. (2016). Introduction to the special issue: Contemporary return migration from the United States to Mexico—focus on children, youth, schools and families. *Mexican Studies/Estudios Mexicanos, 32*(2), 171–198.

Kalman, J., & Rendón V. (2014). Use before know-how: Teaching with technology in a Mexican public school. *International Journal of Qualitative Studies in Education, 27*(8), 974–991.

Kearney, M. (2005). The anthropology of transnational communities and the reframing of immigration research in California: The Mixtec case. In M. Bommes & E. Morawska (Eds.), *International migration research: Constructions, omissions and the promises of interdisciplinarity* (pp. 69–94). Aldershot, UK: Ashgate Publishing Ltd.

Kleyn, T. (Ed.). (2015). *Guía de apoyo a docentes con estudiantes transfronterizos: Alumnos de educación básica y media superior*. Retrieved from https://tatyanakleyn.commons.gc.cuny.edu/files/2013/10/Guia-Final-3-18-16.pdf

Leco Thomas, C. (2015). Migrantes indígenas purépechas: Educación bilingüe México-Estados Unidos. In E. T. Hamann, S. Wortham, & E. G. Murillo (Eds.), *Revisiting education in the New Latino diaspora* (pp. 93–114). Charlotte, NC: Information Age Press.

Masferrer, C., Hamilton, E. R., & Denier, N. (2019). Immigrants in their parental homeland: Half a million U.S.-born minors settle throughout Mexico. *Demography, 56*, 1453–1461.

Meyers, S. V. (2014). *Del otro lado: Literacy and migration across the U.S.-Mexico border*. Carbondale, IL: Southern Illinois University Press.

Olvera, J. J., Doncel J. A., & Muñiz, C. (2014). *Indígenas y educación, diagnóstico del nivel medio superior en Nuevo León*. Monterrey: Fondo Editorial Nuevo León.

Passel, J., Cohn, D. & González-Barrera, A. (2012, April 23). Net migration from Mexico falls to zero and perhaps less. Pew Research Center. Hispanic Trends. Retrieved from http://www.pewhispanic.org/2012/04/23/net-migration-from-mexico-falls-tozero-and-perhaps-less/

Perez, W., Vasquez, R., & Burie, R. (2016). Zapotec, Mixtec, and Purepecha youth: Multilingualism and the marginalization of indigenous immigrants in the United States. In H. S. Alim, J. Rickford, & A. Ball (Eds.), *Raciolinguistics: How language shapes our ideas about race* (pp. 255–271). London: Oxford University Press, 2016.

Proefriedt, W. (2008). *High expectations: The cultural roots of standards reform in American education*. New York: Teachers College Press.

Román González, B., & Carillo, E. (2017). "Bienvenido a la escuela": experiencias escolares de alumnos transnacionales en Morelos, México. *Sinéctica, Revista Electrónica de Educación, 48*. Retrieved from https://sinectica.iteso.mx/index.php/SINECTICA/article/view/667

Romero García, M., & Morfín Stoopen, M. (2009). *Mientras llego a mi escuela* (edición corregida). México: Secretaria de Educación Pública. Retrieved from http://potowski.org/sites/potowski.org/files/MIENTRAS_LLEGO_A_MI_ESCUELA%5B1%5D.pdf

Rubin, H. (2008, September 26). The archer's dilemma, or, Why the question "What will preK-12 students need to know and be able to do in 2028?" is timely and important right now! *Teachers College Record*. Retrieved from http://www.tcrecord.org. ID Number: 15389.

Sánchez García, J., & Hamann, E. T. (2016). Educator responses to migrant children in Mexican schools. *Mexican Studies/Estudios Mexicanos 32*(2), 199–225 [ISSN 0742-9797].

Sánchez García, J., Hamann, E. T., & Zúñiga, V. (2012). What the youngest transnational students have to say about their transition from US schools to Mexican ones. *Diaspora, Indigenous, and Minority Education, 6*(3): 157–171.

Singh, R., Lele, J., & Martohardjono, G. (1988). Communication in a multilingual society: Some missed opportunities. *Language in Society 17*, 43–59.

Stacy, J. (2016). Partnerships through adult education: re-conceptualizing family literacy in the New Latino Diaspora. PhD diss., University of Nebraska-Lincoln. Lincoln, NE. Retrieved from http://digitalcommons.unl.edu/teachlearnstudent/54/

Terán, J. D., Giorguli S. E., & Sánchez, L. (2015). Reconfiguraciones de la geografía del retorno de Estados Unidos a México 2000–2010: un reto para las políticas públicas. In CONAPO *La situación demográfica de México 2015*. Mexico: CONAPO.

Una Vida Dos Paises. (2016). Documentary retrieved from http://www.unavidathe film.com/#watch-the-film

Villenas, S. (2002). Reinventing educación in new Latino communities: Pedagogies of change and continuity in North Carolina. In S. Wortham, E. G. Murillo, & E. T. Hamann (Eds.), *Education in the New Latino diaspora* (pp. 17–36). Westport, CT: Ablex Press.

Wortham, S., Murillo, E. G., & Hamann, E. T. (Eds.). (2002). *Education in the new Latino diaspora: Policy and the politics of identity*. Westport, CT: Ablex Press.

Zúñiga, V., & Hamann, E. T. (2008). Escuelas nacionales, alumnos transnacionales: la migración México/Estados Unidos como fenómeno escolar. *Estudios Sociológicos de El Colegio de México, XXVI* (76), 65–85.

Zúñiga, V., & Hamann, E. T. (2015). Going to a home you have never been to: The return migration of Mexican and American-Mexican children. *Children's Geographies, 13*(6), 643–655.

Zúñiga, V., & Hamann, E. T. (2019). De las escuelas de Estados Unidos a las escuelas de México: Desafíos de política educativa en el marco de la Gran Expulsión. In J. L. Calva (Ed.), *Migración de Mexicanos a Estados Unidos, derechos humanos y desarrollo* (pp. 221–239). México: Juan Pablos Editor/Consejo Nacional de Universitarios. [ISBN 978-607-711-517-5], Retrieved from https://digitalcommons.unl.edu/teachlearnfacpub/367

Zúñiga, V., Hamann, E. T., & Sánchez García, J. (2008). *Alumnos transnacionales: Las escuelas mexicanas frente a la globalización*. Mexico, DF: Secretaria de Educación Pública. Retrieved from http://digitalcommons.unl.edu/teach learnfacpub/97/

Zúñiga, V., & Giorguli, S. E. (2018). *Niñas y niños en la migración de Estados Unidos a México: la generación 0.5*. México: El Colegio de México.

Chapter 5

Preparing Educators for Asset-Based Pedagogies

The Case of Recently Arrived Transnational Students in Central Mexico[1]

Sarah Gallo

Alison[2] sat in her 5th grade classroom in her parents' hometown in Mexico, trying to complete the teacher's dictado [dictation]—four questions students should answer about their poems. Up until a month ago she had attended an English-medium school in North Carolina, where she was born. Alison had many questions on how to write in Spanish what her teacher in Mexico dictated. Eventually he strayed from the traditional dictation—in which the teacher only speaks—and wrote the questions on the white board. Alison, new to writing in Spanish, spent the next 15 minutes carefully copying what he wrote, causing her to miss the whole-group lesson and discussion on consonant and assonant rhyme. When the song that signaled recess blasted over the speaker system and kids joyfully escaped to games of soccer or home-made snacks available for purchase at food stands, Alison stayed behind in her classroom, borrowing a friend's notebook to try and catch up on the dictated content she didn't know how to write in Spanish. (Field Note: 1/26/17)

This field note occurred in a semi-rural elementary school in Puebla, Mexico, and highlights one of the key challenges that newly arrived binational students faced in their Mexican schools: largely undifferentiated pedagogies that required advanced Spanish literacy in order to engage with the content of their classroom lessons. Indeed, newly arrived Alison put her time and energy into writing the assignment questions and missed the actual content of the poetry lesson, as well as opportunities to deepen her social networks during recess. As many in this volume discuss, most educators in Mexico are not prepared to recognize or build upon the multilingual and diverse knowledges that the students we share bring to their classrooms. For instance, Alison's teacher explained how in his 25 years of teaching he had never been trained to work with bilingual students, those new to Mexican schooling, or those developing literacy practices in Spanish. Collaborative work is needed to better support binational students and their teachers for educational success on both sides of the border.

Learning from Students and Teachers in Mexican Schools

This chapter is based on a year-long ethnographic study with 10 recently arrived binational students in five schools, ranging from elementary to high schools, in Puebla, Mexico. By binational students I mean young people who have physically lived and learned in more than one country. This study focused on children from mixed-status Mexican immigrant families in the United States, or families in which some members had official U.S. documentation and others did not, who had relocated to Mexico within the prior two years. Nine of ten of the students in this study were born in the United States and were therefore citizens of both the United States and Mexico, as Mexican citizenship is accessible to anyone with at least one Mexican-national parent. One student was born in Mexico and lived and studied in the United States for seven years before returning to Mexico for his schooling. I adopt the term binational students to focus on students' physical schooling experiences as well as our binational responsibilities—as educators, researchers, and policy makers—for creating spaces for educational success on both sides of the border.

Migration histories and experiences from different regions of Mexico are extremely diverse, and Puebla—located far from the physical U.S.-Mexico border—is a mountainous state in Central Mexico located about two hours from Mexico City. With the exception of the Mixteca region of Puebla, most international migration from the region began in the 1980s and accelerated over the next twenty years[3] (Durand & Massey, 2009). Most people from Puebla left small towns with agricultural economies that offered limited economic opportunities and moved to varying parts of the United States, such as New York City and North Carolina (Binford et al., 2014). Students from this study moved back to their families' small towns in rural Mexico, where their parents usually had constructed a simple home with their earnings while in the United States. Families relocated to Mexico for a range of reasons—some returned to care for ailing family members, others for family reunification after a relative's deportation, while others decided to live in Mexico so that their children could have deeper family networks. Because of limited employment opportunities in these small towns, parents either tried their hand at producing their own crops or started a small business, such as a candy shop or clothing store. Most families talked about the extreme differences in material wealth they experienced once back in Mexico. Although most worked long hours in minimum wage service-industry jobs in the United States, they had had enough money for material items such as clothing and toys for their kids and the occasional family outing to a fast-food restaurant or a movie. Once they returned to their hometowns in rural Mexico, their earnings were usually barely enough for their family to get by, and such material items were a rarity. For example, one family had been able to save and buy a large Expedition truck while in the United States, which they drove back to their town in Mexico. However, because of the costliness of gasoline and their limited income once back in Mexico, they could rarely afford to actually drive it, and it sat unused in their driveway.

Schooling realities were also very different in rural schools in Mexico compared with those in the United States. Unlike in the United States, where public schools must offer supports for qualifying students to develop their English skills as they simultaneously access content for learning (often through English as a second language or bilingual classes), parallel supports for students developing their academic Spanish and literacy were not available in these Mexican schools. By academic Spanish, I mean the school-based forms of language and literacy practices that would permit students to successfully participate in classroom learning. Like school-based language in English in the United States, it is often "particularly difficult to master because it is generally not used outside the classroom, and it draws on new vocabulary, more complex sentence structures, and rhetorical forms not typically encountered in nonacademic settings" (Goldenberg, 2008, p. 13). In these rural schools, there were no separate educators to assist with students' Spanish language development or to teach Spanish literacy, and there were no support professionals—such as literacy coaches, special education teachers, teachers' aides, or separate teachers for specials besides physical education. Each classroom teacher was responsible for teaching every part of the national curriculum to their class and rarely received training on how to differentiate their instruction for students who brought diverse experiences and resources to the classroom. This included binational students who were usually literate in English but had not had the opportunity to develop Spanish for schooling prior to their move to Mexico because of limited opportunities for quality bilingual education in most parts of the United States.

It is important to highlight that there exists a significant learning gap between urban and rural public school students in Mexico, and the findings here are based on Puebla's transnational context, which—like many parts of Mexico experiencing return migration—is largely rural. According to the *Instituto Nacional de Estadística y Geografía* (INEGI), in 2013 45.9% of rural public school sixth graders scored below average on math exams, and 53.5% scored below average on Spanish exams, whereas their urban counterparts scored 36.4% and 37.2% below average, respectively (INEGI). In 2014, Puebla was estimated to educate about 4.6% of Mexico's U.S.-born students in public and private schools, a number that is lower than states closer to the border, such as Chihuahua (11%) or Baja California (9%) (Jacobo Suárez & Espinosa Cárdenas, 2016, p. 181). Just as Latinx immigrant students attending school in Los Angeles compared with small-town Indiana have different schooling experiences, so do binational students in Mexico if they move to urban areas with high concentrations of binational students in places like Tijuana compared with rural Puebla. The limited educational specialists, opportunities for teacher training, and concentration of binational students are shaped by this rural context.

Here I focus on the daily classroom experiences of recently arrived binational students to illustrate the textured realities of teaching and learning related to two key themes that emerged as particularly challenging for binational students and their teachers: dictation practices and social isolation. Ethnography is a type of research in which researchers spend large amounts of time engaged in the routine activities they are looking to better understand. For me, that meant spending one day per week for the 2016–2017 school year in five different Mexican schools working with newly arrived students from the United States. My goal was to understand the complexities that students and teachers faced as they engaged in daily teaching and learning with students who had received their formal education in the United States, and usually in English, until this point. I also conducted interviews with educators, students, and family members to better understand their perspectives and experiences, and paid attention to the types of class materials—such as textbooks and homework assignments—used during class. During each classroom visit, I filmed or observed a single focal student, who was selected because he or she had enrolled in Mexican schools within the past two years and had previously attended school in the United States. As recently arrived students were usually quieter than their Mexican peers, because of their uncertainties of classroom routines and their developing Spanish repertoires, focusing on a single student permitted a window into the ways he or she experienced schooling across the school day, which could otherwise easily be overlooked among the bustle of their lively classroom.

Focal students were from a range of sending contexts in the United States, including newer Mexican immigrant communities in places like North Carolina to more established transnational contexts such as New York City. Because some members of each family did not have official U.S. documentation, a family's return to Mexico for any reason meant that their family planned to stay for an extended amount of time, and their children enrolled in Mexican schools.

Asset-based Pedagogies with Binational Students

I focus on the potential role of asset-based pedagogies to understand these schooling realities. Many education scholars have demonstrated that children develop knowledges and resources across contexts of learning, such as schools, homes, and communities, and that incorporating these resources into schooling could enhance their learning (e.g., González, 2011; Ladson-Billings, 1995; Orellana, 2009). Although more research is needed to pinpoint how the incorporation of specific cultural resources can result in measurable academic gains (see Jensen, Grajeda, & Haertel, 2018), asset-based approaches broadly orient to understanding a wider range of ways of knowing so they can be leveraged for school-based goals. For binational students in Mexico, their range of knowledges are developed through the national curriculum in their Mexican classrooms, among family members, across their multiple communities, via their immigration experiences, and from their time in U.S. schools. Yet in many Mexican classrooms, the only knowledges that are seen as "counting" are those that are part of the national Mexican curriculum that binational students can explain in academic Spanish. In some ways, this parallels the ways that immigrant students in the United States are only tested in English, and, unless educators explicitly look for ways to welcome a range of educational and linguistic resources into their classrooms, forms of knowledge that differ from what is learned in their classrooms are not valued. A key difference is that most educators in Mexico have not received preparation to work with students who speak languages other than Spanish, and for many binational students there are no supports to develop their academic Spanish and literacy in school. I seek to contribute to a dialogue regarding the ways we can better support Mexican teachers to recognize and academically leverage the range of educational resources that binational students bring to their classrooms. The focus is on binational students who move from U.S. to Mexican schools, and in the discussion I provide recommendations for Mexican education policy, Mexican educators, and U.S. educators who also work with the students we share.

Some Educational Challenges in Mexican Schools

El Dictado [Dictation]

One theme that I focus on is the use of "*el dictado,*" or dictation, which is commonly used in Mexican classrooms. It falls within a broader approach to literacy instruction in Mexican schools that emphasizes correct form over authentic communication (Carrasco Altamirano, 2003; Teague, Smith, & Jiménez, 2010). Research in Mexican classrooms has found that despite education reforms oriented to prioritizing meaningful written communication as well as educators' and parents' goals to develop students' authentic literacy practices, the majority of literacy instruction tends to center on dictations, copying, simple texts, neat handwriting, and organized notebooks, prioritizing the prescriptive orthographic conventions of the *Real Academia Española* (Jiménez, Smith, & Martínez-León, 2003). Within these instructional practices, educators rarely incorporate community-based texts, and students are rarely offered opportunities to write from their own experiences or thoughts (Teague, Smith, & Jiménez, 2010). As Jiménez, Smith, and Martínez-León emphasized, "In a sense, the linguistic capital brought by many of our participating students to school . . . was misrecognized as a debit or deficiency and then subjected to a regimen of remediation for its conventions into forms more acceptable to the school, vis-à-vis dominant literacy practices" (2003, p. 505). This was true in public lower-income as well as private middle-class schools they observed (Teague, Smith, & Jiménez, 2010). As these scholars highlight, such rigidly form-focused literacy instruction may be counterproductive to stated literacy goals centered on communicating meaning.

In addition to the centrality of prescriptive norms from the *Real Academia Española*, there are other reasons dictation as a pedagogical practice is common. In Mexican schooling, there is a stronger emphasis on oracy, including oral to print-based connections. Oracy is the language needed to interact with texts that includes a subset of oral language skills and strategies used in academic settings and is often developed through activities such as storytelling, riddles, tongue-twisters, rhymes, and public performances (Escamilla et al., 2014). In contrast to the narrow ways Spanish writing is taught, there is tremendous flexibility and a high value placed on creativity in terms of students' oral contributions (Jiménez, Smith, & Martínez-León, 2003). In addition, printed materials, such as photocopies, are costly and less common in public schooling. This is particularly true in high school, which although on paper has been required in Mexico since 2012, in practice is often inaccessible, especially in rural areas. As the principal at Alison's school emphasized, *"they talk about obligatory education in this country until high school, well if dad has (monetary) possibilities at that time he'll support his kids (to study), but usually there aren't any resources*[4]*"* (Interview 6/13/17). To attend high school in the region, families must be able to afford the school fee, transportation to school, uniform costs, and the costs of all books and materials, which were often beyond families' economic possibilities. Although elementary and middle school students receive free textbooks, at the high school level they are not provided by the Mexican government, and to reduce costs teachers opt to dictate rather than charge families for these materials. Across the grade levels, teachers use dictation to share content, homework assignments, or notes home to families. Teachers usually have a "dictation voice"—it is often slower, deeper, and with regular repetition, so that students write their exact message. These prosodic features often signal to students that it is time for a dictation—and upon hearing it, students tend to stop talking, grab their pencil and notebook, sit up straighter, bow their heads, and focus to write down the precise words of their teacher.

I am not dismissing the utility of *el dictado* [dictation] for certain academic purposes, as many scholars have shown how it can indeed help develop important oracy and print-based literacy skills under certain conditions (e.g., Escamilla et al., 2014). I am, however, questioning the undifferentiated use of *el dictado* with students who have not been supported in learning Spanish literacy, as is the case for most recently arrived binational students. Like in many parts of Mexico, there was no differentiated Spanish literacy instruction for recently arrived students—such as the equivalent of ESL classes or sheltered instruction in the United States—and students were generally left to their own devices to develop reading and writing in Spanish (see also Despagne, 2019; Kleyn, 2017; Panait & Zúñiga, 2016). Dictation—in which students must rely solely on transferring the sounds they hear in Spanish to the correct written grapheme—without visual supports—is very challenging if you have not yet learned the grapheme-phoneme pairings in Spanish, are unsure of other orthographic rules such as accent marks, and have a relatively limited academic vocabulary in Spanish.

In the following interaction, Alison—the recently arrived fifth grader from North Carolina from the opening vignette—tried to learn via el dictado. I selected this interaction because it differs from typical dictations. Generally, teachers were unaware of the challenges that *el dictado* posed to new students. Similarly, many recently arrived students remained silent when they could not complete the dictation, not wanting to draw attention to themselves for being different. In this interaction, in contrast, we see a teacher who looked to differentiate his instruction to a small degree with his new student, as well as a new student who was willing to name her uncertainties. During the lesson below, Alison had been in Profe's classroom for several months. She was sitting next to Katlyn, and called over her friend Frida for help as well.

Example 1: El Dictado[5]

Profe (teacher) **Alison** (binational student) **Katlyn** (tablemate) **Frida** (friend)
WORDS THAT WERE SAID AS PART OF THE DICTATION ARE IN "CAPS"
1. **Profe:** Póngale. La pregunta les dice, "¿Cómo se obtiene su área de trapecio?"
   Put. The question says, "How do you get the area of a trapezoid"?
2. Póngale "SUMANDO." Póngale "SUMANDO." Todos. Estamos viendo de este lado
   Put, "ADDING." Put, "ADDING." Everyone. Are we watching on this side

3. también, todos?
    too, everyone?
((Profe gives the dictation for 40 seconds))
15. **Profe:** Isaih. "SUMANDO LA BASE MAYOR Y MENOR. MULTI-PLICANDO EL RESULTADO POR—"
    Isaih. *"ADDING THE UPPER AND LOWER BASE. MULTIPLYING THE RESULT BY—"*
16. **Alison to Katlyn:** —¿El resultado?—
    —*The result?*—
17. **Profe:** —"LA ALTURA. Y DIVIDIENDOLO ENTRE DOS."
    —*"THE HEIGHT. AND DIVIDING IT BY TWO."*
18. **Alison to herself:** "ENTRE DOS."
    "BY TWO."
19. **Profe:** "¡LA FORMULA QUE RESULTA ES!"
    "THE FORMULA YOU GET IS!"
20. **Alison to herself:** resulta
    results
21. **Students:** ¡Profe! ¡Profe! ¡Yo, yo! ((bidding to answer question))
    Teacher! Teacher! Me, me! ((bidding to answer question))
22. **Alison to herself:** "EL RESULTADO." Frida ((calling over her friend to help))
    "THE RESULT." Frida ((calling over friend to help))
((Profe finishes the dictation for 15 seconds))
29. **Alison to Frida:** Ven.
    Come here.
30. ((Friend comes over))
31. **Alison to Frida:** Aquí, "RESULTANDO?" ((Unsure of what to write))
    Here, "RESULTING?" ((Unsure of what to write))
32. ((Friend runs over to grab her notebook, stops when Profe calls on Alison))
33. **Profe:** Alguna duda díganme. Sí [xxx] Alison.
    Any doubts, tell me. Yes [xxx] Alison.
34. **Alison:** ((unsure)): Síí. ¿Resultado de qué?
    ((unsure)): Yess. Result of what?
35. **Profe:** Es mejor—haz lo que haces. A ver.
    It's better—do what you're doing. Let's see.
36. **Alison:** En—el resultado—
    In—the result—
37. **Profe:** —"SUMANDO." [A ver]. De. De.
    —*"ADDING." [Let's see.] Of. Of.*

38. **Alison:** Sumando la—
    Adding the—
39. **Profe:**—A ver, desde el principio. A ver. "SUMANDO"
    —Let's see, from the beginning. Let's see. "ADDING."
((Profe regives Alison the dictation, which she repeats—60 seconds))

48. ((Profe gets close to Alison's desk to see her work))
49. **Profe:** Eso. Pon dos puntitos. Uno arriba, uno abajo. Eso. Ahora. Una flechita aquí.
    That's it. Put two points. One above, one below. That's it. Now. A little arrow here.
50. ((Takes her pencil to show her)). La vas a poner acá. Espera. Ponle.
    ((Takes her pencil to show her)). You're going to put it here. Wait. Put it.
51. **Profe:** Base mayor se escribe con B mayúscula. No. Con la otra "b." Pero quítale-
    Upper Base is written with an upper-case B. No. With the other "b." But take away
52. es la pura letra. La-
    it's just the letter. The-
53. **Alison:** Ah. ((erases "V"))
54. **Profe:** Eso. "MÁS."
    That's it. "PLUS."
55. ((Alison writes an "x" for "multiply")).
56. **Profe:** No. Más. Esto es "por." No no no no. Es el signo "más" "más" "más."
    No. Plus. This is "times." No no no no. It's the symbol "plus" "plus" plus."
57. **Alison:** ¿Cuál?
    Which one?
58. **Profe:** Una cruz. ((Profe writes it for her))
    A cross ((Profe writes it for her)).
59. ((Alison gasps as she understands, and erases))
60. **Profe:** Es el signo "más." ¿Está bien? Base menor la b minúscula. Adelante. "PORRRR"
    It's the "plus" sign. Is it okay? Lower base with lower-case b. That's it. "TIMESSS"
61. Ahora signo "x" "ALTURA." No no, no me lo hace—pero bueno. Ahora ponle una rayita

Now the symbol "x" "HEIGHT." No no no, you did a—but, ok. Now put a line
62. tooooodo hasta abajo. Hasta allá. Ahora un "dos" abajo. Entre dos. Es la formula.
All the way to the bottom. Until there. Now put "two" below. By two. It's the formula.

Through this interaction, Alison and Profe drew upon various educational strategies to complete this dictation. When I asked Alison what it was like to do *dictados*, she said, "Hard. Like, "How do I do this?" "What's the . . . letter?" What's this and what's that? So like, "Do I do this first? Or not." (Interview 5/26/17). In this class lesson, she drew upon a range of educational resources to complete this task. She first tried to check with her tablemate—to no avail (line 16)—and then tried to call over a friend, who was about to bring her a notebook to copy before Profe interjected (lines 22, 29–32). Alison was also willing to ask questions (lines 34, 57), was vocal about her doubts (line 34), and moved past silences to access support from her teacher and peers (lines 16, 22, 29–32, 33–62). As noted in the opening vignette, she also dedicated her free periods to catching up on the written material, and her family hired a tutor to help develop their children's Spanish literacy at home.

Profe was an exceptional educator who built interpersonal relationships with the students in his classroom. As research in the United States has shown, these relationships of deep care matter for all students, but are particularly important for those from diverse backgrounds (Campano, 2007; Gallo, Link, & Wortham, 2016). Although he had not been trained in ways to provide differentiated instruction through his pre-service or in-service teacher education, he did take notice of his individual students and monitored Alison's progress. During the dictation presented above, he offered Alison feedback along the way—such as kindly correcting her confusion between "b" and "v," which are (nearly) identical sounds in Spanish (lines 51–54), and between the "times" and "plus" symbols (lines 54–60). He also provided written examples in her notebook to reduce the load of writing the dictated content while simultaneously trying to learn it (lines 50, 58).

Across the five schools, newly arrived students demonstrated and talked about the challenges of learning via dictation and developing their Spanish literacy, as they rarely received classroom-based supports. When I talked to educators, they expressed a range of views about *el dictado*.

For example, to illustrate how challenging *el dictado* is for newly arrived students in Spanish, I drew parallels for educators—who usually had rudimentary experiences in English—about what it might be like to learn via dictation in English. Many answered like this principal: *"Gosh, I had never thought about that"* (Principal interview, 6/5/17).

Notably, when teachers were asked if they had ideas about how to adapt their traditional uses of dictation for recently arrived students, the main teacher who offered concrete ideas was one who had lived as an immigrant in the United States for several years, and who drew upon her own language and learning experiences. She reflected, *"Well, look at it like this—[for] anyone who has not mastered a language, dictating to them is death. It's like, 'write what I'm going to tell you,' [but they think], 'I don't even understand what you are saying to me!'"* (Teacher interview, 6/19/17). This teacher had several suggestions for how to better support dictation practices with students who had not yet mastered academic Spanish, such as providing visual cues for students to help contextualize the content, intentionally partnering students with a peer who could help, or finding copies of the text for them to follow.

It is also important to highlight that I am not seeking to blame educators (see also Román González & García Sánchez, Chapter 7). When I asked teachers if they had ever received coursework, trainings, materials, or other resources to help them think through how to work with binational students, they unilaterally answered, *"no—nothing."* Teachers, like Alison's, were teaching the way they had been taught to teach, following a relatively rigid national curriculum and looking for wiggle room within their pedagogy to make adjustments for binational students without larger structural supports. They, like binational students and their families, were left to their own devices. And as this volume discusses, teachers on both sides of the border who work with the students we share need increased supports.

Social Isolation

This relates to a second key challenge binational students faced in their rural Mexican schools: social isolation, or what students and teachers often called bullying. Alison, unlike many students from this study, had a relatively supportive social network in her new school in Mexico. This may have been because she had cousins in her class; both of her parents were originally from the community; her extended family held a prominent position locally; she had a sweet and laid-back personality; or because both her teacher and my research team worked hard to get kids to be open and accepting of her when she arrived halfway through the school year. Many other students—especially in Central Mexico, as Víctor Zúñiga (2016) notes in his research across contexts of reception in Mexico—face social isolation for being different in their Mexican schools (see Despagne, 2019). In this next interaction, at a different school in Puebla, fourth grader Jocelyn, who had recently moved from Brooklyn, New York, tells me a story with her friend about a classmate who tried to convince all of the girls not to hang out with Jocelyn because she was not like them.

Example 2: She's Not Like Us

Vanessa (4th grade classmate) **Jocelyn** (4th grade binational student) **Sarah** (Researcher)

44. **Vanessa:** Y entonces, Diana me dijo. Nos vio y nos reunió a todas . . . Karmen, a
    And so, Diana told me. She saw us and got all of us together . . . Karmen,
45. mí, a Silvia. Menos a Jocelyn. Le dijo que, nos dijo nosotras que—
    me, Silvia. Except for Jocelyn. She told her, she told us that—
46. su mamá es como es muy—
    Her mom is very—
47. **Jocelyn:** Enojona.
    Grumpy.
48. **Vanessa:** No sé como decirlo—no—como muy—presumida.
    I don't know how to say it—no—like very—arrogant.
49. **Sarah:** Ok.
50. **Vanessa:** Y porque su hija—no sé que tanto—y le da todo y—
    And because her daughter—I don't know how much—and gives her everything and—
51. **Sarah:** mmm
52. **Vanessa:** Y Diana le dice [a Jocelyn] . . . nos dijo que no nos juntemos con Jocelyn porque
    And Diana says to her [Jocelyn]—she told us we shouldn't get together with Jocelyn

53. según [Diana] que no es de nuestra clase.
    because according (to Diana) she is not from our class.
54. **Sarah:** ¿Quién dijo eso?
    Who said that?
55. **Vanessa:** Diana. Pero yo—
    Diana. But I—
56. **Sarah:** ¿Qué no es de tu clase?
    That what is not from your class?
57. **Jocelyn:** ((nervous laugh))
58. **Vanessa:** Es que—por ejemplo. De que según de ella nació en Estados Unidos.
    It's that—for example That according to her she [Jocelyn] was born in the United
59. Y nosotras pues acá. Como hemos estado toda nuestra vida. Y ella
    States. And we—well—here. Like we've been here our whole life. And she
60. ((gestures toward Jocelyn)), como nace en Estados Unidos, Diana dice que no nos
    ((gestures toward Jocelyn)), like how she's born in the United States, Diana says we
61. juntemos con ella porque no es de nuestra clase—no es igual que nosotros, dice.
    shouldn't get together with her because she's not from our class—she's not equal to us, she says.
62. **Sarah to Jocelyn:** ¿Y cómo te sentías cuando ella dijo eso?
    And how did you feel when she said this?
63. **Jocelyn:** Mal.
    Bad.
64. **Sarah:** Sí.
    Yeah.
65. **Vanessa:** Luego.
    Then.
66. **Sarah:** ¿Y qué hacemos cuando alguien hace algo así? Porque eso como—en mi—
    And what do we do when someone does something like this? Because it's like—in my—
67. **Vanessa:** Le dije al maestro pero el maestro no le dijo nada.
    I told the teacher but he didn't say anything to her.

68. **Sarah:** Hmmm. Porque tal vez tenemos que tener conversaciones porque—pues—lo que
    Hmmmm. Because maybe we need to have conversations because—well—what
69. pasa es que—todos son diferentes—no? Y para decir solamente por ser diferente es
    happens is that—everyone's different—right? And to say that it's a bad thing just
70. una cosa mala es muy feo, ¿verdad? Y en vez de pensar "aw, es diferente—
    because you're different is nasty, right? And instead of thinking "aw, she's
71. no es parte de nosotros" es pensar "guao—tiene experiencias diferentes
    different—she's not part of us" it's to think "wow—she has different experiences
72. y también iguales y podemos aprender entre nosotros," ¿no?
    and also similar ones and we can learn from each other," right?
73. **Vanessa:** Pero es que—mira—su mamá no le dijo [a Diana] eso.
    But it's that—look—her [Diana's] mom didn't tell her that.

In this interaction, fourth graders attempted to exclude a binational student simply because she was different. Luckily, Jocelyn had a friend, Vanessa, who stood up for her. This was not an isolated incident. For example, Jocelyn shared with me in an interview how a different classmate gave her a card with a similar message: *"And one Valentine's day she gave me a card that said, 'We are equal but we're not from the same class' . . . and then she stopped sitting with me"* (Interview, 5/5/17). Throughout this study, it became clear that it was hard to become socially integrated for many binational students. Jocelyn, for example, had been living in one of the largest urban areas in the world—New York City—and was now in a 5,000-person town at the foot of a volcano. Even in her school uniform, and with physical features similar to those of her peers, the ways she spoke, learned, and interacted, and the accessories she brought to school often set her apart in ways that led to exclusion, violating the importance of enacting *"todos somos iguales"* [we're all the same] that undergirds much of Mexican schooling (Levinson, 2001). The phrase that the students use, that Jocelyn "is not from our class" (lines 53, 61), could be taken up literally. Jocelyn, a newcomer to their school, had not been part of their classroom of students until this year. This is particularly pronounced because in Mexican primary schools, students tend to stay together with the same classmates from first through sixth grade. Yet, as Vanessa's explanations illustrate, the intention behind her classmate's comment was that Jocelyn grew up differently from them and therefore should be excluded (lines 58–61). The message I gave to Vanessa and Jocelyn about how difference should be something exciting so students could learn from one another, not something to be made fun of (lines 68–73), did not appear to form part of schooling for binational students in these rural Mexican schools.

Other students experienced social exclusion as well. Glenda, a high school senior, reflected, "They just always used to say like whatever about me and once they harassed me physically. It was my classmate who was female. Um and the teachers, they didn't do anything . . . when she tried to do that I got aggressive . . . , like I have that idea that I didn't want to be bullied anymore" (Interview, 5/22/17). This also happened in more subtle ways through everyday play among kids. For example, seven-year-old Julián described being excluded by his peers during pickup soccer matches because he was born in the United States: *"Some kids ask me where I was born and I tell them in the US. I don't like to tell them this because sometimes they laugh at me because I am not from here and I feel sad. And sometimes I play soccer and I tell them I want to be on team Mexico. They say, 'No. You are going to play for the US because you were born there.' Lots of kids tell me things like this. I tell them, 'I'm the same as any other person'"* (Interview, 6/27/17). Across age groups, students discussed the ways they faced discrimination because of their binational experiences and how educators rarely intervened in supportive ways. Instead, they often stood up for themselves—through returned aggression for Glenda, using his own words for Julián, or via a friend's support for Jocelyn—to try and counter the social isolation they experienced.

Mexico and the United States have extremely complex shared histories of colonization and conquest, in which Spanish and Mexican knowledges have been devalued vis-à-vis those of the United States (Urrieta, 2016), and students in Mexican small towns—at least those far from the physical border with relatively low density of return migration—may have rejected binational students' ways of talking and knowing because they perceived them as wanting to act superior (Despagne, 2019; Kleyn, 2017). As Adam, a recently arrived high school student, explained, "they'd [his Mexican classmates] try to say that they felt like I had tried to insult them or something like that. They would just tell me that. 'Just because you come from USA, don't think you're better than us.' And I would always say, 'I never said that. I don't even TALK to you guys.'" (Interview, 6/5/17). In addition, this study occurred the year Trump was elected president in the United States, and all students were aware of how Mexicans were negatively positioned in the media and through increasingly anti-immigrant policies. Although Mexican mononational students and educators did not appear to disfavor binational students because of Trump's rhetoric and policies, the political climate fostered even greater tension between Mexico and the United States, and by extension Mexican and U.S. ways of being, speaking, doing, and knowing.

All of this contributed to a context in which Mexican educators appeared to minimally engage in the social worlds of students, including bullying toward binational students. Reactively, when students like Vanessa or Glenda told teachers about mistreatment, teachers did not seem to take action. Preventively, outside of Alison's class, teachers did not appear to seek out ways to welcome and socially orient new students to classrooms or to talk to students about understanding and positively positioning life, language, or schooling experiences that differed from those experienced in their Mexican small towns. It is important to note that a few broader educational resources have been created at the national level for recently arrived students, such as the workbook "Mientras llego a mi escuela" ["As I arrive to my school"],[6] which provides a range of activities to work through their adjustment to school in Mexico compared to the United States. Yet, like most resources for binational students and families, educators in local rural schools did not know about these materials, and no educator from any of the schools ever mentioned their familiarity with these resources. In addition, although there were broad anti-bullying programs in schools throughout Mexico, students excluding others because of their national origin or speaking Spanish differently did not appear to fall into the realm of bullying acts requiring teacher intervention. There were not explicit structural supports—such as guidance counselors, peer-buddy systems, or affiliation groups such as a club for binational students—to help address some of the social challenges binational students faced in these schools. Yet educators also saw the need for change in this area. For example, the high school principal reflected that moving forward she hoped to "implement advisors . . . the work will include getting to know binational students a bit and through this relationship they can tell us what they don't have or what it is they want to keep studying because yes, the change is really hard" (HS Principal Interview, 6/5/17).

Discussion

As Mónica Jacobo's scholarship and activism have illustrated, questions around binational schooling in Mexico tend to focus on the bureaucratic processes of schooling access (e.g., Jacobo Suárez & Espinosa Cárdenas, 2016). Although these are very important, we also need to address broader questions of teacher training and pedagogy. This chapter offers a way to see inside the Mexican classrooms of newly arrived binational students to better understand the realities, challenges, and resourcefulness of educators and students today. Many teachers in Mexico are provided with minimal training and supports. As Jocelyn's teacher noted, when they learn they will have a binational student in their class, they often begin "*temblando*," or shaking in fear (FN 2/1/17). He, like most teachers, felt completely unprepared. As López and Santibáñez (Chapter 8) so clearly illustrate, the more we can prepare educators to work with bilingual and binational students, the better students' long-term educational trajectories will be.

Academically, Jocelyn's teacher was also very surprised by her transition. Jocelyn—unlike most binational students in Mexico—had had the opportunity to attend a bilingual school in Brooklyn, which greatly eased the academic side of her transition. Her teacher noted, "*When she read a paragraph (in Spanish) I said, 'Oh ok, she reads really well, better than some of the most behind students I have'*" (Interview, 6/20/17). Although his reaction illustrates the very low academic expectations he held for Jocelyn when she arrived, her experiences also illustrate how access to bilingual education can better prepare students for their studies on either side of the border. Unfortunately, in Mexico, English-Spanish bilingual schools are largely private, are rarely located in small towns, and are well beyond the financial means of binational working-class families. Although successful transitions across U.S. and Mexican schools are about more than preparing students for the language and literacy demands of their classrooms, opportunities to attend quality bilingual programs can greatly facilitate binational learning.

In 2016, the *Secretaría de Educación Pública* in Mexico passed a law requiring English classes for all first through 12th grade students, which, if implemented carefully, may represent an opportunity for binational students and their linguistic resources to be positively positioned. Although the English taught in these foreign-language classes is not demanding enough to increase binational students' English repertoires (Despagne & Jacobo, 2016), English classes can offer opportunities for binational students to shine as leaders with valuable knowledge (Despagne, 2019; Kleyn, 2017). Yet, as Despagne (2019) also noted, in some cases binational students reported being insulted as *"gringos"* [American white people] and positioned as showing off when speaking in English, illustrating that work is needed to ensure English classes can be a positive space for binational students.

Of the four primary schools in this study, only the one closest to a large city offered English classes once a week via a creative arrangement with an English teacher education program at a nearby university. As the principal at Jocelyn's rural school explained, although a set of English textbooks arrived several years beforehand, there was no room in the budget to hire an English teacher or train their classroom teachers, and no time in their school day (which was split between two shifts of schooling that shared the same building, a common practice) to incorporate English classes into students' schedules. Although she knew of schools closer to urban areas that charged students a weekly fee to pay for an English teacher, they could not convince anyone to come to their remote school because of costs and time. Within this study, the rural context again mattered.

Recommendations

In this final section, I provide recommendations for Mexican education policy, Mexican teachers, and U.S. teachers who work with the students we share.

Recommendations for Mexican Education Policy

1. Create an easily sharable resource (infographic, online training, etc.) that helps Mexican educators understand the basic concept of transfer—how students who already know how to read in English do not have to relearn how to read in Spanish, as the majority of these skills can be applied (Goldenberg, 2008). What students do need to learn are the surface-level differences of letter-sound correspondence between English and Spanish, such as /h/ de *"hombre"* in Spanish (which is silent) vs. "hat" in English and other orthographic rules of written Spanish. Until binational students and their teachers I worked with understood these differences, practices such as dictations were nearly impossible.

2. Carefully analyze student literacy goals and examine if the pedagogical practices emphasized in the national curriculum can achieve them. If authentic written communication is a goal, examine how the literacy curriculum may extend beyond orthographic correctness to include the expression of ideas and experiences (Teague, Smith, & Jiménez, 2010). A unilateral focus on form is particularly challenging for binational students who usually have not had the opportunity to learn these correct forms and who may bring a wider range of literacy knowledges to their Mexican classrooms that go unrecognized.

3. Incorporate coursework into pre-service teaching that trains teachers to work with bilingual students in their Spanish-medium classrooms. Through this coursework, educators can learn to position languages other than Spanish as resources rather than problems, and can build teaching strategies that leverage these linguistic resources to meet academic goals. Competencies might include building students' metalinguistic awareness, understanding key differences in Spanish and English phonological systems, and highlighting differences in approaches to literacy instruction across both countries. Teachers do not have to be bilingual themselves to engage in these pedagogical approaches (see Gallo, 2017).

4. Create certificates that train practicing classroom teachers to offer Spanish as a second language supports and literacy instruction across the grade levels (as described in #3), including incentives for educators to complete these certificates.

5. Linguistic diversity and intercultural communication form part of Mexico's education policies and reform, but usually reference bilingual and bicultural education for indigenous communities. Proactively seek to include English-speaking binational students in these agendas, policies, and schooling practices.

6. Pilot public, cost-free dual-immersion schools in areas with significant binational student populations, such as border cities like Tijuana. The proximity to the border may also offer a useful point of departure, as it is likely easier to find

and train bilingual teachers in these areas. This schooling model permits Spanish-dominant and English-dominant students to develop their bilingual and biliteracy skills in both languages. This would help move access to bilingual education in Mexico from elite bilingualism for high-income families who can afford private schooling or bilingual programs for indigenous populations to also include working-class binational students. This could also be a robust way to support the *Programa Nacional de Inglés* in Mexico, which strives to offer English language instruction across public 1-12 schooling.

7. Offer both pre-service and in-service training on how educators can position different experiences as resources rather than deficits, with an emphasis on interrupting discriminatory behavior among students. Educators should be better prepared to work with students so they do not discriminate based on national origin, language, or other forms of difference. Such training does not just matter for binational students, but for all forms of difference.

Recommendations for Mexican Educators

1. Carefully monitor new students and make them feel comfortable. As was clear in Alison's dictation interaction, her teacher did this effectively.

2. Implement a buddy system for newly arrived students. Schooling procedures are very different in Mexico, and binational students can benefit from a kind classmate who can show them the ropes of day-to-day practices.

3. Create procedures to welcome new students to your classroom, and look for opportunities for them to share—when they seem comfortable—about their life and schooling experiences in the United States. Some materials such as "Mientras llego a mi escuela" (described above) may already exist, so part of this strategy includes better promoting and sharing resources that have been utilized throughout Mexico.

4. Like teachers in the United States working with newcomers, seek to adjust your instruction (vocabulary, rate of speech, sentence complexity) and provide redundant key information via visual cues, pictures, physical gestures (Goldenberg, 2008, p, 20).

5. In most Mexican schools, there are robust opportunities for oral expression and for students to "count" as legitimate speakers. Instead of only prioritizing correct orthography, think about how to create literacy practices that also permit a wide range of reading and writing skills to be recognized and built upon to broaden who "counts" as a legitimate writer (Jiménez, Smith, & Martínez-León, 2003).

6. Be cognizant of how you use dictation practices in your teaching, and try out adaptations for binational students. This may include lending them a copy of the text to visually support their writing or pairing them with a kind classmate who will help them.

7. Look for ways to create classroom activities besides teacher-fronted whole group instruction. It can be intimidating for binational students who are unsure of their academic Spanish, the Mexican curriculum, or Mexican classroom procedures to answer in front of the entire group. Smaller-group activities or pair work provides more comfortable spaces for binational students to try things out and provides lower-stakes interactions for them to meaningfully draw upon academic and social language in Spanish with peers (Goldenberg, 2008).

8. Work with other educators at your school to collaboratively create Spanish literacy tutoring sessions for newly arrived students during lunch or outside of school hours. Or work with students' families to find qualified local resources (such as a retired teacher) who could help guide students in their Spanish literacy instruction.

9. Work with colleagues at your school to create a club for binational students so that they can navigate their experiences with the support of one another and educators from

the school, rather than alone. Consider opportunities to invite mononational students as allies into this club as well.

10. Raise your awareness of how students position binational students in terms of their differences and interrupt discriminatory behavior each and every time you witness it, no matter how minor the insult appears.

Recommendations for U.S. Educators

Many of the recommendations for Mexican educators can also apply to U.S. educators welcoming newly arrived immigrant students to their classrooms.

1. Advocate for additive bilingual education opportunities for students from immigrant families. Depending on your local context, this may be through formal programs such as dual-immersion schools, via lunchtime or after-school clubs that help develop students' academic Spanish, or by encouraging families to develop their children's academic Spanish in outside spaces, such as Latinx community centers or religious institutions.

2. The current political climate has made topics related to national origin, language, immigration, and undocumented status feel more polemic than ever. Yet rather than remaining silent when you hear discriminatory comments among students related to these topics, it is increasingly important that you speak up to interrupt talk that makes students from immigrant families feel unwelcome or unimportant. Schools are meant to be safe spaces for learning for all students, which requires educators to serve as role models who proactively seek out ways to keep these spaces safe within the current political context.

3. Some immigrant families may consider relocating to their home country and may come to you to discuss the academic transition for their child. The following resource kit (http://www.colorincolorado.org/toolkit-mexican-schools) provides some ideas of how to engage in a supportive conversation with caregivers about this topic.

It is important to emphasize the cyclical nature of the students we share. The students I knew in Puebla lived far from the physical border and were not just students with U.S. schooling who now went to school in Mexico. It became clear that they or their families often had concrete plans for their U.S.-born children to return to the United States for schooling. Indeed, one of the most common questions I received from students' caregivers was what was the best age to send their kids back to the United States for schooling success. Jocelyn, for example, imagined herself moving back to live with extended family members in New York after she completed primary or middle school. Thus, as this volume highlights, we cannot simply engage in conversations about adaptations to Mexican schooling for the students we share. We need to be thinking about the complex trajectories of bidirectional movement that students experience across these two national schooling systems, and how we can better support them and their teachers to achieve their academic goals.

Notes

1. I would like to thank Andrea Ortiz, who served as my research assistant on this study. I would also like to thank Fulbright and the National Academy of Education and Spencer foundations for funding to support this study.
2. All names are pseudonyms.
3. Unlike other regions of Puebla, U.S. agriculture heavily recruited workers in the Mixteca region for the Bracero program beginning in the 1960s, and there has been a robust, relatively uninterrupted flow of migration from this region since that time.
4. Italicized quotations are translations from Spanish completed by the researcher.
5. See Appendix for transcription conventions.
6. This workbook can be found at https://www.yumpu.com/es/document/read/36711129/mientras-llego-a-mi-escuela.

References

Binford, L., D'Aubeterre, M. E., & Rivermar, M. L. (2014). Preguntas, coordenadas teóricas y procedimientos. In D'Aubeterre & Rivermar (Eds.), *Todos vuelven? Migración acelerada, crisis de la economía estadounidense y retorno en cuatro localidades del estado de Puebla, México* (11–42). Puebla, México: Benemérita Universidad Autónoma de Puebla.

Campano, G. (2007). *Immigrant students and literacy: Reading, writing, and remembering*. New York: Teachers College Press.

Carrasco Altamirano, A. (2003). La escuela puede enseñar estrategias de lectura y promover su regular empleo. *Revista Mexicana de Investigación Educativa, 8*(17), 129–142.

Despagne, C. (2019). "Language is what makes everything easier": The awareness of semiotic resources of Mexican transnational students in Mexican schools. *International Multilingual Research Journal.*

Despagne, C., & Jacobo, M. (2016). Desafíos actuales de la escuela monolítica Mexicana: El caso de los alumnos migrantes transnacionales. *Sinéctica, 47.*

Durand, J., & Massey, D. (2009). *Clandestinos: Migración México-Estados Unidos en los albores del siglo XXI.* Zacatecas, Universidad Autónoma de Zacatecas.

Escamilla, K., Hopewell, S., Butvilofsky, S., Sparrow, W., Soltero-González, L., Ruiz-Figueroa, O., & Escamilla, M. (2014). *Biliteracy from the start.* Philadelphia, PA: Caslon Publishing.

Gallo, S. (2017). *Mi padre: Mexican immigrant fathers and their children's education.* New York: Teachers College Press.

Gallo, S., Link, H., & Wortham, S. (2017). "Qué las maestras hablaran más con ellos": Children grappling with documentation status in school. In S. Salas & P. Portes (Eds.), *US Latinization: Education and the New Latino South* (pp. 123–140). Albany, NY: State University of New York Press.

Goldenberg, C. (2008). Teaching English language learners: What the research does—and does not—say. *American Educator, 32*(2), 8–43.

González, N. (2011, February). Immigration and migration in dynamic times and spaces. Presented at Ethnography and Education Research Forum, Philadelphia, PA.

INEGI. Catalogo de Indicadores. Retrieved from http://www3.inegi.org.mx/sistemas/cni/indicadores.aspx?idOrden=1.1

Jacobo Suárez, M., & Espinosa Cárdenas, F. (2016). Retos al acceso educativo en el contexto de migración de retorno en México: el caso de la dispensa de la apostille del acta de nacimiento extranjera. In G. C. Valdéz Gardea & I. García Castro (Eds.), *Tránsito y retorno de la niñez migrante: Epílogo en la administración Trump* (pp. 175–203). Sonora, Mexico: El Colegio de Sonora.

Jensen, B., Grajeda, S., & Haertel, E. (2018). Measuring cultural dimensions of classroom interactions. *Educational Assessment, 23*(4), 250–276.

Jímenez, R., Smith, P., & Martínez-León, N. (2003). Freedom and form: The language and literacy practices of two Mexican schools. *Reading Research Quarterly, 38*(4), 488–508.

Kleyn, T. (2017). Centering transborder students: Perspectives on identity, languaging, and schooling between the U.S. and Mexico. *Multicultural Perspectives, 19*(2), 76–84.

Ladson-Billings, G. (1995). Toward a theory of culturally relevant pedagogy. *American Educational Research Journal, 32*(3), 465–491.

Levinson, B. A. U. (2001). *We are all equal: Student culture and identity at a Mexican secondary school.* Durham, NC: Duke University Press.

Orellana, M. F. (2009). *Translating childhoods: Immigrant youth, language, and culture.* New Brunswick, NJ: Rutgers University Press.

Panait, C., & Zúñiga, V. (2016). Children circulating between the U.S. and Mexico: Fractured schooling and linguistic ruptures. *Mexican Studies/Estudios Mexicanos, 32*(2), 226–251.

Teague, B., Smith, P., & Jiménez, R. (2010). Learning to write in a Mexican school. *Journal of Language and Literacy Education, 6*(1), 1–19.

Urrieta, L. (2016). Diasporic community smartness: *saberes* (knowings) beyond schooling and borders. *Race Ethnicity and Education, 19*(6), 1186–1199.

Zúñiga, V. (2016). *Dos fortalezas de la colección de trabajos reunidos en el libro editado por H. Romo y O. Mogollon-Lopez.* Presentation at the Universidad de las Américas Puebla, October 18, 2016.

Chapter 6

Equitable Teaching Enhances Achievement Opportunity for the Students We Share[1]

Bryant Jensen

Opportunities to learn are not evenly distributed across schools and classrooms. For the 9 million primary and secondary students that we share between Mexico and the United States, achievement[2] opportunities are weaker than for their more privileged peers. Entrenched institutional challenges in both countries undermine transnational students' opportunities to learn. In the United States, transnational students are likelier to live in segregated neighborhoods and attend segregated, undersourced schools (e.g., Orfield, Kucsera, & Siegel-Hawley, 2012). In Mexico, transnational children are likelier to attend rural or semi-rural schools, which are more underresourced than urban schools (Jensen & Jacobo, 2019; Treviño, 2013).

In this chapter, I address "equitable teaching" to enhance achievement opportunity for the students we share between the United States and Mexico. I define equitable teaching as high-quality instruction that resonates with students' lived experiences, values, and cultural knowledge, practices, and identities (Jensen, Grajeda, & Haertel, 2018; Jensen, Pérez Martínez, & Aguilar Escobar, 2016). I provide illustrations of equitable teaching in classrooms in both countries, mostly at the primary level, and conclude with a series of recommendations for U.S. and Mexican educators, teacher educators, researchers, and policy makers to collaborate in pursuit of an equitable teaching agenda.

My focus on classroom teaching and learning takes into account the significance of other factors that bear on achievement opportunity for transnational students as well. I frame teaching as inextricably embedded within broader structures of achievement opportunity, such as segregation or the uneven distribution of resources. Even after accounting for these multiplier influences, teaching matters. International studies and research in Mexico and the United States confirm that qualities of teaching, among school factors, have the strongest effect on student achievement opportunity (INEE, 2007, 2009, 2015; Riddell, 2008; Rivkin, Hanushek, & Kain, 2005; Willms, 2006). With adequate support, strong teachers can help students to learn two years or more worth of academic material in a single school year (Hanushek, 2016).

There is an essential distinction between *high-quality* teaching and *equitable* teaching. The way colleagues and I use "equity" to characterize a particular type of teaching includes, but is more than, just universal aspects (Jensen & García, 2019; Jensen, Mejía Arauz, & Aguilar Zepeda, 2017), such as asking analytic questions (Saunders, Goldenberg, & Hamann, 1992), providing clear behavioral expectations (Emmer & Stough, 2001), or engendering warm, respectful, and enthusiastic relationships with students (Roorda, Koomen, Spilt, & Oort, 2011). Many consider these aspects of teaching to be "universal" because they are important for all students to learn, regardless of context.

Equitable teaching is instruction, lesson planning, teacher-child relationships, and parental engagement that connect meaningfully with what children know and do outside school—with family, friends, and others in their communities. It integrates the cultural practices and identities of underserved children, like the "students we share." Meaningful connections with students' everyday lives are equitable because they acknowledge and accommodate sociocultural differences rather than ignore or minimize them for the sake of "equality."

Reese, Jensen, and Ramirez (2014) found in K-2 classrooms in a rural agricultural community in California that teachers communicated emotional support, a universal feature of effective teaching, by using children's native language (Spanish). Teachers in highly supportive classrooms used Spanish more than six times as often as those in less supportive classrooms to provide comfort, assistance, and to address learning problems. Spanish use, a cultural feature, was a medium through which teachers communicated strong affective support, a universal feature. Equitable teaching is meant to be both effective (universal) *and* meaningful (cultural). I see these two values as mutually reinforcing—as different sides of the same coin.

The transnational students we share between the United States and Mexico are an especially important case to examine the notion of equitable teaching. Though a very large and diverse group in terms of language, social class, race, and immigrant experiences, the students we share, as a single demographic, demonstrate "paradoxical development" (Fuller & García Coll, 2010; Jensen, Reese, Hall-Kenyon, & Bennett, 2015): strong social-behavioral competencies like collaboration, respect, and composure, though weak performance on standard academic measures across school curricula. Scholars have argued that this developmental profile is "paradoxical" (Fuller et al., 2009) because in mainstream U.S. society, children who perform well socially also tend to demonstrate high academic achievement (Denham, 2006). Equitable teaching, understood and replicated across thousands of classrooms, promises to ameliorate the paradoxical development of the students we share by drawing on their social-behavioral strengths in classroom activities to improve their academic learning opportunities.

Throughout the chapter, I make comparisons between U.S. and Mexican schools regarding teaching and achievement opportunity. The purpose of these comparisons is to envision possibilities for improvement, rather than make claims about superiority or inferiority. Indeed, there are relative strengths and weaknesses to education systems in both countries, and there is certainly more variation in teaching quality within than between countries (Jensen & Sawyer, 2013). The organization of schooling in the United States is different than in Mexico, as Santibañez demonstrates in Chapter 1. For example, even with recent reforms, Mexican education is largely managed by the central government, whereas U.S. education is run by states and local districts. Differences like these have important implications for any kind of binational recommendation for educational improvement. I engage implications of these differences—in the spirit of learning from and with one another—to enhance equitable teaching for the students we share.

Bien Educados and Achievement Opportunity

For teacher-student interactions to be equitable, it is the job of every teacher to know who their students are and the patterns of behaviors and related values that they exhibit. For those teaching Mexican-origin students from transnational families, decades of research suggest a critical finding that is important for teachers to understand. Mexican immigrant parents are greatly concerned to raise up children who are *bien educados*—respectful, loyal to family, collaborative, and hardworking (Bridges et al., 2012). *Bien educado* parental practices are based on agrarian family values (LeVine & White, 1986; Reese, Balzano, Gallimore, & Goldenberg, 1995), reflected in common social graces in Mexico and in phrases like *para servirle* [at your service] or *¿mande usted?* [could you please repeat that?]. When they talk with their child's teacher, in either country, Mexican-origin parents express great interest in and responsibility for their child's comportment in class and at school (Valdés, 1996). They ask, "Is my daughter/son behaving properly, respectful, helpful, and obedient?"

Social competencies associated with being *bien educados* have direct implications for achievement opportunities of transnational students (Galindo & Fuller, 2010). Understanding this fact, capitalizing on the parents' efforts to raise "well-behaved" children, is a good starting point for examining equitable teaching of transnational students of Mexican origins. It helps identify some of the challenges that must be addressed.

For example, despite a focus in the United States on social competencies that enable student engagement in academic tasks (Malecki & Elliott, 2002; Denham & Brown, 2010), educators are often blind to the social competencies of children from Mexican immigrant households (Bridges et al., 2012). They fail to perceive social competencies like *respeto* or *cooperación* because they are "culturally bounded" (Fuller & García Coll, 2010, p. 560). Many U.S. educators characterize "cooperation" as following class rules. The same concept in many Mexican immigrant households (*cooperación* in Spanish), however, refers to being accommodating and working well with others (Bridges et al., 2012).

It is difficult for children who are *bien educados* to be integrated into classrooms when their developmental strengths do not map onto educators' ways of seeing/valuing competence (Jensen, Reese, Hall-Kenyon, & Bennett, 2015). Children raised to have *respeto* for persons in authority can be viewed by U.S. educators as taciturn. Children socialized to be collaborative can be seen as lacking initiative or independence. Often as educators, we see children and their development more as *we* are than as *they* are, which can undermine their opportunity to achieve. If our lenses keep us from seeing/valuing children's strengths, then it is very difficult to integrate them into classrooms to organize and motivate academic engagement and learning.

Bien educado values and practices in Mexican classrooms, on the other hand, are part of daily life, especially in public schools. As long as children remain in the same community, they remain in the same *grupo escolar* throughout elementary school, from first until sixth grade. *Grupo*

1ºB in first grade becomes *2ºB* in second grade, *3ºB* in third grade, and so on (Jensen, 2005). Each school year the teacher changes, but the student group remains the same. This way, children in public schools—nearly 9 in 10 of all Mexican children—are socialized to be familiar with and to help each other. They identify with one another's success and well-being (Schmelkes, Mosso, & Reyes, 2010). The *grupo* identity in many ways supersedes individual identities (Levinson, 2001). Being *bien educados* in Mexican classrooms is a scholastic advantage.

At the same time, some teaching practices associated with *bien educados* can be less effective in the universal sense. *Bien educados* and related agrarian values can lead to an emphasis on rote learning practices like *el dictado* (see Gallo, Chapter 5) or deference to teacher authority, which can limit student opportunities to ask unsolicited questions, lead a discussion, or express their own ideas. Equitable opportunities for underserved students to achieve require interweaving high-quality classroom instruction with the knowledge, values, and practices of students' cultural communities. Both are necessary for equitable teaching.

Equitable Teaching for the Students We Share

Teaching for all students, transnational or otherwise, is inevitably contextual (Jensen, Wallace, et al., 2019). This is because students, like all of us, learn and make meaning in terms of what we know and have experienced in specific (or local) settings. The implications of this are profound. What works in one classroom could paradoxically decrease achievement opportunity for the students we share in another. For example, an emphasis on students using precise mathematical language to convey mathematical ideas (e.g., Hill et al., 2008) can unwittingly ignore—or, worse yet, dismiss as inappropriate—the everyday language practices (e.g., in Spanish) of students we share (Moschkovich, 2010), detrimentally affecting their academic identities, engagement, and achievement (Flores & Rosa, 2015). Disciplinary and everyday language practices interact; they are not mutually exclusive (Jensen & Thompson, 2020).

The alternative is equitable teaching that is both rigorous *and* culturally situated. Learning is enhanced by incorporating—rather than ignoring or rejecting—what children and youth from underserved communities know and do outside school, including the ways they are socialized in their cultural communities. Equity in teaching is the interaction of effective and locally meaningful practices. Instead of a binary choice between teaching effectively and attending to contextual variations, I argue for addressing both—the combination of generic and cultural aspects (Jensen, Grajeda, & Haertel, 2018).

Jensen, Pérez Martínez, and Aguilar Escobar (2016) discuss three elements of equitable teaching that shape marginalized students' opportunity to learn in classrooms. These elements are critical to the achievement opportunity for the students we share (Jensen, Mejía Arauz, & Aguilar Zepeda, 2017). I summarize these elements in Table 6.1, including some

Table 6.1. Elements of Equitable Teaching and Associated Factors and Variables

Elements	Factors	Associated Variables
Instructional Time Essential Question: How *much* is taught?	Institutional Efficiency	Number of school days per year Length of school day School closures
	Classroom Efficiency	Teacher attendance Student attendance Use of class time
Generic Quality Essential Question: How *well* is the content taught?	Affective Support	Positive climate Negative climate Teacher sensitivity
	Organization	Behavior management Productivity Instructional formats
	Instructional Support	Concept development Quality of feedback Academc language
Local Quality Essential Question: How *meaningfully* is the content taught?	Life Applications	Language use Content connections Equity
	Self in Group	Competition Peer collaboration Social organization
	Agency	Autonomy Role flexibility Equitable expectations

associated factors and variables. Though I draw from interdisciplinary research in both countries to propose this list, these variables are not meant to be exhaustive. Moreover, the factors are not specific to teaching particular academic content; I recognize that features of effective instruction can vary by content (Shulman, 1987). The purpose of specifying these elements, including associated factors and variables, is to discuss how they affect achievement opportunity for the students we share, as well as to examine how they relate with one another.

Instructional Time. It is no surprise that school learning depends on the amount of time children engage in deliberate practice of academic knowledge and skills (Bloom, 1974). Basic institutional (in)efficiencies, thus, have a direct effect on student achievement opportunity (Stallings, Knight, & Markham, 2014). Instructional time depends on the number of intended instructional hours, reflected in the school schedule (i.e., number of school days, length of school day), as well as the efficient use of scheduled time. Several types of inefficiencies in school can widen the gap between intended and actual instructional time (Abadzi, 2009)—e.g., unscheduled school closures, teacher absenteeism, student absenteeism, as well as lengthy transitions or managerial tasks, regular disruptions, and unclear expectations in classroom tasks.

Inadequate instructional time is a major issue in underresourced schools across Latin America (Schiefelbein & McGinn, 2008). Ezpeleta and Weiss (1996) found in rural schools in the Mexican states of Guerrero and Oaxaca that of the 200 scheduled days, only 100 were provided in terms of actual instructional hours. Actual instructional time, in which students were engaged in instructional activity, was 60 to 90 minutes per day, on average. Authors found that teacher absenteeism, impromptu faculty meetings, and bureaucratic demands significantly reduced instructional time and, thus, student achievement opportunity. Given that transnational students are likelier than their peers in Mexico to attend a rural or semi-rural (rather than an urban) school, they are less likely to have instructional time they need to achieve. Adequate time in instructional activity is necessary but certainly not sufficient to enhance achievement opportunity for the students we share (Martinic & Vergara, 2007; Schiefelbein & McGinn, 2008).

Generic Quality. "Generic quality" in teaching refers to aspects that are important for all children to learn, regardless of students' socioeconomic, cultural, or linguistic backgrounds. In Table 6.1, I identify three broad factors of generic teaching quality. Affective support refers to the extent to which students experience comfort, positivity, and enthusiasm in their relationships with peers and the teacher in the classroom (Denham, 2006). Positive affect, demonstrated through respectful and joyful relationships, helps students take risks and accept difficult academic and social challenges (Blair, 2002; Roorda et al., 2011). Organization refers to how well teachers help students to regulate their own behavior to get the most out of each school day and maintain interest in learning activities (Emmer & Stough, 2001) through positive redirection of misbehavior (Doyle, 1986), clear expectations, productive routines, etc. Last, instructional support concerns how well teachers develop students' problem-solving and critical thinking skills through modeling, questions, correction, conversations, and other interactions in the classroom. The most consequential instructional interactions support students' reasoning, critical thinking, and conceptual understanding, rather than memorizing facts (Bransford, Brown, & Cocking, 2000). This occurs through regular analytic discourse (Goldenberg, 1992), specific and individualized feedback (Martínez Rizo, 2012), and developing proficiency in the language practices of academic disciplines (Snow & Uccelli, 2009).

Studies in both Mexico and the United States show that generic qualities of teaching affect the achievement opportunities of the students we share (e.g., Downer et al., 2012; Goldenberg, 2008; Guevara et al., 2005; Reese, Jensen, & Ramirez, 2014; Schmelkes et al., 2010). Acknowledging that there are generic or universal features of teaching quality (e.g., Stigler & Hiebert, 2009), however, is not to say that there are not also important differences or considerations for teaching quality across academic content. Indeed, Grossman et al. (2014) find instructional features specific to teaching language arts, and Hill et al. (2008) identify instructional qualities for teaching mathematics. There are overlaps as well as important divergences between generic and content-specific instructional quality (Blazar et al., 2017).

Local Quality. As mentioned earlier, I also argue that it is vital to distinguish between generic and cultural aspects of teaching. To be clear, generic aspects of teaching are never "acultural." There is no such thing. Default ways of thinking, talking, feeling, and presenting; as well as organizing and motivating student participation in classroom activities tend to privilege normative, even hegemonic, ways of being. This is just the way that social institutions like schools evolve. They are designed to instantiate the values and practices of those in power. In the United States, the content and form of teaching and learning in school privilege White, middle-class ways of interacting. In Mexico, the situation is not as different as one might think. Schooling in both countries tends to perpetuate privilege for the reasons I mentioned earlier: 1) underrepresented students are much more likely to attend underresourced schools with underprepared teachers; and 2) the content and form of school interactions favor children from privileged families and communities.

By addressing cultural aspects of teaching, we can address this second disadvantage faced by the students we share. Equitable teaching is generic quality instantiated in culturally meaningful ways. We should separate the aim of high-quality teaching from the ways it may inadvertently privilege some children over others. For example, competitive activities like Jeopardy games are often used in U.S. classroom to review concepts and integrate them with new ones (McInerney, Roche, McInerney, & Marsh, 1997). Researchers have found that these activities tend to engage White, middle-class children, while marginalizing children from underrepresented—and especially indigenous—communities (Rogoff, 2003, pp. 229–235; Suina & Smolkin, 1994). Competition is not a universal motivator for learning, and for some it is culturally incompatible. Whereas integrating concepts with prior knowledge is important for all students to achieve (i.e., generic quality), the ways we practice this should be culturally meaningful (i.e., local quality).

Colleagues and I have proposed three domains of local quality in teaching (Jensen, 2014; Jensen, Reese, Rueda, & Garcia, 2014)—ways to make local adjustments to provide learning opportunities that resonate with what the students we share know, do, and identify with outside school (Jensen, Mejía Arauz, et al., 2019; Jensen, Mejía Arauz, & Aguilar Zepeda, 2017) (see Table 6.1). First, Life Applications: the extent to which teaching explores and integrates aspects of students' lives (e.g., routines, practices, relationships, values, interests). This includes how teachers and children use non-school languages (e.g., codes, style, vernacular) to enhance learning and social relationships (García, 2005), connect out-of-school knowledge and experiences with instructional content (Tharp, Estrada, Dalton, & Yamauchi, 2000, pp. 26–29), and examine and explore resolutions to social justice issues (Banks & Banks, 1995; Ogbu, 1992).

Second, Self in Group refers to how teaching socializes students to work and identify with peers to organize learning and motivate participation in classroom activity (Paradise, 1996; Webb & Farivar, 1994). This domain has particular significance for students we share who are raised to be *bien educados*—to value comportment, collaboration, respect, and negotiation over individualistic practices like competition or the use of external rewards (Rogoff et al., 2015). It examines the extent to which opportunities are provided to students to coordinate their participation in classroom activities with peers—to assist and support one another, to build on each other's contributions, and to work toward a common objective. Some research shows that collaborative organization for learning is especially meaningful for children of color in the United States (Slavin, 2010; Webb & Farvivar, 1994), as well as for Mexican students from rural, indigenous, and low-socioeconomic status (SES) communities (Mejía Arauz, 2001). In upper-elementary, Latino-majority classrooms in Salt Lake City, controlling for generic quality, I recently found that more peer collaboration significantly predicted gains in students' disciplinary language development (Jensen, 2018).

Last, Agency concerns how student choice and freedom are managed in the classroom. It refers to the extent to which all students have opportunities to have a responsibility, ask their own questions, lead an activity, and internalize high expectations. Bazán, Martínez, and Trejo (2009) found that more agency support from first-grade teachers in Sonora, Mexico, enriched children's literacy engagement and learning. Adair, Colegrove, and McManus (2018) found that early educators in a Texas school near the U.S.-Mexico border restricted child agency in classrooms because of deficit perspectives they had toward immigrant children and families.

Recommendations to Foster Equitable Teaching

Advocating equitable teaching for the students we share implies a need for change in commonly used and traditional instructional practices—in both countries. By this, I do not mean to blame teachers for students' underperformance. Indeed, I believe it is vital to distinguish teach*ers* from the complex act of teach*ing* (Jensen, Wallace, et al., 2019; Shulman, 1987). Introducing and refining equitable teaching does not rest on teachers alone. Teaching quality and changes in instructional practices depend on several influences that are within *and* beyond the classroom. Teaching and learning occur within institutions that are inequitable by design, apparent in their histories and organization, as I describe in the section below on "caveats."

Teaching includes lesson planning, instruction, classroom organization, and connections with students and their family and community. It involves not only what teachers do and know, but who they are in terms of dispositions, identities, and backgrounds. Teaching is a relational process—between teacher and students, among students, and that the teachers and students have with the content they are learning (Ball, Thames, & Phelps, 2008). It also depends on infrastructural supports like manageable student-to-teacher ratios or adequate instructional materials or technologies that are outside of what a teacher alone can provide (Jensen, Pérez Martínez, & Aguilar Escobar, 2016). Thus, improving teaching is a shared obligation of us all: administrators, legislators, researchers, students, teachers, and teacher educators.

Efforts to make teaching and learning more equitable for the students we share must grapple with the ways instructional time and generic and local quality interact across classroom settings. Attending to these three elements on their own is necessary, but insufficient. Equitable achievement opportunity is found in combinations of these elements. For example, in 160 video segments of 40 public early education classrooms in the state of Aguascalientes, colleagues and I found a strong, statistically significant relationship between instructional support (generic quality) and "social organization" (local quality)—the use of social relatedness and authentic incentives to organize learning (Jensen, Pérez Martínez, Johnstun, & Hernandez, 2018). Teachers used the inherent value of analytic, critical-thinking tasks to motivate child participation, in collaboration with peers. In one classroom, the teacher provided extensive feedback in back-and-forth exchanges with two boys working together on addition word problems.

T: "*A ver, tú puedes explicar a él por qué sacaste ocho. A ver, explícale. Tú le puedes ayudar a él*" ["Let's see, you can explain to him how you got eight. Explain it. You can help him."]

In this interaction, the teacher gave personalized feedback while orienting the first student to help the second. After listening to them talk together about their answers, the teacher helped the children identify their respective errors by learning from one another. The teacher socialized peer engagement and social learning *in order to* teach deeper understanding of math concepts. The teacher drew on the social strengths of her students to enhance an achievement opportunity.

How can we as educators, teacher educators, researchers, and policy makers in Mexico and in the United States provide more equitable learning opportunities like this one for the students we share? It would be disingenuous for me to say that we know all we need to know to enhance achievement opportunities through equitable teaching for the students we share. Yet we know enough from existing scholarship to offer some suggestions. My recommendations are meant to apply what we already know to foster equitable teaching as well as to deepen what we know through collaborations between educators, researchers, and other stakeholders in both countries.

Educators. Learn about and from your transnational students in order to connect the academic content that you teach with what your students already know and do in their daily lives. Home visits are certainly a useful way of accomplishing this (González, Moll, & Amanti, 2005). Replacing our teacher hat with a learner hat, we can glean a lot of helpful information by observing family routines, interactions, and traditions in home settings. Referencing what you learn from these visits in your classroom teaching with students can enhance their interest in academic content and the impact of classroom activities on their achievement.

You can also interview transnational children and their family members. Be sensitive, of course, but do not shy away from asking questions about their transnational experiences, especially when they have attended school in the other country. They learn a lot of content, particularly in civics, in one country that is often "invisible" to educators in the other (Zúñiga & Hamann, 2013). You can have conversations about the knowledge and experiences of students we share during class time as well. Sharing about yourself with them (e.g., background, hobbies, recent trips, family traditions) can encourage students to share and ask questions of each other. This requires a classroom culture that appreciates student differences as a means for increasing classroom solidarity, participation, and achievement.

Last, educators—teachers and administrators alike—should foster a collaborative climate of instructional improvement in their schools (Gallimore, Ermeling, Saunders, & Goldenberg, 2009). Some of the aspects of teaching that I have identified in my characterization of equity are fairly nuanced. It is not enough to talk about them. Teachers need to be able to see them in practice (their own and others') and have adequate time and support to analyze them in collegial teams to foster improvement (Jensen, Haertel, & Gomez, 2020). In these teams, teachers establish joint goals and observe key learning moments in one another's teaching to improve student learning opportunities (Ermeling, Gallimore, & Hiebert, 2017).

Teacher Educators. Teaching is a demanding profession. It is not possible for teachers in their first year of teaching to know and be able to do all that is required to be an equitable educator (Bullough & Baughman, 1997). A lot of teacher learning must happen on the job (Borko, 2004). As teacher educators, we build a foundation for lifelong professional learning. Thus, between the varied requirements for teacher licensure in

Mexico and in the United States—content knowledge, teaching methods, lesson planning, assessment, ethics, etc.—teacher educators should build a foundation of dispositional development in pre-service teachers. Dispositions are underlying orientations to self, others, and society that shape how we think and act. In the teaching profession, dispositions are related inseparably with "knowledge and skills to teach particular content in particular ways" (Borko, Liston, & Whitcomb, 2007, p. 361).

Colleagues and I have identified and empirically validated three dispositions to develop in pre-service teachers in order for them to foster equitable learning opportunities for underserved students (Jensen, Feinauer Whiting, & Chapman, 2018), like those we share between Mexico and the United States. First is social awareness—the ability for teachers to understand their own and others' social positions as well as the structures of privilege in society. Self-awareness precedes social awareness. Aware educators understand what leads to ethnic or socioeconomic segregation in communities, neighborhoods, and schools. They understand how the form of schooling often perpetuates rather than changes structures of societal privilege.

Second is meekness—the ability to be curious, teachable, and even-tempered to learn from sociocultural differences and to persist through ambiguity and discomfort to communicate well across these differences. Meekness is openness, but it is more than that (Pettigrove, 2012). Meek educators communicate their views without speaking down to those who disagree. They seek to learn from those with differing experiences and perspectives. They are willing to be uncomfortable to have hard conversations (e.g., about unauthorized migration).

Finally, the third disposition for equitable educators to develop is advocacy for students—a personal commitment to go out of our way to make schooling fairer for all students. Advocate educators position the students we share as knowers. They find ways to help them help us and the others in the classroom better understand what it is like to speak another language or attend school in another country. They go out of their way to find the resources students need to succeed, and they enrich instructional activities by discussing hard social issues like poverty or discrimination. These three interrelated dispositions—social awareness, meekness, and advocacy for students—are critical for equitable pre-service teachers to develop in both countries. They will help educators see teaching as more than a technical profession, and will lead them to wonder, reflect, innovate, and collaborate to better meet the needs of the students we share.

Researchers. We need more evidence about what constitutes equitable teaching and learning and how to more systematically implement it across academic content and sociocultural contexts. Colleagues and I have argued that this requires interdisciplinary frameworks, multiple analytic methods, and a pragmatic approach to "evidence" that values subjective meaning-making in local contexts, as well as objective trends in teaching quality across settings (Haertel, Moss, Pullin, & Gee, 2008; Jensen, Grajeda, & Haertel, 2018; Moss & Haertel, 2016). I identify two ways researchers can foster more equitable teaching and learning for the students we share.

First, researchers should design more products to foster equitable teaching and learning. Product design is research activity to the extent that it is iterative and seeks through analytic rigor to uncover and refine principles of teaching and learning (Cobb, Confrey, diSessa, Lehrer, & Schauble, 2003). Research-based products include curricula, instructional guides, measures of teaching, and professional development programs. For example, colleagues and I developed a classroom observational system designed to measure three dozen indicators of the three domains of local quality mentioned in Table 6.1 (Jensen, Mejía Arauz, et al., 2019; Jensen, Grajeda, & Haertel, 2018). Referred to as the Classroom Assessment of Sociocultural Interactions (CASI), this measure can be used to rate live or videoed classroom observation segments 15 to 20 minutes in length. While observing, certified raters gather descriptive field notes in relation to CASI indicators. Immediately following the observation, raters examine their field notes alongside CASI rubrics to assign a score. Designed for research and as a formative tool for teachers, the CASI demonstrates strong internal structure and adequate reliability across multiple raters and observation occasions.

Second, more research is needed to test the effects of equitable teaching on the achievement opportunity of the students we share. This includes examining relationships between teaching factors identified in Table 6.1 and the academic achievement gains of students we share, as well as studies on the efficacy of products designed to support implementation of equitable teaching practices. Currently, Mexican colleagues and I are designing a collaborative professional learning experience called *Matemáticas Equitativas* to enhance equitable math teaching for American-Mexican children in rural classrooms in Morelos. We incorporate two measures of teaching into the professional development: the CASI and *El Protocolo de Observación de las Actividades de Enseñanza en Matemáticas* (POAEM; Rodríguez Martínez, 2018). Eventually we will test the efficacy of this professional development on the math achievement gains of American-Mexican students.

Policy makers. Erasing gaps between intended and actual instructional time due to institutional inefficiencies remains a pressing education policy issue throughout Latin America (Bruns & Luque, 2014; Schiefelbein & McGinn, 2008). Mexican policy makers should enact and enforce laws to enhance instructional time by reducing institutional (e.g., reduce unscheduled school closures, extend the school day) and classroom (e.g., substitute teacher system) inefficiencies. Initiatives like eliminating the double shift of Mexican schools, whereby school days are abbreviated and students are further segregated by socioeconomic status (Cárdenas, 2011), can help with this.

Second, more state and federal funding is needed for collaborative research between Mexican and U.S. educators and scholars to understand and improve equitable teaching and learning for the students we share (Jacobo & Jensen, 2018). There are precedents to these collaborations. Several binational education programs were launched over the past 35 years to support Mexican immigrants and their children (Martínez-Wenzl, 2013). At least part of the funds for these initiatives should be reallocated as research investments to address how U.S. and Mexican educators develop the knowledge, practices, and dispositions needed to teach equitably. A focus on professional development programs and their dissemination is especially needed—on formative rather than summative evaluations of teaching (Jensen, Wallace, et al., 2019).

Some Caveats: Structural Inequities

It is vital to acknowledge that efforts to enhance equitable teaching within classrooms alone cannot totally equalize achievement opportunities for most transnational students. Teaching inextricably occurs within a structural context, and structural inequities loom large. For example, achievement opportunities are associated with school segregation for transnational students, which is associated with teacher segregation. In both countries, better-prepared teachers work in schools that are more privileged in terms of student backgrounds and resource supports (e.g., Frankenberg, 2009; INEE, 2015). These patterns of segregation are a primary mechanism through which social and economic inequities are reproduced (Anyon, 1981; Schmelkes, 2005).

Transnational students we share face a double disadvantage in U.S. and Mexican schools. First, because of the segregated communities they tend to live in and the schools they attend, they are less likely than their more privileged peers to receive high-quality instruction by teachers who are well prepared (INEE, 2015; Orfield, 2014). They enjoy fewer material and human resources. This issue is even more dire in Mexico; a recent cross-national study demonstrates glaring differences in teacher quality between rather than within schools in Mexico (Luschei & Jeong, 2018). Second, they are less likely than their more privileged peers to enjoy classroom activities and interactions that resonate with their knowledge, experiences, and identities outside school. This includes experiences with transnationalism. In their work in Jalisco, Nuevo León, Puebla, and Zacatecas, Zúñiga and Hamann (2013) found that teachers lacked basic knowledge in English or about migration or the curriculum of U.S. schools to meet the educational needs of American-Mexican students in Mexican schools.

This double disadvantage is systematic rather than coincidental. In the United States, for example, children and youth from Mexican immigrant families are more likely to receive English-only than bilingual instruction (Gándara, 2017), even though we know well from decades of research that bilingual programs are more effective than monolingual programs at fostering academic achievement in English (e.g., Cheung & Slavin, 2012). State laws were passed in the 1990s and 2000s to restrict bilingual instruction, despite the evidence (Gándara & Hopkins, 2010). In recent years, attitudes about bilingual programs are changing once again. Dual-immersion programs are especially growing in popularity (Adamy, 2016). However, many new programs provide foreign- (one-way) rather than heritage-language (two-way) instruction, designed for monolingual, middle-class Whites rather than immigrant families (e.g., Valdez, Delavan, & Freire, 2016).

Indeed, immigrant status in the United States is systematically associated with inequitable opportunity to achieve in school. Though we see achievement gains between second (i.e., children with a Mexican-born parent) and third generations (i.e., children with a Mexican-born grandparent), we do not see significant gains between first and second generations (Galindo, 2013; Reardon & Galindo, 2009). Average differences in achievement between first- and second-generation Mexican-origin students and their White, non-Hispanic peers is about three-fourths of a standard deviation, compared to a third of a standard deviation for third-generation students.

Much of this intergenerational improvement is due to socioeconomic mobility, but achievement disparities between Mexican-American students and their White, non-Hispanic peers persist *within* socioeconomic strata as well. Reardon and Galindo (2009) found a Hispanic-White reading achievement gap of a third of a standard deviation in a nationally representative sample of middle-class students, and two-fifths of a standard deviation gap in math achievement between middle-class Hispanics and middle-class Whites. Inequitable achievement opportunity is not simply about socioeconomic mobility or immigrant adaptation.

Additional work has found that the documentation status of immigrant students in the United States and that of their parents also affect their achievement opportunity in school (Yoshikawa & Kholoptseva, 2013). The uncertainty of being—or having a family member who is—undocumented creates stress that makes it difficult to focus on schoolwork to perform well (Suarez-Orozco, Yoshikawa, Teranishi, & Suarez-Orozco, 2011). As Sugarman asserts in Chapter 9 of this volume, this uncertainty and stress increased during the Trump era.

In Mexico, urbanicity plays a fundamental role in systems of inequitable achievement opportunity for students we share (e.g., INEE, 2013). Average achievement outcomes between rural and urban schools are woefully disparate (i.e., more than a full standard deviation) because of unequal resource distributions to rural schools (INEE, 2016). Efforts to expand school access in recent decades, mostly by building many more middle schools in rural communities, had a tremendous effect on enrollments. In 2000, half of 15-year-olds in Mexico were enrolled in school, compared to well over 80% of 15-year-olds by 2017 (INEE, 2018). This rapid expansion, though positive, expanded variation in achievement opportunity and, thus, outcomes (Pérez Martínez, Ruiz Cuellar, & García Cabrero, 2013; Schmelkes, 2005). The quality and quantity of teaching in rural schools is lower than in more-resourced urban schools (Schiefelbein & McGinn, 2008). Rural communities tend to be poorer and have less infrastructure than urban communities, and transnational students are more likely than their peers in Mexico to attend a rural or semi-rural (rather than an urban) school (Giorguli et al., 2014). (Semi-)rural schools have shorter days, fewer resources, and teachers with less preparation (Solís, 2010).

Some evidence also indicates that achievement opportunity in Mexico is affected by international migration (Jensen, Giorguli, & Hernández, 2018), though more research has addressed migration relationships with attainment (i.e., years of schooling) than achievement. Scholars, for example, have found that remittances from an immigrant parent in the United States can improve school enrollment and attainment for their children who remain in Mexico (Kandel & Kao, 2001). This boost, however, can be undermined by the negative impact of family separation (caused by migration) on school enrollment (McKenzie & Rapoport, 2006). The relationship between family migration and the educational aspirations of Mexican youth with an emigrant parent in the United States is also mixed. That is, having a parent in the United States while attending school in Mexico can increase resources and youths' aspirations for education, but it also fosters aspirations in youth to migrate themselves (Kandel & Massey, 2002). Kandel and Kao (2000) find that education and migration, rather than being complementary, are "distinct pathways to mobility" (p. 16).

In a nationally representative study of ninth grade students in Mexico, colleagues and I examined relationships between family migration, youth migration aspirations, and Spanish literacy achievement (Jensen, Giorguli, & Hernández, 2018). Our findings confirmed that parent migration exposure was associated with more immediate plans of youth to migrate themselves. We also found that the immediacy of their migration plans affected their achievement: More immediate plans to migrate to the United States (i.e., before completing high school) were associated with lower performance, and this effect was strongest for those in low-SES communities.

Less research has been done on achievement opportunity for students in Mexico with prior experiences in the United States. As mentioned, we know that "American-Mexican" students in Mexico are more likely than their peers to attend a rural school and that this affects their opportunity to achieve (Jensen & Jacobo, 2019). We also know that American Mexicans face challenges adapting to school in Mexico—e.g., limited Spanish proficiency, gaps in curricular knowledge, acculturation—that can affect achievement opportunity (Zúñiga & Hamann, 2013). Hamann, Zúñiga, and Sánchez García (2010) found that these challenges led American-Mexican students in Zacatecas and Nuevo León to be three times likelier than their Mexican peers to be held back a grade in school. This is alarming given the strong negative effect of grade retention on student achievement in general in Mexico (e.g., Jensen, Giorguli, & Hernández, 2018).

Conclusion

The students we share between Mexico and the United States are a large and diverse group. Their learning needs undoubtedly vary. However, I argue that there is an overwhelming need to enhance the achievement opportunity for these 9 million children and youth by providing them with more equitable teaching. I have defined and illustrated what I mean by "equitable teaching" and provided some steps for moving forward. My recommendations—directed at educators, teacher educators, researchers, and policy makers in both countries—are meant to respond to rather than ignore broader systematic structures of educational inequity in the United States and in Mexico, such as segregation or unequal resource distribution. I focus on teaching because it is a powerful and the most proximate institutional cause of inequitable achievement. To be clear, arguing for actions to support more equitable teaching is not meant to somehow blame educators for the underperformance of Mexican immigrants and their children. I mean it as a call for greater collaborations with educators to understand and to improve classroom teaching and learning. *Teaching*—a shared responsibility of legislators, administrators, researchers, students, teachers, and teacher educators—rather than *teachers*, has been my focus for improvement in this chapter.

Through a combination of elements—i.e., instructional time, generic quality, local quality—equitable teaching is a distinct way of being to connect academic learning with the lives, hearts, and minds of the students we share. It simultaneously upends tradition in classroom practice while preparing all students for professional success and civic participation in the 21st century. Equitable teaching is effective and meaningful—high-quality instruction situated in the local practices, customs, and values of students' families and communities. Preparing equitable educators for the students we share requires us to understand the significance of raising children to be *bien educados*—to eliminate deficit ways of perceiving Mexican immigrants and their children and provide connected and communal activities and interactions in classrooms to enhance achievement opportunities for all students.

Notes

1. I acknowledge and thank Bruce Fuller, Patricia Gándara, Ronald Gallimore, and Leslie Reese for their generous and astute feedback to earlier drafts of this chapter.

2. My use of "achievement" is meant to reflect a broad notion of learning that incorporates traditional competencies (e.g., reading, writing, mathematics, understanding of the natural and social world) as well as intrapersonal (e.g., initiative, self-reflection, adaptability, self-regulation) and interpersonal (e.g., communication, collaboration, empathy, negotiation) competencies (National

Research Council, 2012). I see "achievement" as the development of knowledge, skills, identities, and character that contribute to a lifetime of excellence in terms of citizenship, career choice, and economic mobility.

References

Abadzi, H. (2009). Instructional time loss in developing countries: Concepts, measurement, and implications. *The World Bank Research Observer, 24*(2), 267–290.

Adair, J. K., Colegrove, K. S. S., & McManus, M. (2018). Troubling messages: Agency and learning in the early schooling experiences of children of Latina/o immigrants. *Teachers College Record, 120*(6).

Adamy, J. (2016, April 1). Dual-language classes for kids grow in popularity. *Wall Street Journal*.

Anyon, J. (1981). Social class and school knowledge. *Curriculum Inquiry, 11*(1), 3–42.

Backhoff, E., Bouzas, A., Hernández, E., & García, M. (2007). *Aprendizaje y desigualdad social en México: Implicaciones de política educativa en el nivel básico*. México, DF: INEE.

Ball, D. L., Thames, M. H., & Phelps, G. (2008). Content knowledge for teaching: What makes it special? *Journal of Teacher Education, 59*(5), 389–407.

Banks, C. A., & Banks, J. A. (1995). Equity pedagogy: An essential component of multicultural education. *Theory Into Practice, 34*(3), 152–158.

Bazán, A., Martínez, X. V., & Trejo, M. (2009). Análisis de interacciones en clases de Español de primer grado de primaria. *Revista Interamericana de Psicología, 43*, 466–478.

Blair, C. (2002). School readiness: Integrating cognition and emotion in a neurobiological conceptualization of children's functioning at school entry. *American Psychologist, 57*(2), 111–127.

Blazar, D., Braslow, D., Charalambous, C. Y., & Hill, H. C. (2017). Attending to general and mathematics-specific dimensions of teaching: Exploring factors across two observation instruments. *Educational Assessment, 22*(2), 71–94.

Bloom, B. (1974). Time and learning. *American Psychologist, 29*(9), 682–688.

Borko, H. (2004). Professional development and teacher learning: Mapping the terrain. *Educational Researcher, 33*(8), 3–15.

Borko, H., Liston, D., & Whitcomb, J. A. (2007). Apples and fishes: The debate over dispositions in teacher education. *Journal of Teacher Education, 58*(5), 359–364.

Bransford, J. D., Brown, A. L., & Cocking, R. R. (2000). *How people learn: Brain, mind experience, and school*. Washington, DC: National Academies Press.

Bridges, M., Cohen, S. R., McGuire, L. W., Yamada, H., Fuller, B., Mireles, L., & Scott, L. (2012). Measuring the social behavior of Mexican American children. *Early Childhood Research Quarterly, 27*, 555–567.

Bruns, B., & Luque, J. (2014). *Great teachers: How to raise student learning in Latin America and the Caribbean.* Washington, DC: The World Bank.

Bullough, R. V., & Baughman, K. (1997). *"First-year teacher" eight years later: An inquiry into teacher development.* New York, NY: Teachers College Press.

Cárdenas, S. (2011). Escuelas de doble turno en México: Una estimación de diferencias asociadas con su implementación. *Revista Mexicana de Investigación Educativa, 16*, 801–827.

Cheung, A. C., & Slavin, R. E. (2012). Effective reading programs for Spanish-dominant English language learners (ELLs) in the elementary grades: A synthesis of research. *Review of Educational Research, 82*(4), 351–395.

Cobb, P., Confrey, J., DiSessa, A., Lehrer, R., & Schauble, L. (2003). Design experiments in educational research. *Educational Researcher, 32*(1), 9–13.

Denham, S. (2006). Social-emotional competence as support for school readiness: What is it and how do we assess it? *Early Education and Development, 17*(1), 57–89.

Denham, S., & Brown, C. (2010). "Plays nice with others": Social-emotional learning and academic success. *Early Education and Development, 21*(5), 652–680.

Downer, J. T., López, M. L., Grimm, K. J., Hamagami, A., Pianta, R. C., & Howes, C. (2012). Observations of teacher–child interactions in classrooms serving Latinos and dual language learners: Applicability of the Classroom Assessment Scoring System in diverse settings. *Early Childhood Research Quarterly, 27*(1), 21–32.

Doyle, W. (1986). Classroom organization and management. In M. C. Wittrock (Ed.), *Handbook of research on teaching* (3rd ed). New York: Macmillan.

Emmer, E. T., & Stough, L. M. (2001). Classroom management: A critical part of educational psychology, with implications for teacher education. *Educational Psychologist, 36*(2), 103–112.

Ermeling, B. A., Gallimore, R., & Hiebert, J. (2017). Making teaching visible through learning opportunities. *Phi Delta Kappan, 98*(8), 54–58.

Ezpeleta, J., & Weiss, E. (1996). Las escuelas rurales en zonas de pobreza y sus maestros: tramas preexistentes y políticas innovadoras. *Revista Mexicana de Investigación Educativa, 1*(1), 53–69.

Flores, N., & Rosa, J. (2015). Undoing appropriateness: Raciolinguistic ideologies and language diversity in education. *Harvard Educational Review, 85*(2), 149–171.

Frankenberg, E. (2009). The segregation of American teachers. *Education Policy Analysis Archives, 17*(1).

Fuller, B., & García Coll, C. (2010). Learning from Latinos: Contexts, families, and child development in motion. *Developmental Psychology, 46*(3), 559–565.

Fuller, B., Bridges, M., Bein, E., Jang, H., Jung, S., Rabe-Hesketh, S., Halfon, N., & Kuo, A. (2009). The health and cognitive growth of Latino toddlers: At risk or immigrant paradox? *Maternal and Child Health Journal, 13*(6).

Galindo, C. (2013). Math performance of young Mexican-origin children in the United States: Socioeconomic status, immigrant generation, and English proficiency. In B. Jensen & A. Sawyer (Eds.), *Regarding Educación: Mexican-American Schooling, Immigration, and Bi-national Improvement*. New York, NY: Teachers College Press.

Galindo, C., & Fuller, B. (2010). The social competence of Latino kindergartners and growth in mathematical understanding. *Developmental Psychology, 46*(3), 579.

Gallimore, R., Ermeling, B. A., Saunders, W. M., & Goldenberg, C. (2009). Moving the learning of teaching closer to practice: Teacher education implications of school-based inquiry teams. *The Elementary School Journal, 109*(5), 537–553.

Gallo, S. (2021). Preparing educators for asset-based pedagogies: The case of recently-arrived transnational students in Central Mexico. In P. Gándara and B. Jensen (Eds.), *The Students We Share: Preparing US and Mexican Educators for Our Transnational Future*. Albany, NY: State University of New York Press.

Gándara, P. (2017). The potential and promise of Latino students. *American Educator, 41*(1), 4–11.

Gándara, P., & Hopkins, M. (Eds.). (2010). *Forbidden language: English learners and restrictive language policies*. New York, NY: Teachers College Press.

García, E. (2005). *Teaching and learning in two languages: Bilingualism and schooling in the United States*. New York, NY: Teachers College Press.

Giorguli, S., Jensen, B., Bean, F., Brown, S., Sawyer, A., & Zúñiga, V. (2014). El bienestar educativo de niños de inmigrantes mexicanos en los Estados Unidos y en México. In A. Escobar, L. Lowell, & S. Martin (Eds.), *Dialogo binacional sobre migrantes Mexicanos en Estados Unidos y México*. Guadalajara, México: Centro de Investigaciones y Estudios Superiores en Antropología Social.

Goldenberg, C. (1992). Instructional conversations: Promoting comprehension through discussion. *The Reading teacher, 46*(4), 316–326.

Goldenberg, C. (2008). Teaching English language learners: What the research does—and does not—say. *American Educator, 32*(2), 8–44.

González, N., Moll, L., & Amanti, C. (Eds.). (2005). *Funds of knowledge: Theorizing practices, households, communities, and classrooms*. Mahwah, NJ: Lawrence Erlbaum Associates.

Grossman, P., Cohen, J., Ronfeldt, M., & Brown, L. (2014). The test matters: The relationship between classroom observation scores and teacher value added on multiple types of assessment. *Educational Researcher, 43*(6), 293–303.

Guerrero, A. D., Fuller, B., Chu, L., Kim, A., Franke, T., Bridges, M., & Kuo, A. (2013). Early growth of Mexican-American children: Lagging in preliteracy skills but not social development. *Maternal and Child Health Journal*, *17*(9), 1701–1711.

Guevara, Y., Mares, G., Rueda, E., Rivas, O., Sánchez, B., Rocha, H. (2005). Niveles de interacción que se propician en alumnos de educación primaria durante la enseñanza de la materia español. *Revista Mexicana de Análisis de la Conducta*, *31*(5), 23–45.

Haertel, E. H., Moss, P. A., Pullin, D. C., & Gee, J. P. (2008). Introduction. In P. Moss et al. (Eds.), *Assessment, Equity, and Opportunity to Learn*. New York, NY: Cambridge University Press.

Hamann, E. T., Zúñiga, V., & García, J. S. (2010). Transnational students' perspectives on schooling in the United States and Mexico: The salience of school experience and country of birth. In M. O. Ensor & E. M. Gozdziak (Eds.), *Children and migration: At the crossroads of resiliency and vulnerability*. London, UK: Palgrave Macmillan.

Hanushek, E. A. (2016). What matters for student achievement. *Education Next*, *16*(2), 19–26.

Hill, H. C., Blunk, M. L., Charalambous, C. Y., Lewis, J. M., Phelps, G. C., Sleep, L., & Ball, D. L. (2008). Mathematical knowledge for teaching and the mathematical quality of instruction: An exploratory study. *Cognition and Instruction*, *26*(4), 430–511.

Instituto Nacional para la Evaluación de la Educación (INEE). (2007). *Aprendizaje y desigualdad social en México*. México, DF: INEE.

Instituto Nacional para la Evaluación de la Educación (INEE). (2009). *El aprendizaje en tercero de secundaria en México*. México, DF: INEE.

Instituto Nacional para la Evaluación de la Educación (INEE). (2010). *La Educación Preescolar en México. Condiciones para la enseñanza y el aprendizaje*. México, DF: INEE.

Instituto Nacional para la Evaluación de la Educación (INEE). (2013). *Panorama educativo de México: Indicadores del sistema educativo nacional*. México, DF: INEE.

Instituto Nacional para la Evaluación de la Educación (2015). Los docentes en México: Informe 2015. México, DF: INEE.

Instituto Nacional para la Evaluación de la Educación. (2016). *Aprendizaje en tercero de secundaria en México. Informe de resultados*. México, DF: INEE.

Instituto Nacional para la Evaluación de la Educación (INEE). (2018). *Panorama educativo de México: Indicadores del sistema educativo nacional*. México, DF: INEE.

Jacobo, M., & Jensen, B. (2018). *Schooling for US-citizen students in Mexico*. Los Angeles, CA: The Civil Rights Project/Proyecto Derechos Civiles.

Jensen B. (2005). Culture and practice of Mexican primary schooling: Implications for improving policy and practice in the U.S. *Current Issues in Education, 8*(25).

Jensen, B. (2013). Finding synergy to improve learning opportunities for Mexican-origin students. In B. Jensen & A. Sawyer (Eds.), *Regarding educación: Mexican American schooling, immigration, and binational improvement* (pp. 299–324). New York, NY: Teachers College Press.

Jensen, B. (2014). Framing sociocultural interactions to design equitable learning environments. In J. Polman et al. (Eds.), *Learning and becoming in practice: The International Conference of the Learning Sciences* (ICLS) (Vol. 2., pp. 903–910). Boulder, CO: International Society of the Learning Sciences.

Jensen, B. (2018). *Equitable classroom interactions and Latino academic language development in upper elementary grades.* Paper presented at the annual meeting for the American Educational Research Associate, New York City.

Jensen, B., Feinauer Whiting, E., & Chapman, S. (2018). Measuring multicultural dispositions of preservice teachers. *Journal of Psychoeducational Assessment, 36*(2), 120–135.

Jensen, B., & García, E. (2019). Fostering equitable developmental opportunities for dual-language learners in early education settings. In V. L. Gadsden, B. Graue, F. J. Levine, & S. K. Ryan (Eds.), *Diversity issues in early education* [tentative title]. Washington, DC: American Educational Research Association.

Jensen, B., Giorguli, S., & Hernández, E. (2018). International migration and the academic performance of Mexican adolescents. *International Migration Review, 52*(2), 559–596.

Jensen, B., Grajeda, S., & Haertel, E. (2015). Measuring cultural dimensions of classroom interactions. *Educational Assessment, 23*(4), 250–276.

Jensen, B., Haertel, E., & Gomez, L. (2020). *Validating formative uses of measures of teaching quality for school improvement.* Manuscript under review.

Jensen, B., & Jacobo-Suárez, M. (2019). Integrating American-Mexican students in Mexican classrooms. *Kappa Delta Pi Record.*

Jensen, B., Mejía Arauz, R., & Aguilar Zepeda, R. (2017). Equitable teaching for returnee children in Mexico. *Sinéctica, 48*, 1–20.

Jensen, B., Mejía Arauz, R., Grajeda, S., García Toranzo, S., Encinas, J., & Larsen, R. (2019). Measuring cultural aspects of teacher-child interactions to foster equitable developmental opportunities for young Latino children. *Early Childhood Research Quarterly, 52*, 112–123.

Jensen, B., Pérez Martínez, G. M., & Aguilar Escobar, A. (2016). Framing and assessing classroom opportunity to learn: The case of Mexico. *Assessment in Education: Principles, Policy & Practice, 23*(1), 149–172.

Jensen, B., Pérez Martínez, M. G., Johnstun, K., & Hernández, J. (2018). *Equitable teaching for young children in Central Mexico.* Paper presented at the annual meeting for the Comparative and International Education Society, Mexico City.

Jensen, B., Reese, L., Hall-Kenyon, K., & Bennett, C. (2015). Social competencies and oral language development for young Latino children of immigrants. *Early Education & Development, 26*(7), 933–955.

Jensen, B., Rueda, R., Reese, L., & Garcia, E. (2014). *Designing sociocultural interactions to improve relevant learning opportunities for underperforming minority students.* Unpublished manuscript.

Jensen, B., & Sawyer, A. (2013). Regarding educación: A vision for school improvement. In B. Jensen, B., & Sawyer, A. (Eds.), *Regarding educación: Mexican American schooling, immigration, and binational improvement.* New York, NY: Teachers College Press.

Jensen, B., & Thompson, G. A. (2020). Equity in teaching academic language—an interdisciplinary approach. *Theory Into Practice, 59*(1), 1–7.

Jensen, B., Wallace, T. L., Steinberg, M. P., Gabriel, R., Dietiker, L., Davis, D., Kelcey, B., Covay, E., Halpin, P., & Rui, N. (2019). Complexity and scale in teaching effectiveness research: Reflections from the MET study. *Education Policy Analysis Archives, 27*(7).

Kandel, W., & Kao, G. (2000). Shifting orientations: How US labor migration affects children's aspirations in Mexican migrant communities. *Social Science Quarterly*, 16–32.

Kandel, W., & Kao, G. (2001). The impact of temporary labor migration on Mexican children's educational aspirations and performance. *International Migration Review, 35*(4), 1205–1231.

Kandel, W., & Massey, D. S. (2002). The culture of Mexican migration: A theoretical and empirical analysis. *Social Forces, 80*(3), 981–1004.

LeVine, R. A., & White, M. I. (2017). *Human conditions: The cultural basis of educational developments.* New York, NY: Routledge.

Levinson, B. U. (2001). *We are all equal: Student culture and identity at a Mexican secondary school, 1988–1998.* Durham, NC: Duke University Press.

Luschei, T. F., & Jeong, D. W. (2018). Is teacher sorting a global phenomenon? Cross-national evidence on the nature and correlates of teacher quality opportunity gaps. *Educational Researcher, 47*(9), 556–576.

Malecki, C. K., & Elliott, S. N. (2002). Children's social behaviors as predictors of academic achievement: A longitudinal analysis. *School Psychology Quarterly, 17*(1), 1–23.

Martínez, R. A. (2010). "Spanglish" as literacy tool: Toward an understanding of the potential role of Spanish-English code-switching in the development of academic literacy. *Research in the Teaching of English, 45*(2), 124–149.

Martínez Rizo, F. (2012). Investigación empírica sobre el impacto de la evaluación formativa: Revisión de literatura. *Revista Electrónica de Investigación Educativa, 14*(1).

Martínez-Wenzl, M. (2013). Bi-national education initiatives: A brief history. In B. Jensen & A. Sawyer (Eds.), *Regarding educación: Mexican-American schooling, immigration and bi-national improvement*. New York, NY: Teachers College Press.

Martinic, S., & Vergara, C. (2007). Gestión del tiempo e interacción del profesor-alumno en la sala de clases de establecimientos con Jornada Escolar Completa en Chile. *REICE–Revista Iberoamericana sobre Calidad, Eficacia y Cambio en Educación, 5*(5), 3–20.

McInerney, D. M., Roche, L. A., McInerney, V., & Marsh, H. W. (1997). Cultural perspectives on school motivation: The relevance and application of goal theory. *American Educational Research Journal, 34*(1), 207–236.

McKenzie, D., & Rapoport, H. (2006). *Can migration reduce educational attainment? Evidence from Mexico*. Washington, DC: The World Bank.

Mejía Arauz, R. (2001). El desarrollo de la intersubjetividad y la colaboración. *Cultura y Educación, 13*(4), 355–371.

Moschkovich, J. N. (Ed.). (2010). *Language and mathematics education: Multiple perspectives and directions for research*. Charlotte, NC: Information Age Publishing.

Moss, P. A., & Haertel, E. H. (2016). Engaging methodological pluralism. In D. H. Gitomer & C. A. Bell (Eds.), *Handbook of research on teaching* (5th ed., pp. 127–247). Washington, DC: American Educational Research Association.

National Research Council (2012). *Education for life and work: Developing transferrable knowledge and skills in the 21st century*. Washington, DC: National Academies Press.

Ogbu, J. (1992). Understanding cultural diversity and learning. *Educational Researcher, 21*(8), 5–24.

Orfield, G. (2014). A new civil rights agenda for American Education. *Educational Researcher, 43*(6), 273–292.

Orfield, G., Kucsera, J., & Siegel-Hawley, G. (2012). *"E pluribus" . . . separation: Deepening double segregation for more students*. Los Angeles, CA: Civil Rights Project/Proyecto Derechos Civiles.

Paradise, R. (1996). Passivity or tacit collaboration: Mazahua interaction in cultural context. *Learning and Instruction, 6*(4), 379–389.

Pérez Martínez, M. G., Ruiz Cuellar, G., & García Cabrero, B. (2013). Challenges to improving preschool quality in Mexico. In B. Jensen & A. Sawyer (Eds.), *Regarding educación: Mexican-American schooling, immigration, and bi-national improvement*. New York: Teachers College Press.

Pettigrove, G. (2012). Meekness and "moral" anger. *Ethics, 122*, 341–370.

Reardon, S. (2011). The widening academic achievement gaps between the rich and poor: New evidence and possible explanations. In G. Duncan & R. Murnane (Eds.), *Whither opportunity? Rising inequality, schools, and children's life chances*. New York, NY: Russell Sage Foundation.

Reardon, S. F., & Galindo, C. (2009). The Hispanic-White achievement gap in math and reading in the elementary grades. *American Educational Research Journal, 46*, 853–891.

Reese, L. (2013). Cultural change and continuity in U.S. and Mexican settings. In B. Jensen & A. Sawyer (Eds.), *Regarding educación: Mexican American schooling, immigration, bi-national improvement*. New York: Teachers College Press.

Reese, L., Balzano, S., Gallimore, R., & Goldenberg, C. (1995). The concept of "educación": Latino family values and American schooling. *International Journal of Education Research, 23*(1), 57–81.

Reese, L., Jensen, B., & Ramirez, D. (2014). Emotionally supportive classroom contexts for young Latino children in rural California. *The Elementary School Journal, 114*(4), 501–526.

Riddell, A. (2008). *Factors influencing educational quality and effectiveness in developing countries: A review of research*. Berlin, Germany: German Federal Ministry for Economic Cooperation and Development.

Rivkin, S., Hanushek, E., & Kain, J. (2005). Teachers, schools, and academic achievement. *Econometrica, 73*(2), 417–458.

Rodríguez Martínez, L. Y. (2018). *Diseño y validación de un protocolo de observación para evaluar las actividades de enseñanza en quinto grado de primaria en la asignatura de matemáticas*. Unpublished doctoral dissertation. Aguascalientes, México: Universidad Autónoma de Aguascalientes.

Rogoff, B. (2003). *The cultural nature of human development*. New York: Oxford University.

Rogoff, B., Mejía Arauz, R., & Correa-Chávez, M. (2015). A cultural paradigm— Learning by observing and pitching in. *Advances in Child Development and Behavior, 49*, 1–22.

Roorda, D. L., Koomen, H. M. Y., Spilt, J. L., & Oort, F. J. (2011). The influence of affective teacher-student relationships on students' school engagement and achievement: A meta-analytic approach. *Review of Educational Research, 81*(4), 493–529.

Saunders, W., Goldenberg, C., & Hamann, J. (1992). Instructional conversations beget instructional conversations. *Teaching and Teacher Education, 8*(2), 199–218.

Santibañez, L. (2021). Contrasting realities: How differences between the Mexican and US education systems affect transnational students. In P. Gándara & B. Jensen (Eds.), *The students we share: Preparing US and Mexican teachers for our transnational future*. Albany, NY: State University of New York Press.

Schiefelbein, E., & McGinn, N. F. (2008). *Learning to educate: Proposals for the reconstruction of education in Latin America*. UNESCO & International Bureau of Education.

Schmelkes, S. (2005). La desigualdad en la calidad de la educación primaria. *Revista Latinoamericana de Estudios Educativos, 35*(3–4), 9–33.

Schmelkes, S., Mosso, T., & Reyes, M. (2010). Colectivo, valores, lengua y cultura: Componentes de la calidad en la Escuela Intercultural Bilingüe El Progreso, *Gestión y calidad de la educación básica. Casos ejemplares de las escuelas públicas mexicanas*, 174–197.

Shulman, L. S. (1987). Knowledge and teaching: Foundations of the new reform. *Harvard Educational Review, 57*(1), 1–23.

Slavin, R. E. (2010). Instruction based on cooperative learning. In R. E. Mayer & P. A. Alexander (Eds.), *Handbook of research on learning and instruction*. New York, NY: Routledge.

Snow, C. E., & Uccelli, P. (2009). The challenge of academic language. In D. R. Olson & N. Torrance (Eds.), *The Cambridge handbook of literacy* (pp. 112–133). Cambridge: Cambridge University Press.

Solís, P. (2010). La desigualdad de oportunidades y las brechas de escolaridad. In A. Arnaut & S. Giorguli (Eds.), *Los grandes problemas de México: Educación*. México, DF: El Colegio de México.

Stallings, J. A., Knight, S. L., & Markham, D. (2014). *Using the Stallings Observation System to investigate time on task in four countries*. Washington, DC: World Bank Group.

Stigler, J. W., & Hiebert, J. (2009). *The teaching gap: Best ideas from the world's teachers for improving education in the classroom*. New York: Free Press.

Suárez-Orozco, C., Yoshikawa, H., Teranishi, R., & Suárez-Orozco, M. (2011). Growing up in the shadows: The developmental implications of unauthorized status. *Harvard Educational Review, 81*(3), 438–473.

Sugarman, J. (2021). From *Plyler* to sanctuary: U.S. policy and public school access and implications for educators of transnational students. In P. Gándara and B. Jensen (Eds.), *The students we share: Preparing U.S. and Mexican educators for our transnational future*. Albany, NY: State University of New York Press.

Suina, J. H., & Smolkin, L. B. (1994). From natal culture to school culture to dominant society culture: Supporting transitions for Pueblo Indian students. In P. Greenfield & R. Cocking (Eds.), *Cross-cultural roots of minority child development*. Hillsdale, NJ: Erlbaum.

Treviño, E. (2013). Learning inequality among indigenous students in Mexico. In B. Jensen and A. Sawyer (Eds.), *Regarding educación: Mexican-American schooling, immigration, and bi-national improvement*. New York: Teachers College Press.

Valdés, G. (1996). *Con respeto: Bridging the differences between culturally diverse families and schools*. New York, NY: Teachers College Press.

Valdez, V. E., Delavan, G., & Freire, J. A. (2016). The marketing of dual language education policy in Utah print media. *Educational Policy, 30*(6), 849–883.

Webb, N. M., & Farivar, S. (1994). Promoting helping behavior in cooperative small groups in middle school mathematics. *American Educational Research Journal, 31*(2), 369–395.

Willms, J. D. (2006). *Learning divides: Ten policy questions about the performance and equity of schools and schooling systems*. Montreal, Quebec: UNESCO Institute for Statistics.

Yoshikawa, H., & Kholoptseva, J. (2013). *Unauthorized immigrant parents and their children's development*. Washington, DC: Migration Policy Institute.

Zúñiga, V., & Hamann, T. (2013). Understanding American-Mexican children. In B. Jensen and A. Sawyer (Eds.), *Regarding educación: Mexican-American schooling, immigration, and bi-national improvement*. New York, NY: Teachers College Press.

Chapter 7

Mirroring Students' and Teachers' Classroom Experiences to Address the Challenges of Transnationalism in Mexican Schools

Betsabé Román González and Juan Sánchez García[1]

The challenges of integrating students with U.S. experiences into Mexican schools have been well documented over the last 15 years. Some scholars refer to these students as "invisible" because their U.S.-based knowledge, experiences, and identities often go unacknowledged (e.g., Zúñiga & Hamann, 2009). Yet teachers can also become invisible when administrators prioritize students' or other voices and implement new strategies without consulting them as central actors in classrooms (Sánchez García & Hamann, 2016). Therefore, in this chapter, we examine the perspectives of students and teachers who mirror the challenges of transnationalism in Mexican schools. Igoa (1995) recognized the need for immigrant children to find a "reflection" of themselves in other people, such as their classmates and/or teachers, with the hope that the child has a form of acquaintance with the new environment. Additionally, Marks and Abo-Zena (2015) emphasize that a "social reflection" is needed to help child migrants in their educational transitions. As a result, mirroring the experiences of transnational students and their Mexican teachers, in the educational process, allows us to recognize the internal and external worlds where students and teachers are constantly interacting; additionally, we will be able to make suggestions that are oriented toward teacher training in a context of migratory trajectories.

Teachers are one of the first links between these students and their new contexts. Consequently, their pedagogical practices should reflect the cultural beliefs and knowledge of a binational society. In turn, transnational students are living a new experience in another country (UNICEF, 2008; 2017). We argue that seeing students *and* teachers as protagonists in teaching and learning processes is necessary to meet the different challenges of transnational education—and the opportunities that students' transnationalism bring into classrooms.

Between 2005 and 2010, but particularly in the second half of this period during the "Great Recession" years, about 1 million Mexican citizens returned to Mexico from the United States; 25% of them were children and teenagers (Giorguli & Gutiérrez, 2011). Since that time, each year has brought more and more children as "return" migrants to Mexico, even though many are encountering Mexico for the first time, having been born in the United States. This movement/repatriation has meant families are being separated and have had to deal with different social, economic, and educational challenges because of that separation, including going to school in both countries. Therefore, the migration of children and teenagers between Mexico and the United States can be understood within the framework of families separated by borders (Dreby, 2010) and/or the transition processes of children where families are separated on one side and reunited on the other (Suárez-Orozco, 2015).

Using "transnational schooling" to refer to scenarios where teachers, or more commonly students, bring experience from more than one country into the classroom, we want to emphasize that transnational schooling involves different actors, communities, and situations. Each story that we share exemplifies dynamics encountered by some or most of the thousands of students who move to Mexico from U.S. schools every year. Their teachers and principals do not always know where they went or if they are ever coming back. Some return to the United States the next school year, and others they never see again.

In Mexico, the story is similar. There are students who return or arrive for the first time from the United States to their parents' homeland. Most of the teachers, principals, and classmates do not know where they are coming from, who they are, what academic preparation they have had, and/or whether or not they will stay through the whole school year.

Schools are meant to give children the tools to build relationships and become social actors who can contribute to the greater society (Berger & Luckmann, 2003), but they cannot do so when they know little about the migratory and educational trajectories of their transnational students. This lack of recognition from teachers, institutions, and educational authorities can be interpreted as a "moral blindness" and a lack of sensitivity toward the vulnerability of these children (Bauman & Donskis, 2013).

We acknowledge that those are serious allegations, and teachers may not willfully ignore the plight of these students, though attending to the needs and promise of children as they come of age is serious and important work. Our goal in this chapter is to provoke dialogues between all the actors involved in the education process, especially the teachers on both sides of the border. At the end, we provide recommendations for better teaching-learning practices in transnational classrooms, and for the professional development of both American and Mexican teachers from the perspective of inclusion and attention to diversity. As a point of departure, we start with five assertions:

1. Children have the right to quality education and equality in both countries, the United States and Mexico.

2. Families and children are vulnerable, and at risk, in transborder contexts.

3. Schools are social institutions where children should interact and learn about different social contexts.

4. Teachers should be experts in pedagogy and curriculum and should establish inclusive classroom strategies where student heterogeneity is seen as a pedagogical and curricular asset.

5. Such teaching should pay special attention to diversity and consider students' transnational school and community experiences as educational resources.

The Data Set

The empirical information for this chapter comes from semi-structured interviews with transnational students and Mexican teachers. We follow, document, and write about the lives of 10 boys and girls who arrived in Morelos (a state just south of Mexico City) between 2010 and 2012. These were children between the ages of eight and 13 who had previous educational experiences in the United States. They were enrolled from third grade of *primaria* (elementary school) up to the first year of *secundaria* (i.e., the first year of junior high, or seventh grade) (Table 7.1).

Each case was selected to illuminate different voluntary and non-voluntary migration experiences from the United States to Mexico. This is a longitudinal study in which the interviews take place in schools and homes (in both countries).

From the teacher side, we interviewed 12 teachers and the state coordinator of the *Programa Binacional de Educación Migrante* (PROBEM)[2] in elementary and middle schools in the state of Morelos (Table 7.2).

These interviews were designed to explore the challenges and understandings that teachers have when transnational students arrive in their classrooms and to consider their pedagogical responses to migrant students and their contexts. For this work, we took into account previous studies about transnational education in both countries (e.g., Hamann, Zúñiga, & Sánchez, 2018; Román González, 2017; Román González & Carrillo Cantú, 2017; Sánchez & Hamann, 2016; Sánchez y Zúñiga, 2010, Zúñiga, Hamann, & Sánchez, 2008; 2010). These provided us with further background on international migration and schooling.

For this chapter, we take excerpts of interviews with students who have had formal schooling in both countries and juxtapose them with

Table 7.1. Children Interviewed in the State of Morelos

*Name	Country of birth	Age of arrival to Mexico	Place of departure in the United States	Place of arrival in Morelos, Mexico
Astrid	U.S.	10	Porterville, CA	Jiutepec
Luis	U.S.	14	Porterville, CA	Jiutepec
Salvador	U.S.	13	Porterville, CA	Jiutepec
Flor	U.S.	11	Portland, OR	Jiutepec
Quique	U.S.	13	Chicago, IL	Jiutepec
Marco	Mexico	8	Chicago, IL	Cuernavaca
Lulú	U.S.	13	Los Angeles, CA	Tlaltizapán
Sofía	U.S.	15	Los Angeles, CA	Tlaltizapán
Elena	U.S.	9	Los Angeles, CA	Tlaltizapán
Beto	Mexico	15	Santa Ana, CA	Temixco

*Names have been changed for pseudonyms to protect children's identities.

Table 7.2. Interviews with Teachers, Principals, and PROBEM's Director in the State of Morelos

*Name	Job Title
Eleine	Elementary school teacher
Margarita and José Antonio	Elementary school teachers
Angélica	Elementary school teacher
Xóchitl	Elementary school principal
Maricruz	Elementary school teacher
Monserrat	Elementary school teacher
Virginia	Elementary school teacher
Omar	Secondary school teacher (7th–9th grade)
María de la Luz, Alicia, and Consuelo	Secondary school teachers (7th–9th grade)
Ana	PROBEM's Director

*Names have been changed to pseudonyms to protect subjects' identities.

experiences of Mexican teachers who have received them in their classrooms. Doing so, we found three themes related to mirroring: I) transnational families, II) educational transitions, and III) future aspirations in one or both countries.

I. Transnational Families

Students' Perspectives

One of the main reasons children say they moved to Mexico is "to be together as a family." In most cases, younger children and teenagers are the ones who move around with their parents, while older siblings stay in the United States to work or study. Some older siblings are even married and have a family of their own. Transnational families are not homogeneous. Nonetheless, one characteristic that these families might share is that, at some point, they were divided by the border or are still divided now. From our study on children's narratives, we sketch three general types of transnational families in Mexico.

The first type is *returned families*. These are families where both parents and children were born in Mexico and were undocumented when they were in the United States. After living in the United States for a few years, these families decided to return to Mexico, for different reasons, and stay. Sometimes children were too young to remember when they moved to the United States. When they moved back to Mexico, students in these families usually had some proficiency in conversational Spanish, which was learned at home, but many did not receive formal Spanish instruction in the United States before moving to Mexico. As a result, these students' abilities to read or write Spanish were limited. They also have difficulties with other subjects such as Mexican history.

Beto, for example, moved to the United States with his mother to reunite with his father, when he was two years old. He proudly considered himself a "Californian" until twelve years later, when in Mexico, he found out he was Mexican. For Beto, it felt like he was in Mexico for the first time; he could only recall from pictures what his parents' home looked like; and, after the summer, he wanted to go back to his home in California. Unfortunately, his parents had returned to Mexico to stay. He was devastated: "I felt really bad and started crying, I didn't say bye to my friends, there were so many things I had planned with them, and here I was not being able to go back home." Beto did not know his parents fled the United States to avoid death threats from a gang member.

The second type of transnational family is the *mixed-status family* living in Mexico. These are families where parents are Mexican-born, and at least some of the children are U.S.-born. Unlike returnees, most American children have never been to Mexico before, and it is their first time in the Mexican school system. Lulú's family exemplifies this situation. Lulú and her three sisters were born in the United States. Her parents were undocumented immigrants in the United States and were denied legal residency several times. The family decided to move to Mexico before one of the parents was deported to avoid separation from their daughters. The girls have double nationality and can return to the United States at any moment. Even though at the beginning it was hard for them to integrate into Mexican schools and communities, they preferred staying with their parents and keeping the family together. In Lulú's words: "We are here as a family, that's what's important. We might not have all the possessions and commodities we used to have over there [United States], but the six of us, we are doing well . . . having our family together, and being healthy, and having food and a home, that's enough."

The third type of transnational family is the *divided (by borders) family*. These are families whose parents are Mexican-born and whose children are either Mexican- or U.S.-born. Just like other mixed-status families who move to Mexico, there is a big chance that the undocumented parents will never go back to the United States. However, their American children have the opportunity to go back if they decide to do so. When binational children find themselves "stuck" in school or feel like their future plans will be obstructed if they stay in Mexico, they move back to the States with older siblings, relatives, or friends.

For example, Quique was nine when he moved to Mexico with his parents after his father's deportation. In his first year of middle school, he started smoking cigarettes, drinking alcohol, and doing other drugs, while getting into fights to gain "respect" among his classmates. He recalls: "in this school it was the first time I tried drugs. I had never done it, but everyone does it (t)here, I have friends that give them (drugs) to me." When his father found him at home sniffing rubbing alcohol, the family decided it was time for him to go back to the United States. He moved to Chicago when he was 13 years old and stayed with his older sibling and his mother's best friend. Quique has been back to Mexico only once in almost four years to visit his parents and younger brother.

Teachers' Perspectives

In the conversations with elementary and middle school teachers and principals, they shared their insights on transnational schooling and migration and how they reacted to new situations, to their students' aspirations, and to new teacher preparation. These interviews also gave insight into dynamics at their schools for student inclusion and exclusion.

In the interviews, Mexican educators recognized the presence of international migration in Morelos. Historically, Morelos had a modest record of return migration (Durand & Massey, 2003). However, in the last decade teachers had observed an increase in the number of transnational students in their schools. The majority of teachers commented that migration to the United States is very common in Mexico and that both countries are interconnected. They talked about how people from Morelos can move to California, Nevada, Texas, Illinois, or Minnesota one day, build relationships there, and then, suddenly, return to Mexico. A few teachers observed that each family was different.

One teacher, Mrs. Monserrat, expressed that she had been working with children who lived and studied in the United States. Some of her students told her "their father had to go back [to the United States], and/or that their mother was still there [United States] working but had sent them back to Mexico to go to school." Mrs. Monserrat explained that it is very common that while parents are in the United States, grandparents take care of the children in Mexico (a dynamic also detailed by Dreby [2010] for nearby Puebla and Oaxaca).

Other students had returned to the area with their whole families, especially those who had been deported. She remembered a student who had one parent in the United States and the other in Mexico: "There is a boy that lives only with his mom. His dad is over there. I think they (boy and mother) are moving over there when he is 16 years old, because he was born there [United States] . . . the ones that are born there, they dream of going back."

Teachers also talked about family separation because of the border. Another teacher, Eleine, described parents who leave Mexico and never come back. She explained that one girl in her class lived alone with her mother in Mexico, and they had no idea where her father was; he had left for the United States when she was a baby.

Another teacher named Omar commented about situations where U.S.-born children return to the United States without their parents:

> Some of them, when they finish middle school [in Mexico] go and continue studying on the "other side" [United States] . . . those who are not sure about their future plans, they let go and are influenced by bad people and the environment, and that is where they stay.

Mirroring

The perceptions of transnational students and the vision of Mexican teachers coincide in presenting a panorama of families negotiating borders in various ways. While students recount the different types of families that represent significant social and linguistic diversity, many teachers seem well informed about various migratory phenomena as well. Giving voice to both students and teachers manifests, on one hand, the challenges that children's migratory trajectories bring along, while, on the other hand, it explores the areas of opportunity where school systems and their curriculums could work toward a better integration of child migrants in the schools and classrooms.

For example, in their testimonies, students talk about the difficulties of adjusting to a new community, culture, and even their own relatives. Teachers, however, even though they are aware of the most common migratory trajectories (especially of families migrating to the United States), are not aware of the new migration patterns that involve a return and/or circularity. These new patterns usually hide the heterogeneity of migrant families, their children, and the particularities of their sociocultural experiences.

González, Moll, and Amanti (2005) consider that when teachers learn about their students' cultural backgrounds, they can revise their curricula to implement better teaching strategies that take advantage of the diversity in their classrooms. They can also better incorporate parents into the educational endeavor, providing an important resource for these students.

II. Educational Transitions

Students' Perspectives

First days at school can be challenging when you are in a country and attending school there for the first time, have not mastered the spoken language, and do not know what to expect from teachers and classmates. When we met newly arrived transnational students in Mexican schools, they regularly compare their new school with American schools and often express that they wish they were back in the United States. When we meet those who had been in Mexico a little longer, they are speaking, reading, and writing Spanish more fluently; have learned new materials; and have figured out how to get around in the school and how to talk to teachers. Little by little, they adapt to their new environments, and comparisons with their schools in the United States subside.

Beto's first impression, for instance, was that his new schools were too small: "My *secundaria* in Cuentepec (Morelos, Mexico) is like four times smaller than McFadden (in California), and this high school is bigger than the one in Cuentepec, but when you go to California, you'll see that McFadden it's even bigger." Beto's school was indeed very small, even compared with other Mexican schools. There were only nine groups/classrooms, three for each grade level of *secundaria* (seventh-ninth grade). Although there was electricity, the classrooms were dark and had no fans or air conditioners. There were only two other rooms beside the classrooms, the library/computer center and the principal's office. The school had a soccer field behind the first grade of *secundaria* classrooms and a basketball court covered by a big tent roof by the entrance. Teachers and students used the basketball court to salute the Mexican flag on Mondays and to exercise during their PE (physical education) classes.

For Lulú, lack of skill in Spanish was her main problem in her Mexican school. During the implementation of our survey at her school, a teacher pointed her out and said, "She does not know Spanish, she just got here." Once we had a chance to talk to her in the principal's office, she explained: "I can't read in Spanish, or in English, because of my problem, but if you read me the questions I can answer." She later told us that she had been diagnosed with dyslexia in the United States. On top of that, her lack of Spanish skills made her very uncomfortable. Lulú felt very "frustrated" about being in Mexico and in a new school: "They (teachers) think I'm from here, but I'm not. They don't know. They ask me to work the same as everyone else, but I can't. I don't get it."

For Quique, the teaching strategies at his school were not aligned with his previous experience, especially while he was trying to learn Spanish. He recalled trying to write down a dictation in Spanish (see Gallo, "Preparing Educators for Asset-Based Pedagogies: The Case of Recently-Arrived Transnational Students in Central Mexico," Chapter 5 in this volume), but thinking in English:

> I was used to the pronunciation in English, and so whenever the teachers were dictating it was so hard! I was hearing something and writing something totally different, that was it for me, that was the hard part . . . Once I got a hold of it, it became easier . . . Here, look, my notebooks have red all over it, that's how teachers here grade writing, and they gave me a lot of *"planas"* (lists of words) for homework, man! It was so boring!

Beto and Sofía (Lulú's older sister) both described their interactions with teachers in the United States and Mexico as very different. Beto, for example, said that in California he felt free to ask his teachers questions and participate in class, while in Cuentepec he felt lost. For him, it was harder to speak to his teacher here, and he had new school rules:

> I didn't know how to talk to teachers, not like in Spanish, but like if I needed something, like going to the restroom. For example, in the States they only give you like three passes for the whole semester, and here I didn't know if I had to ask or

just go or what. It was so confusing . . . and then, I didn't know about grades, over there they use letters like A for excellent and F for fail. Here, they use numbers, I didn't know if I was doing good or bad, I had to ask my parents.

Sofía's words resembled those of Beto's:

Here (Mexico) it is different; they (teachers) don't listen to the students. Over there, the students have power, we can speak up, we can say what we are thinking or if the teacher is not a good teacher. Here, teachers have more power. It is different; they get to stay even if what they did is not correct.

Sofía failed her first English class in Mexico for talking back to her teacher and trying to correct her in front of the other students. "At the end of the semester she gave me a forty (out of a hundred). I turned in all my homework and did everything she wanted, and still, I failed, it's not fair!"

Last, our interviewed students agreed that in Mexico teachers expect them to learn new rules, activities, and school material in a matter of days, without taking into account that they are coming from another country and/or that they speak another language. Sofía told us that the most difficult subject for her was history. She explained:

I know History from the United States; we were born there. I know the American anthem and pledge to the flag, but here, I didn't know anything about Mexico and their anthem and the *juramento a la bandera* (pledge to the flag). I know I am smart and . . . I ended up learning it.

Teachers' Perspectives

Transnational mobility is a process where students encounter discontinuities and educational and social ruptures (Hamann & Zúñiga, 2011). There are challenges when it comes to adapting to schools, to interaction with teachers and classmates, and to doing so in a new or less familiar language. A teacher named Virginia explained that she could relate to how students negotiated differences between the schools in both countries because she had worked in California a few years earlier:

> I can grasp that attitude of the children, of how they want to go back to their roots. I think it is because they are in a country with a very different culture . . . what I mean is that our customs and traditions are rooted in us, and that is part of our identity, it is something we should and cannot get rid of.

Another teacher, Eleine, believed that another difference students find has to do with the school's infrastructure. She commented that a boy in her class had adaptation problems because of this. She wondered whether or not schools in the United States had "another form of life" and might be better than Mexican ones. For example, she said that the boy told her that some schools had swimming pools. She also mentioned that one of her students liked American schools more because they would give her lunch.

During an interview with two teachers, José Antonio and Margarita, José Antonio told us about a transnational girl who was his student in fourth grade. She had trouble adapting to school. She would tell him that in the United States they had free breakfast, while in Mexico they had to eat at home before going to school. Another difference was that schools in the United States were "really nice," while in Mexico the ceiling had leaks when it rained. There were also fewer students in each classroom in the United States, and they would move from room to room, and finish school at 3:00 p.m., instead of 1:00 p.m. (in Mexico). Margarita observed that grading was different too. In the United States they used letters to grade students; they took fewer subjects and had lockers and transportation, while in Mexico they used numbers to grade and did not have those other things.

Teacher Maricruz agreed with her colleagues and elaborated that the changes in the environment can obstruct a child's learning skills:

> It's a brutal change from civilization, from nice classrooms, and here they come to a world that they don't understand. As much as we want to explain, they won't understand . . . as much as I wanted to integrate them, I couldn't because they didn't speak Spanish.

Many teachers agreed with Maricruz's final statement; language is a major challenge for transnational students. Maricruz remembered a girl she had in her class who initially had language problems and how, with time, she started getting better at Spanish while keeping her English skills:

> She arrived in second grade and had a lot of trouble with the language. She would only speak in English. Her teacher and classmates didn't understand her because they didn't speak English. It was hard for her to adapt. In third grade, she was a bit more sociable and had more friends. In fourth grade, she already knew a lot of Spanish. Because of the language it was hard for her to keep up with school subjects. Nonetheless, she was very active in the English class; she loved it! We teach English here from fourth grade on.

According to English teacher Mrs. Monserrat, children have difficulties with the Spanish language when parents "do not teach them at home"; this is a common thought that teachers share even though parents claim to speak Spanish at home all the time. Because she taught the English class, she felt it was not as hard for her to include transnational students as it was for her fellow coworkers:

> Well, maybe in other subjects [they have problems]; if they don't learn Spanish at home, when they get here, they suffer a "shock." They stop, and there are some challenges they have to overcome to be at the same level as their classmates. Besides that, I haven't found any other difficulties—maybe some spelling problems—but in general they are good students.

Nonetheless, Mrs. Monserrat underlined that having English-speaking skills has some advantages, such as being able to help their classmates with their work. She, for example, asks transnational students to help her with the English class:

> The goal is to try to pronounce English words as well as they do it. I've never been to the United States; my preparation has been in schools here. I have worked with them [i.e., transnational students] as monitors. They are the ones that help me. They like presenting in front of the class. When they finish their activities, they help me with the other teams. They are like my small teachers.

Another teacher, Omar, does not teach English, but he explained how the skills that transnational students bring with them could be useful in other subjects: "The majority of them have good studying skills and work well, they help others that are not doing so well, I use them as monitors."

One advantage that most teachers observed about migrant families was that transnational parents were very participative and responsible. They never had problems contacting them about their sons' and daughters' schooling. There were some cases when the child was living with his or her grandparents or other relatives. In those cases, teachers observed a lack of participation from the adults in the child's education. Teachers also explained that the educational level of the parents made a difference in how much they got involved with their children's education.

Mirroring

Comparing schools in both countries is common among both transnational students and their teachers. Both describe difficulties that arise when children join a new educational environment. Above all, linguistic discontinuities are mentioned. The better conditions of the schools' infrastructure in the United States are also highlighted and can cause students to feel disappointed with their new school.

In students' interviews, it is recurrent that language acquisition, especially reading and writing in Spanish, is the most difficult task to learn. Additionally, subjects such as Mexican history and math are in the top three. Students also recognize that their interactions with Mexican teachers differ from those with their American teachers; in their own words, "teachers in Mexico are good, but they are not very patient" and are not considerate of their linguistic and cultural backgrounds. They also observe that Mexican teachers have certain "power" and are authoritarian.

For their part, teachers declare that when the school authorities do not mention that the new student comes from the United States, it is hard for them to point them out in the classroom. Nonetheless, when they discover who they are, teachers learn about different forms of assessment in American schools and how students receive extra support in classrooms to learn the English language. It is important to note that teachers acknowledged some advantages from school migration, with the higher educational participation of the parents just one of the items highlighted, but one that can be a critical resource for the students, as well as additional support for teachers.

These two points of view make us wonder what else could be done to recognize transnational students and their trajectories in Mexican schools. What kind of actions are needed to have successful school transitions where students feel welcomed and decide to stay and continue with their studies? And how can Mexican schools take advantage of different practices in U.S. schools, such as incorporating parents more in their children's schooling?

III. Future Aspirations

Students' Perspectives

Perhaps reflecting educational aspirations influenced by their time in the United States, as well as increases in obligatory years of schooling in Mexico, in most transnational families, these younger children will be the first generation to finish middle school (*secundaria*), high school (*preparatoria*), and maybe even go to college. We have observed that transnational parents are more actively involved in their children's schools and often go above and beyond to find the economic and moral resources to assist their children's educational trajectories. Additionally, transnational students are aware of the challenges and sacrifices their parents go through to help them finish school and strive to live up to their expectations, while facing their own academic, social, and cultural challenges. Students are also aware that their legal citizenship(s) can either obstruct or encourage their career and labor aspirations in one or both countries. In other words, Mexican-born *retornado* children cannot return to the United States without a visa, while American-born children can travel back and forth between the two countries because of their birthright.

Beto, even though he was a Mexican returnee, told us he still dreams of going back to California someday. He acknowledged he needs certain documents to do so and is constantly asking about the possibility of either studying or working in the United States. "How can I go back to the States? What do I need? Is it hard to get (a visa)?" He also thinks that it is important to maintain his English language skills in order to succeed in the United States:

> This is what I'm gonna do, finish high school, go to college, and then find a really good job where they will send me to

the States legally. Then I will stay there and send money to my parents or even try to bring them back to the States . . . In the meantime, I don't want to forget [the language] for when I go back.

In contrast, for students like Lulú, Sofía, and Quique, visa papers were not an issue. When Lulú stopped going to school in Mexico because she did not feel accepted, she saw the United States as an option to keep studying:

I want to go back (to school), but now I am older than the other students and maybe they will make fun of me . . . I could go to adult school too, but I will be the only teenager there . . . A third option is to go back to the United States, I can enroll over there.

Sofía at some point went back to California with the dream of finishing high school and working to send money to her parents. However, it took her only two months to realize that she wanted to be in Mexico instead, and that even though she was American, she "felt more Mexican" now.

Finally, Quique's plans changed when he went back to the United States. He agrees that being in the United States changed his life for the better; he stopped doing drugs and started doing sports and going to school again. His primary plan was to finish high school and start working to support his parents in Mexico and bring them to the United States. Nonetheless, studying and working at the same time became a major challenge for him, and he decided to stop going to school for some time. Additionally, when Donald Trump became president, he realized that bringing his parents back to the United States would be much harder. He still wants to finish high school and have his family together and is working and sending money to his parents whenever he can.

I know that (finishing school) would make my parents very proud, and it is a priority for me, but I can't stop working right now. My younger brother will come here to live with me and I have to save money for when he is here. I won't let my parents down, I am working very hard to build something there (Mexico), if they cannot be here with me, I will do everything in my hands to go back and be with them.

Teachers' Perspectives

Mexican teachers recognized that transnational students are a heterogeneous group with binational experiences in the United States and Mexico, for the most part. They believed that there is a high probability that U.S.-born students will take advantage of their American citizenship, with multicultural and multilinguistic elements, and go back to that country to study or work.

Even though having dual citizenship gives American students certain advantages over those who only have Mexican citizenship, teachers believe that these American-born students struggle more to find an identity of their own. Some children tell their teachers that they are American and that they would like to go back to their country of birth. Teachers said other children, who are born in Mexico but started schooling in the United States, often feel more Mexican. Yet they too sometimes still dream of going back to the States someday. For example, teacher José Antonio commented that one of his students has the goal to go back to the United States and finish studying there. This girl, he says, "knows the school system over there very well; she lived through it and liked it. She has the possibility to go back. Her father lives there, and she is a citizen. She has been telling me that she leaves in a month."

Another teacher, Virginia, explained that transnational children have a complex identity:

> If the child had things in the United States and he or she liked it, and if they have the possibility to go back, they are going to do it. They might even try to go back undocumented. They are going to keep trying in different ways. However, if they have a solid family and support here, he or she will remain here in Mexico. This country is beautiful and when you are away, you miss it. You love your country and everything in it, [even] corruption, dirt . . . You love it because it is your identity. I am worried about those who go back and forth, they don't know where they fit anymore, and they don't have a place to stay. They are there and want to be here or are here and want to be there. They lose their identity, their country and their sense of belonging.

Maricruz (another teacher) elaborated on her sense of how transnational students contemplate the geographies of their future:

> Besides Guadalupe and Gerardo, there is another girl named Paulina. She has a double nationality. She says that as soon as she finishes middle and high school she will go back to the United States. I think she is a very smart girl. She has a high IQ. So, I think she can make it, her objectives are clear. Everyone has the same opportunities; they just have to work hard for their dreams. She always told me she liked it more over there [United States]. I truly think she'll do better over there than here.

Teacher Omar also observed that students' decisions to migrate depend on whether students have clear aspirations for their future:

> Some, when they finish middle school, move to other places to study. There are others, who as soon as they finish middle school, they go back to the United States. And there are others, those who do not have clear expectations, who are absorbed by their environment and stay.

Mrs. Monserrat talked about the importance of having strong family ties in one or both countries:

> We, as teachers, know when the child is here with one or both parents. The ones with both parents here are the ones that tend to have aspirations; but there are cases where the whole family has some type of business (like selling different products) and the child wants to follow those footsteps. They don't have an example of higher aspirations.

Mirroring

On the aspiration of transnational life, there are clear similarities in the perceptions of children and teachers. To return to live in the United States, to continue their studies, and to work are ingrained ideas, especially in cases where they have a dual nationality. A binational future is perceived in their narratives.

Both binational students and Mexican teachers agree that dual citizenship is an advantage over mononational peers. Being able to travel back and forth will not only allow them to have multicultural experiences, master two or more languages, and have broader networks, but it also will open the way for a better future and better job opportunities in both countries. Unfortunately, neither schools nor communities are ready to promote a global citizenship that is embedded in their curricula and that answers to the pedagogical challenges that transnational children face in their early education, which obscures their future goals and dreams.

Recommendations Expressed by Students and Teachers

Findings from our interviews with transnational students and their Mexican teachers suggest a series of recommendations to better receive, guide, and support the transition of transnational children to either Mexican or American schools.

From students' perspectives, teachers and school administrators should (1) learn about the educational and migratory trajectories of transnational students to improve welcome protocols to the school and their classrooms; (2) establish educational programs that rescue and promote the cultural background of migrant families in their lesson plans and teaching modules; and (3) promote a transitional curriculum with linguistic, pedagogical, content, and evaluative procedures.

From the perspectives of Mexican teachers, it would be desirable (1) to learn about their students' trajectories and how these can shape their students' school performance to be able to readapt their teaching practices and promote respect and teamwork among peer students; (2) to establish, along with transnational and mononational students, strategies for a global citizenship in the classroom; and (3) to create initial teacher education curricula that target educational inclusiveness, with a focus on multicultural pedagogy with attention to diversity.

Specifically for teachers in the United States, it would be helpful (1) to understand transnationalism from the perspective of students as the source of information; (2) to take advantage of the transnational experiences of students from a multicultural perspective by sharing them with their peers and connecting their stories with class material; (3) to educate for and from a globalized ontology; (4) to publish guidebooks in Spanish to facilitate inclusion to schools in both countries; (5) to develop curricular resources in English and Spanish to use in the teaching-learning processes; (6) to learn about the curricula and organization of schooling in Mexico in order to facilitate students' transitions; (7) to have access to continuous distance-technology-enabled teacher education to help with school challenges such as diversity; and (8) to increase the number of bilingual teachers in all schools by making Spanish, or other languages, part of the curriculum in teacher preparation institutions.

Conclusions

The current conditions in both countries of expulsion in the global economy (Sassen, 2015) show that the population of students with transnational experiences will continue to grow and intensify in the coming years. As a result, transnational schooling should be part of our agendas toward the development of better global societies (see Chapter 2 by Hamann and Zúñiga). Transnational students are part of a new era, one in which full citizenship requires a deeper social understanding of transnational exchange (Gándara, 2016, 2020).

These students share knowledge of two educational systems, two cultures, and two or more languages, which, if effectively supported and cultivated, give them the tools to succeed in many settings. Transnational students can go above and beyond the borders that might separate their families, their schooling, and their cultures. However, we are still far behind recognizing this potential in our schools. Immediate educational policies and actions are needed to capture what is possible and desirable for the students Mexico and the United States share.

We recommend two strategies to support transnational students in Mexican schools. First, there is a need for school-based programs that support learning Spanish as a second language (SSL). In this regard, Reimers (2006) affirms that though SSL resources are sometimes available in classrooms (targeting indigenous students), we found no evidence in our study that SSL materials were used to teach Spanish or to help transition from English to Spanish for transnational students. Second, school principals and teachers should take advantage of the school culture that returned parents bring along from the United States to get them involved in their children's education and their learning performance (see Chapter 1 by Santibañez).

The mirroring experiences of the two most important actors at the teaching/learning interface—i.e., students and teachers—need to be dually considered to understand the educational and migratory trajectories of transnational children and the challenges and gaps that we need to target. Transnational students bring with them sets of skills—linguistic, social, and cultural—that their classmates can benefit from. Therefore, we strongly believe that students with migratory experiences in other countries should not be seen as a burden in the classroom, but rather as assets who can contribute to the teachers' and the classmates' views of the world. Of course, this will only happen if teachers are prepared to receive these students and are taught how to perceive, appreciate, and take advantage of their assets.

Transnational students turn obstacles and challenges into opportunities that allow them to move back and forth between the two countries, using their understandings of both systems and their social networks (Román González, Carrillo Cantú, & Hernández-León, 2016). Therefore, it is important that we, as teachers, appreciate these students' experiences and how they can encourage a sense of community, love, friendship, and companionship in our classrooms. It is our duty to do the best we can to better include them in our schools (Nieto, 2005; 2015).

By juxtaposing the views of Mexican teachers and transnational students, we have learned that schools and school systems can pay better attention to diversity under multicultural frameworks that allow transnational students to share their experiences with mononational students. We believe that these mirroring experiences will benefit the dialogues and interactions between students and teachers. As Octavio Paz (2004), Mexican poet, wrote in his poem "Piedra de Sol" [Sunstone]: ". . . el mundo cambia si dos se miran y se reconocen . . ." [. . . the world changes if two (people) look at each other and recognize themselves. . . .]

Notes

1. We thank Dr. Víctor Zúñiga and Dr. Edmund T. Hamann, who have been colleagues and mentors in our projects.
2. PROBEM is the federal Mexican program that attends to students who move transnationally.

References

Bauman, Z., & Donskis, L. (2013). *Moral blindness. The loss of sensibility in liquid modernity*. USA: Wiley.
Berger, P. L., & Luckmann, T. (2003). *La construcción de la realidad social*. Buenos Aires: Amorrortu.

Dreby, J. (2010). *Divided by borders. Mexican migrants and their children.* USA: University of California Press.

Durand, J., & Massey, D. S. (2003). *Clandestinos. Migración México-Estados Unidos en los albores del siglo XXI.* México: Universidad Autónoma de Zacatecas y Porrúa.

Fondo de Naciones Unidas para la Infancia (UNICEF). (2017). *Niños y niñas migrantes y refugiados. Proteger a los niños y las niñas en tránsito contra la violencia, el abuso y la explotación.* Resumen ejecutivo. New York, NY: UNICEF.

Gallo, S. (2021). Preparing educators for asset-based pedagogies: The case of recently-arrived transnational students in Central Mexico. In P. Gándara & B. Jensen (Eds.), *The students we share: Preparing US and Mexican educators for our transnational future.* Albany, NY: State University of New York Press.

Gándara, P. (2016). Policy report. The students we share. *Mexican Studies/Estudios Mexicanos. 32*(2), 357–378.

Gándara, P. (2020). The students we share: falling through the cracks on both sides of the US-Mexico border. *Ethnic and Racial Studies, 43*(1), 38–59.

Giorguli Saucedo, S., & Gutiérrez Vázquez, E. (2011). Niños y jóvenes en el contexto de la migración internacional entre México y Estados Unidos. *Coyuntura Demográfica,* N.° 1, 21–25.

González, N., Moll, L., & Amanti, C. (Eds.). (2005). *Funds of knowledge: Theorizing practices in households, communities, and classrooms.* Mahwah, NJ: Lawrence Erlbaum Associates, Publishers.

Hamann, E. T., & Zúñiga, V. (2011). Schooling and the everyday ruptures transnational children encounter in the United States and Mexico. In C. Coe, R. Reynolds, D. Boehm, J. M. Hess, & H. Rae-Espinoza (Eds.), *Everyday ruptures: Children and migration in global perspective* (pp. 141–160). Nashville, TN: Vanderbilt University Press.

Hamann, E. T., Zúñiga, V., & Sánchez, J. (2018). Where should my child go to school? Parent and child considerations in binational families. In M. R. T. de Guzman, J. Brown, & C. P. Edwards (Eds.), *Parenting from afar and the reconfiguration of family across distance* (pp. 339–350). United Kingdom: Oxford Press.

Igoa, C. (1995). *The inner world of the immigrant child.* Mahwah, NJ: Lawrence Erlbaum Associates, Publishers.

Marks, A.K., & Abo-Zena, M.M. (2015). Process of development. In C. Suárez-Orozco, M. M. Abo-Zena, & A. K. Marks (Eds.), *Transitions: The development of children of immigrants* (pp. 199–223). New York, NY: New York University Press.

Nieto, S. (2005). *Why we teach.* New York, NY: Teachers College Press.

Nieto, S. (2015). *Why we teach now.* New York, NY: Teachers College Press.

Paz, O. (2004). Obra poética I (1935–1970). Obras completas. Edición del autor. México: Círculo de Lectores y Fondo de Cultura Económica.

Reimers, F. (2006). Las condiciones para el desarrollo de competencias lectoras y de escritura en el aula. El impacto del PNL, Los libros de texto y el programa de actualización. In Fernando Reimers (Ed.), *Aprender más y Mejor. Políticas, programas y oportunidades de aprendizaje en educación básica en México* (pp. 245–303). México, DF: Secretaría de Educación Pública, Fondo de Cultura Económica, Instituto Latinoamericano de la Comunicación Educativa y Escuela de Postgrado en Educación de la Universidad de Harvard.

Román González, B. (2017). *Pa´cuando me regrese, can we speak in English?: Trayectorias de menores migrantes que llegan a México.* Tesis para obtener el grado de Doctor en Ciencias Sociales. Monterrey, Nuevo León: Instituto Tecnológico y de Estudios Superiores de Monterrey.

Román González, B., & Carrillo, E. (2017). "Bienvenido a la escuela": The school experiences of transnational students in Morelos, Mexico. *Sinéctica, 48*, 2–17.

Román González, B., Carrillo, E., & Hernández-León, R. (2016). Moving to the "Homeland." Children's narratives of migration from the United States to Mexico. *Mexican Studies/Estudios Mexicanos, 32*(2), 252–275.

Sassen, S. (2015). *Expulsiones. Brutalidad y complejidad en la economía global.* España: Katz.

Sánchez García, J., & Zúñiga, V. (2010). Trayectorias de alumnos transnacionales en México. Propuesta de educación intercultural de atención educativa. *Revista Trayectorias, 12,* 5–23.

Sánchez García, J., & Hamann, E. (2016). Educator responses to migrant children in Mexican schools. *Mexican Studies/Estudios Mexicanos, 32*(2), 199–225.

Santibañez, L. (2021). Teacher education policy in Mexico and the quality of teaching for transnational students. In P. Gándara & B. Jensen (Eds.), *The students we share: Preparing US and Mexican educators for our transnational future.* Albany, NY: State University of New York Press.

Suárez-Orozco, C. (2015). Family separations and reunifications. In C. Suárez-Orozco, M. M. Abo-Zena, & A. K. Marks (Eds.), *Transitions: The development of children of immigrants* (pp. 69–94). New York, NY: New York University Press.

UNICEF. (2006). *Estado mundial de la infancia 2006. Excluidos e invisibles.* New York: UNICEF.

Zúñiga, V., & Hamann, E.T. (2009). Sojourners in Mexico with U.S. school experience: A new taxonomy for transnational students. *Comparative Education Review, 53*(3): 329–353. Retrieved from http://digitalcommons.unl.edu/teachlearnfacpub/91/

Zúñiga, V., Hamann, E. T., & Sánchez García, J. (2008 y 2010). *Alumnos transnacionales: Las escuelas mexicanas frente a la globalización.* México: Secretaría de Educación Pública. Primera edición y primera reimpresión.

Part 3

Bridging Policies

Chapter 8

Language and Cultural Skills of U.S. Teachers

Informing Policy to Meet the Needs of Transnational Bilingual Students

Francesca López and Lucrecia Santibañez

In 2016, there were 43 million immigrants in the United States, making up 13% of the total population. More than 55% of those immigrants come from Mexico. Immigrants leave their homes to access better opportunities for themselves and their families, to escape violence, and to join family members who left, along with many other reasons. Immigration follows haphazard patterns: Mothers and/or fathers move to another country and leave their children behind; children sometimes follow them accompanied by other family members or making the journey on their own; new siblings born in the United States result in "mixed-status families." Sometimes things don't quite work out. Whether family members are deported or elect to return to their home country, these moves can be profoundly disruptive. Children must adapt to new situations and conditions such as a different language, culture, social structure, and, crucially, different norms and expectations for educational behavior and performance. Youth who experience schooling in both the United States and Mexico are known as *transnational students*, sometimes referred to as sojourners to reflect the continuous migration not fully captured by terms such as migrant and immigrant (Zúñiga & Hamann, 2009). Dramatic changes in the learning environment that introduce added stress can threaten not only transnational students' academic development, but also their *socio-emotional learning*

(SEL), which collectively refers to knowledge, attitudes, and skills about the self and others (Bronfenbrenner, 1979, 1989; Sandstrom & Huerta, 2013; Wright & Masten, 2005). This poses extraordinary challenges for the teachers who teach them. What should teachers of transnational students know and do to meet their unique needs?

There is an extensive body of research focused on how teachers can support the language needs of students whose home language differs from the dominant language used in schools. In the United States, these students are often classified as *English learners* (ELs), and most often speak Spanish as their home language. To reflect the cultural and linguistic assets shared by these students, some have argued that *emergent bilingual* should replace terms that ignore students' linguistic potential (e.g., García, 2009), but others have pointed to the limitations implicit in a term that continues to reflect what students *do not yet have*. Here, we use the terms *dual language learners* (DLLs) to reflect more accurately the linguistic realities of students in the United States whose home language is not English and *transnational dual language learners* (TDLLs) to refer to students the United States and Mexico share.[1]

The unique needs of our transnational students have largely been ignored by research because of an assumption that students—both those whose families have been in the United States for generations and those who are more recent arrivals—are here to stay. Yet there are a large number of TDLLs who are in U.S. schools and will leave, some of whom likely will return. Accordingly, while TDLLs share many needs with other DLLs, they also have unique needs introduced by their transnational experiences. This chapter begins with a review of the research on the kind of knowledge teachers must have about language and SEL needs of DLLs. Then we discuss some of the unique considerations introduced by the contexts navigated by TDLLs.

Teachers' Knowledge About Language and SEL

An examination of DLLs' overall performance on the National Assessment of Educational Progress (NAEP) over the past 16 years suggests that U.S. schools, on average, do not engage in practices that are effective in promoting their academic learning outcomes. There are, however, marked differences across states in EL student performance. Among fourth graders between 2005 and 2015, Arizona DLLs perform about 1 *SD* lower than their peers in California, who in turn perform about 1 *SD* lower than their peers in Texas.[2] Some may wonder whether different curricular standards across states are a source of these differences; however, students who are *not* labeled as "English learners" across the three states perform similarly to each other, suggesting that curricular differences across states are not a likely source of the variation. What explains this variation?

We assert that state-level policies are the primary mechanism that influences DLL achievement. This is because state-level policies, which vary from state to state, prescribe the kind of knowledge teachers are required to have. Although there are many Language Instruction Educational Policies (LIEP) used in the United States, with wide variation within states as well as across states, LIEPs generally either incorporate DLLs' home language in instruction to build content knowledge as DLLs acquire proficiency in English, or rely on instruction in English to build English proficiency in anticipation that content knowledge will follow (see Table 8.1).

This required knowledge, in turn, contributes to teachers' *self-efficacy*, which includes perceptions about their capacity to affect student performance and influence how well students learn. We highlight self-efficacy over other metrics of teacher quality related to student achievement given that teacher self-efficacy has demonstrated powerful links with student outcomes in research (e.g., Caprara et al., 2006; Klassen & Chiu, 2011; Tschannen-Moran & Hoy, 2001) (see Figure 8.1).

Table 8.1. Range of Language Instruction Educational Programs and Their Respective Language of Instruction and Goals

Language Instruction Educational Program (LIEP)	Structured English Immersion	English as a Second Language	Transitional Bilingual Education	Dual Language
Language of instruction	English	English	Bilingual	Bilingual
Goal	Proficiency in English	Proficiency in English	Proficiency in English	Bilingualism/ Biliteracy

Note: Adapted from Scanlan, M., & López, F. (2014). *Organizing schools to serve linguistically and culturally diverse students*. New York: Routledge.

Definitions are provided in footnotes 11 and 12.

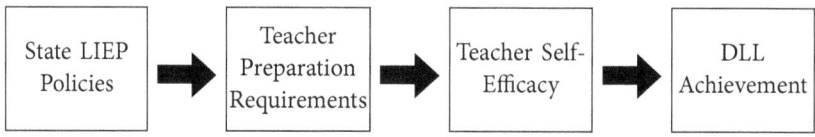

Figure 8.1. Conceptual Framework Representing Teacher Preparation and Teacher Self-Efficacy as Mediators of Policy on DLLS' Achievement Outcomes.

Although state policies "exert significant influence on the pre-service training teachers receive prior to entering the classroom as the teacher of record" (Loeb & Miller, 2006, p. 8), state LIEP policies play a particularly salient role in the training teachers of DLLs receive (López, Scanlan, & Gundrum, 2013). For example, prior to restrictive LIEPs in Arizona and California, the two states and Texas had roughly the same proportion of teachers with bilingual/ESL training.[3] Between 2000 and 2012, when both Arizona and California had anti-bilingual education legislation, the proportion of teachers with bilingual/ESL training in the three states begins to diverge (see Figure 8.2). In Texas, the proportion of teachers who are bilingual/ESL certified increased, whereas in both Arizona and California, the proportion of teachers with this training declined. Given that pre-service teachers receive essential knowledge through required coursework (see Darling-Hammond, 2000; Darling-Hammond & Bransford, 2005)

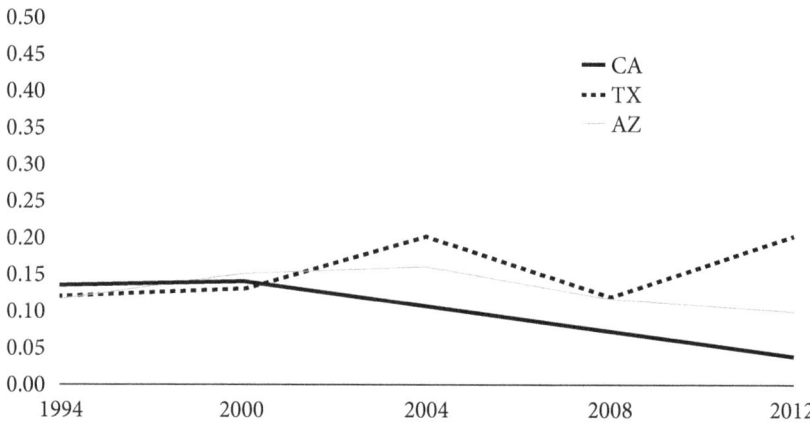

Figure 8.2. Percentage of New Teachers with Bilingual and/or ESL Training over Time.

and that more rigorous coursework leading to specialist certification in bilingual education[4] and/or ESL[5] is related to better outcomes for DLLs (López et al., 2013), it is useful to identify discrete teacher skills associated with DLLs' achievement to inform teacher education policies.

Requisite Teacher Skills to Meet the Needs of DLLs

Although many scholars have proposed frameworks to describe the knowledge and skills teachers of DLLs should develop (for a review, see López & Santibañez, 2018), here we describe research undergirding the most comprehensive theoretical framework we identified. The framework was created nearly two decades ago with input from experts at American Association of Colleges for Teacher Education (AACTE), as well as the National Center for Bilingual Education; the Center for Research on Education, Diversity, and Excellence; and the Teachers of English to Speakers of Other Languages Pre-K-12 Teacher Education ESL Standards Committee (Menken & Antunez, 2001) and consists of three domains: *knowledge of pedagogy, knowledge of linguistics,* and *knowledge of cultural and linguistic diversity.* In consideration of the critiques raised by a contemporary review by Faltis and Valdés (2016) (e.g., some of the scholarship and empirical research that frequently has been used in teacher preparation is often extraneous to K-12 populations and thus is not applicable to teacher preparation), we briefly summarize the research reflected in the three domains below, updated with the essential knowledge and critiques raised by Faltis and Valdés (2016).

Knowledge of Pedagogy

Teachers' knowledge of pedagogy should reflect research focused on DLLs' home language literacy, language acquisition and bilingualism, and the particular language practices and language demands of different subjects. It includes a focus on the importance of teachers acquiring various scaffolding strategies to accommodate variability in DLLs' language needs with the goal of ensuring that DLLs engage "in communicative interaction to build meaning (vocabulary and language practices), interpretation of talk and text, and performance using newly learned language and knowledge to show understanding of content" (Faltis & Valdés, 2016, p. 573).

Home language literacy. Although opponents of bilingual approaches claim that DLLs are prevented from learning English in settings that promote literacy in students' home language, ample research supports the notion that "knowledge and skills developed in the first language will transfer to the other" (Hakuta, 1990, p. 50). Indeed, researchers have found that DLLs' use of their home language to process a second language, both in print and orally, is associated with DLLs' English literacy (August & Shanahan, 2006; Genesee, Geva, Dressler, & Kamil, 2008). Moreover, teachers with skills that allow them to nurture DLLs' home language literacy, exposing them to *high quality* disciplinary language instruction and modeling, not only prevent DLLs from falling behind in content as they acquire English (August, Carlo, Dressler, & Snow, 2005), but also provide DLLs with the academic advantages associated with bilingualism (Adesope, Lavin, Thompson, & Ungerleider, 2010; Peal & Lambert, 1962). Accordingly, teachers who understand the role of DLLs' home language literacy in the development of a second language are more inclined to incorporate and/or accommodate bilingual strategies that reflect an asset-view of students' home language proficiency. Although there are many settings where teachers do not share DLLs' first language, this knowledge is instrumental in the ways in which they view language and the extent to which they can encourage literacy practices in students' first language (Faltis & Valdés, 2016).

ESL/ELD. It often can take DLLs up to seven years to develop the variations of English needed to be successful in school, but the time it takes varies as a function of the individual, how English proficiency is defined and assessed, the educational setting, and the kind of instructional support received. Although most DLLs are reclassified as English proficient after seven years, up to one-third of DLLs take longer and are identified as *long-term English learners* (LTEL). LTELs often have not received ideal instructional support (Menken, Kleyn, & Chae, 2012), which underscores the importance of teachers possessing the skills to deliver instruction that supports the development of subject matter understanding as DLLs develop English proficiency. This includes skills in the delivery of sheltered English approaches that emphasize English acquisition via content with support provided for students as necessary (Echevarria & Graves, 2010; Goldenberg, 2013). These skills, often described as scaffolding approaches, include awareness of the level of English that should be used with students to ensure comprehension, while supporting DLLs' "communicative interaction to build meaning (vocabulary and language practices), interpretation of talk and text, and performance using newly learned language and knowledge to show understanding of content" (Faltis & Valdés, 2016, p. 573).

Curriculum. Given the scarcity of curricular resources aimed specifically at DLLs, teachers must be able "to adapt the existing curricula and materials" to meet DLLs' needs (Menken & Antunez, 2001, p. 10). The current policy landscape is no exception: the Common Core State Standards (CCSS) and the Next Generation Science Standards (NGSS) have been criticized for ignoring the linguistic and cultural diversity of our students (e.g., Bale, 2015). Until curricula reflect the needs of DLLs, teachers must be able to align culturally sensitive content and standards to disciplinary language standards to ensure DLLs have equitable access.

Assessment. In addition to understanding how they can assess what their students know, it is imperative that teachers of DLLs understand the limits of the assessments their DLL students are often required to take. In many states, DLLs are assessed in English despite the fact that by definition, their English proficiency is developing and, as such, scores from these exams are not valid reflections of what students know. Thus, for many DLLs, assessment in their developing language often reflects more about where they are in their proficiency trajectory than what they know about content (Butler & Stevens, 2001). One of the most promising practices that reduces (but does not eliminate) this kind of assessment bias involves the use of linguistic modifications and pop-up glossaries (Abedi, 2002; Abedi, Hofstetter, & Lord, 2001), which are consistent with the kind of sheltered support teachers should provide in instruction. When teachers have knowledge about ways to assess DLL students more accurately, they can better inform their instruction to meet students' needs. Given that these types of linguistic accommodations often are *not* provided, and under the best of circumstances do not eliminate bias, it is imperative that teachers have an understanding of the limitations of assessments that are often interpreted incorrectly, yet can have very high stakes for students.

Practicum. Although the extant literature is explicit that teachers of DLLs should have field experiences that help them apply and further develop the knowledge they have acquired within culturally diverse settings, too often pre-service teachers have field experiences in schools that do not provide the opportunity to work with culturally and linguistically diverse students. This precludes pre-service teachers from applying the very skills they learn in their programs, which limits the extent to which they can practice and enhance their skills before they become teachers. Some states, like California, require a year- or two-year-long induction program to "clear" a credential. Research has found that although the induction phase presents a unique opportunity for teachers to hone their skills teaching DLLs with the help of a coach, this does not always happen. The induction process in California, for example, is structured in a way that does not require that teachers demonstrate proficiency teaching DLLs as the diverse group that they are in order to obtain a permanent, "clear" credential (Santibañez & Snyder, 2018).

Knowledge of Linguistics

Assumptions about language acquisition, such as the more DLLs in the United States inhibit the use of their home language, the more quickly they will acquire English; dedicated grammar practice will enhance language acquisition; and "conversational English" is not as cognitively demanding as "academic English," all reflect commonly held beliefs in the United States. Unfortunately, these and other views about language are not based on research and are deleterious to DLLs. To counter these and other widely held assumptions about language acquisition, Faltis and Valdés (2016) assert that, at the very minimum, teachers of DLLs require an understanding of the research focused on language structure (*linguistics*), language use as a function of specific contexts as well as nonstandard language varieties and code switching (*sociolinguistics*; see Alfaro & Bartolomé, 2017; Potowski & Shin, 2019; Valdés, 2005), as well as research on the psychological processes of language acquisition (*psycholinguistics*) to gain an appreciation of students' affect toward their home language and English, the role of home language in acquiring English, and the ways teachers can promote students' "full communicative repertoires" (Faltis & Valdés, 2016, p. 570).

This broad language-based knowledge is essential in preventing erroneous views of language and language acquisition, particularly for students who engage with multiple languages in their contexts or nonstandard varieties. Teachers should have the requisite knowledge and "ideological clarity" as described in Alfaro and Bartolomé (2017) to understand and appreciate these varieties while at the same building students' linguistic repertoires in formal variants. Without this knowledge, teachers can succumb to deficiency-based assumptions about language varieties used in different contexts that have been shown to have deleterious consequences for DLLs.

Knowledge of Cultural and Linguistic Diversity

In the third domain of their matrix, Menken and Antunez (2001) include policy, history, legislation, and other foundations on DLL instruction, as well as multiculturalism and parent involvement, as essential knowledge for teachers of DLLs. These dimensions are consistent with prior work that has established the importance of developing (1) teachers' foundational understanding of the sociohistorical context of traditionally marginalized youth (Gay, 2005; Hollins & Torres-Guzman, 2005; Milner, 2010; Morrison, Robbins, & Rose, 2008; Valenzuela, 2016); (2) cultural competencies of teachers so they are able to bring the diversity of students' and families' experiences into the learning and teaching process (Butvilofsky & Sparrow, 2012; González, Moll, & Amanti, 2005); and (3) an understanding of their own cultural, class, and linguistic identities (Faltis & Valdés, 2016; Pray & Marx, 2010). Notably, coursework that covers these dimensions has been shown to reduce teacher biases (Kumar & Hamer, 2013), which can have a marked influence on marginalized student achievement (López, 2017; McKown & Weinstein, 2002; Tenenbaum & Ruck, 2001).

The empirical support for requiring specialized teacher training (i.e. bilingual and/or ESL training) has suggested better academic outcomes for DLLs in mathematics (Master, Loeb, Whitney, & Wyckoff, 2012) and reading (López et al., 2013). It should be noted that specialized teacher preparation programs that include (albeit to varying degrees) the competencies we have reviewed require more time (sometimes as much as an additional semester of coursework or more). Given the shortage of teachers with specialized training, this presents a dilemma. Can programs incorporate this knowledge in more efficient ways? How can we prepare teachers with this knowledge while balancing the other teacher preparation needs they have? This dilemma notwithstanding, to understand why more rigorous teacher training may be associated with better academic outcomes among DLLs, we now turn to one of the factors that is directly associated with the kind of preparation teachers receive: teacher self-efficacy.

Teacher Self-efficacy

We conceptualize teacher self-efficacy as the extent to which teachers feel they have the capacity to affect student performance and influence how well students learn, including students who may be unmotivated, or present unique learning challenges (Klassen & Chiu, 2011; Berman, McLaughlin, Bass, Pauly, & Zellman, 1977; Rotter, 1966; Guskey & Passaro, 1994). Work in the area of teacher self-efficacy finds a high degree of correlation between self-efficacy ratings and preparedness ratings (Tschannen-Moran, Woolfok Hoy, & Hoy 1998; Raudenbush, Rowen, & Cheong, 1992) and enthusiasm for teaching and positive interactions with students (see Tschannen-Moran & Hoy, 2001). The strong relationship between teacher self-efficacy and satisfaction with teaching is especially relevant because it is related to job performance (Caprara, Barbaranelli, Borgogni, & Steca, 2003; Judge, Thoresen, Bono, & Patton, 2001; Klassen & Chiu, 2011). In addition to consequential teacher outcomes, there is also a solid research base linking teacher efficacy constructs to student motivation (Caprara, Barbaranelli, Steca, & Malone, 2006; Skaalvik & Skaalvik, 2007) and student achievement (Caprara et al., 2006; Klassen & Chiu, 2011; Tschannen-Moran & Hoy, 2001).

Many scholars have argued that teachers are not currently being adequately prepared to meet the needs of DLLs (Gándara & Santibañez, 2016; Faltis & Valdés, 2016; Menken & Antunez, 2001; Santibañez & Snyder, 2018). This is a particularly salient concern not only because teachers report being significantly less confident about teaching DLLs compared with non-DLLs (Ballantyne et al., 2008; Gándara, Maxwell-Jolly, & Driscoll, 2005; Karabenick & Noda, 2004), but also because teachers can develop negative attitudes toward DLLs when they have not received specialized training to be effective with them (Walker, Shafer, & Iiams, 2004). Although low self-efficacy among teachers of DLLs is often attributed to the absence of specialist certification, even specialist certified teachers report feeling "inept in meeting the needs of bilingual learners" (Flores, 2001, p. 269) when certified through alternative routes.

Specialist certification, as well as ongoing learning opportunities through professional development focused on the needs of DLLs, is associated with higher levels of teacher self-efficacy and student achievement outcomes (Master et al., 2012). Notably, teachers with these additional experiences who report higher preferences to work with DLLs are also markedly more effective (Master et al., 2012). Taken together, pre-service and in-service training are paramount in teacher self-efficacy, as well as teachers' satisfaction and teachers' desire to work with DLLs. All of these factors have important implications for DLLs' outcomes and must inform policy deliberations surrounding the kind of training teachers of DLLs should have.

In their examination of differences in teacher self-efficacy among teachers in Arizona, California, and Texas, López and Santibañez (2018) found that bilingual/ESL training is associated with markedly higher self-efficacy for novice teachers in Arizona and California, suggesting that teachers in contexts with weaker preparation requirements who choose to receive more rigorous training have enhanced self-efficacy. That is, the more rigorous training allows teachers to draw from a robust repertoire of knowledge to attenuate obstacles introduced by restrictive policies (e.g., the inability to use DLL's home language as a resource to scaffold instruction), which enhances their self-efficacy. This research is consistent with prior studies that have found that teachers with bilingual/ESL certification possess skills that enable them to navigate LIEP restrictions to address their DLLs' needs in these more complex situations (e.g., Lillie et al., 2012; Harper & de Jong, 2009). [Hopkins (2013) also found that bilingual teachers had more confidence in reaching out to parents of DLLs and therefore were more knowledgeable about their students' circumstances.] López and Santibañez additionally examined teachers' feelings of preparedness and found that bilingual-/ESL-trained new teachers with at least one DLL in their classrooms felt substantially (and significantly) more prepared than non-bilingually trained teachers. Overall, however, teachers feel underprepared to teach DLLs and many continue to develop their skills teaching DLLs through in-service professional development. A study of secondary teachers in the Los Angeles Unified School District (LAUSD) found that a significant proportion of teachers with DLLs in their classroom felt that professional development was a useful way to remedy gaps in training not received during pre-service (Santibañez & Gándara, 2018).

Given that the vast majority of teachers feel underprepared to meet the needs of students who speak a language other than English at home (Ballantyne, Sanderman, & Levy, 2008; Faltis & Valdés, 2016) and that teachers' beliefs about their competencies are associated with both student (e.g., learning) and teacher (e.g., turnover) outcomes (see Klassen & Chiu, 2011), ensuring that teachers are provided with skills that promote their sense of efficacy should be an important goal of teacher preparation.

Socioemotional Learning

Transnational students face not only challenges associated with learning a new language (in most cases) and learning academic content—often in mainstream English-only programs that don't take advantage of their linguistic and cultural assets—but also challenges associated with learning a new culture and environment. Adapting to the new context can prove extraordinarily difficult for TDLLs and requires deft and caring attention by teachers, administrators, and families. Teachers and administrators who lack an understanding of the unique challenges TDLLs face, however, may have unrealistic expectations of them, such as knowing basic routines (e.g., the Pledge of Allegiance) as well as norms around civic culture and basic U.S. historical or cultural references. TDLLs also may be completely unprepared to meet classroom norms around willingness to speak up in class and to challenge an opinion (see Chapter 1 by Santibañez for more on the norms in Mexican schools). One way to capture the additional learning and skills that these students develop in school is through socioemotional learning (SEL).

The Collaborative for Academic, Social and Emotional Learning (2013) describes SEL as comprising five domains: self-awareness, self-management, social awareness, relationship skills, and responsible decision making (CASEL, 2013). The past decades have seen burgeoning research examining student SEL outcomes. A comprehensive review of this research carried out by the RAND Corporation points to self-awareness (referred to as *intrapersonal*) and relationship (referred to as *interpersonal*) skills as the most promising SEL skills for improving academic outcomes (Grant et al., 2017). This growing body of evidence contributed to the introduction of the Academic, Social, and Emotional Learning Act of 2013 (HR 1875), which would have expanded SEL into teacher and principal training, as well as into the school curriculum. Although the bill did not become law, many states have begun to implement policies on SEL anyway. For example, several school districts in Texas have been piloting the integration of SEL for both student outcomes and teacher training; in February 2018, the California State Schools Chief released SEL guidelines for students, teachers, and administrators. Here, we briefly describe some of the research that has focused explicitly on DLLs and the interpersonal and intrapersonal dimensions of SEL.

In a review of research focused on SEL and DLLs, Halle et al. (2014) explains that several studies found DLLs to have enhanced interpersonal and intrapersonal SEL skills and explained that the challenges associated with learning language and content may contribute to heightening these SEL skills among DLLs. Despite the positive SEL effects introduced by challenging circumstances, there is also prior research that has found various intrapersonal dimensions including academic self-concept and ethnic identity to be negatively related to contexts that do not support DLLs' language and culture (López 2010, 2017). Another study found that among DLLs, *social-emotional problems* (a dimension of the interpersonal domain) were negatively related to academic outcomes and academic self-concept (Niehaus & Adelson, 2014). Collectively, this research suggests that DLLs and TDLLs have numerous advantages—both linguistic and those related to SEL—but teachers must be aware of the ways they can build on these students' assets to mitigate experiences that negatively influence SEL skills.

Discussion

Although there is a paucity of research focused on the specific needs of TDLLs, there is much that can be extrapolated from the extant research. For instance, we know that content and pedagogical knowledge are necessary but insufficient given the unique linguistic needs of students who are in multilingual contexts. We also know that colonization, assimilation, segregation, and inferior schooling all form part of the lasting legacy of schooling of minoritized youth in the United States, and many transnational students, though ethnically and racially diverse, will share these experiences with other minoritized youth. While historical knowledge that can assist teachers in better meeting the needs of students has been documented in the literature, it too is insufficient for TDLLs. Their unique experiences, and stress that comes along with such a monumental change in circumstances, require additional knowledge among teachers.

Earlier in this chapter, we asserted that state-level policies are the primary mechanism that influences DLL achievement given that state policies prescribe the kind of knowledge teachers are required to have. This holds true for TDLLs as well. The more policies align with the unique needs of TDLLs, the more likely achievement of TDLLs is enhanced. To wit, although Arizona, California, and Texas all consider bilingual/ESL teacher endorsement to meet the minimum requirements to teach DLLs, the three states have markedly disparate policies on the requirements for teachers of DLLs that have influenced the extent to which teachers seek out specialist endorsement. It is lamentable that states would continue to adhere to LIEP policies that promote this more rigorous training disparately (see Figure 8.2) given that these policies do appear to align with student outcomes across the three states we profile here. As such, these policies are particularly important for TDLLs who require teachers with more nuanced understandings about the challenges these students face.

Taken together, the evidence we discussed here has implications not only for revisions to Arizona's LIEP, but for all states with multilingual students. Rigorous knowledge is particularly necessary given that the vast majority of pre-service teachers come from backgrounds that are dissimilar to the students they will serve. Although specialist training may seem untenable given the numerous languages represented in schools, it is important to keep in mind that hypersegregation has resulted in 70% of DLLs—most of whom share the same home language—to be represented in just 10% of schools (Faltis & Valdés, 2016). Thus, states without rigorous requirements for teachers of DLLs should be compelled to revise their LIEP policy, which would serve to increase pre-service teacher requirements. States should consider the case of Texas, which requires bilingual/ESL certification in situations where a critical mass of DLLs share a home language, and ESL in other situations. Considering that DLLs may still require some support after reclassification to the status of English proficient, however, it makes sense to ensure *all* teachers have some knowledge about the particular needs of DLLs (Lucas, Villegas, & Freedson-Gonzalez., 2008; Santos, Darling-Hammond, & Cheuk, 2012). This approach, however, cannot replace more rigorous training that does require more time and resources.

In addition to more robust teacher requirements, it is imperative that states consider the access DLLs have to bilingualism, biculturalism, and biliteracy. The framework and the evidence we review suggest that LIEPs, like that of Texas, serve to provide opportunities that would not exist if they were not driven by policy. This is particularly important for TDLLs who face the challenge of adapting to a new country and whose assets may be completely overlooked—given their perceived linguistic and social deficits.

Accordingly, LIEPs must be forceful in ensuring that they reflect not only the kind of knowledge teachers must have to comply with state requirements, but that DLLs have access to learning opportunities that take advantage of teachers' expertise. Moreover, LIEPs should consider the variation within DLLs that include TDLLs, and ways teachers must consider their unique needs.

States are slowly catching up to the reality that other outcomes beyond academic test scores (e.g., non-cognitive outcomes) need to be measured and reported. SEL includes a set of domains that characterize a set of skills and dispositions that help students succeed not only in school, but also personally. We know very little about TDLLs' SEL and how schools/districts attempt to monitor these students' needs, particularly beyond the academic. Nevertheless, it is a welcome sign that some states such as California and Texas have begun to formally incorporate SEL into their district reporting and accountability frameworks and might be a function of the federal education law: Every Student Succeeds Act. Identifying who is a TDLL in these reporting systems, something that to our knowledge is not currently done in any state, would possibly go a long way toward better identifying and understanding their needs and monitoring their progress.

Conclusion

Although state-level language instruction education policies and teacher preparation requirements vary substantially from state to state, there are clear advantages to teachers in states that require knowledge of best practices for the students we share. When teachers have knowledge specific to the linguistic, cultural, and SEL needs of TDLLs, there are sure to be advantages to teachers' self-efficacy and satisfaction as well as TDLLs' achievement and SEL skills. Accordingly, although TDLLs are currently ignored in policy debates, policies should reflect the assets TDLLs introduce into classrooms and ensure that teachers can capitalize on their potential throughout compulsory schooling—both in the United States and Mexico. Although some states, like California, are moving in the right direction by repealing policies that have failed to fully meet the needs of DLLs, others remain woefully behind. The evidence we review here can inform debates about teacher preparation—particularly because TDLLs are unlikely to have teachers who are prepared to meet their needs. To that end, the findings across teacher preparation requirements, self-efficacy, achievement trends, and SEL point to the importance of rigorous teacher preparation for *all* teachers, and specialized training for teachers of DLLs in the early stages of their U.S. education.

Despite the evidence we do have, the unique needs of TDLLs present additional challenges to teacher preparation programs across the nation. Do teachers need to know anything about the system of education transnational students have experienced and/or might experience in the future? What about how educational and behavioral expectations differ in the United States and Mexico? While we know quite a bit about the importance of teacher understanding of the linguistic needs of transnational students, less is known about the ways culture, history, prior experience, and national contexts might demand teacher knowledge that is not usually part of pre-service training. For example, the increasingly hostile climate toward immigrants in the United States offered no respite from the hostility transnational students may encounter in Mexico in anti-U.S. contexts. What might these experiences do to shape transnational students' sense of belonging and identity? And how does this translate into future challenges incorporating these youth into a society that has, at best, ignored them and, at worst, rejected them? Draconian immigration policies that threaten family separation create countless difficulties that included limited access to proper nutrition and/or health care. Is this knowledge germane to educational expectations in the United States? If a sense of belonging and identity has any bearing on educational outcomes (and we know it does), then transnational students' experiences—both past and future—are essential in informing what teachers of these students should know and be able to do.

Notes

1. We retain terminology used by U.S. states when describing classification based on state criteria.

2. Source: U.S. Department of Education, Institute of Education Sciences, National Center for Education Statistics, National Assessment of Educational Progress.

3. We define bilingually trained teachers as those with a bilingual education or ESL certification, B.A. with bilingual education or ESL as major field of study, and/or M.A. in bilingual education or ESL. The reasons for this include the fact that the US Department of Education School and Staffing Survey does not distinguish between bilingual and ESL endorsement. In the three states we examine here the requirements are very similar for both ESL and bilingual endorsement, with one key exception: bilingual authorizations require that teachers demonstrate language proficiency and take coursework including bilingual pedagogies. Note that in California, the ESL-endorsement is obtained through the "World Languages-ELD" credential. Any credential in California issued after 2002 received an "embedded" EL authorization. This EL-authorization authorizes teachers to teach integrated-ELD (ELD that happens within the regular classes in all content areas), but not designated-ELD (specific ELD that happens during specific pro-

tected time or as part of a separate course intended to develop English language proficiency, e.g. ESL). Teachers with a bilingual authorization in California may teach designated-ELD, but teachers with an EL-authorization must obtain the World Languages-ELD credential. For more information see here: https://www.ctc.ca.gov/docs/default-source/leaflets/cl628b.pdf. The fact that SASS groups combine bilingual and ESL-endorsements is a limitation of the data that we cannot overcome. Findings should be interpreted with this in mind.

4. Transitional bilingual programs are the most prevalent bilingual programs in the U.S. and require teachers to hold bilingual certification and have fluency in emergent bilingual students' home language (López et al., 2013).

5. English as a second language (ESL) programs used in the United States tend to be either (1) pull-out, whereby students are removed from their mainstream (English-only) classroom during a designated time(s) and day(s) and are provided with focused English instruction in a small-group setting; or (2) instruction in a content area (e.g., science) that emphasizes the acquisition of English within the content area.

References

Abedi, J. (2002). Assessing and accommodations of English language learners: Issues, concerns and recommendations. *Journal of School Improvement, 3,* 83–89.

Abedi, J., Hofstetter, C., & Lord, C. (2004). Assessment accommodations for English language learners: Implications for policy-based research. *Review of Educational Research, 74,* 1–28.

Adesope, O. O., Lavin, T., Thompson, T., & Ungerleider, C. (2010). A systematic review and meta-analysis of the cognitive correlates of bilingualism. *Review of Educational Research, 80,* 207–245.

Alfaro, C., & Bartolomé, L. (2017). Preparing ideologically clear bilingual teachers: Honoring working-class non-standard language use in the bilingual education classroom. *Issues in Teacher Education, 26*(2), 11–34.

August, D., Carlo, M., Dressler, C., & Snow, C. (2005). The critical role of vocabulary development for English language learners. *Learning Disabilities Research & Practice, 20,* 50–57.

August, D., & Shanahan, T. (2006). *Developing literacy in second-language learners: Report of the national literacy panel on language minority children and youth.* Mahwah, NJ: Lawrence Erlbaum Associates.

Bale, J. (2015). English-only to the core: What the Common Core means for emergent bilingual youth. *Rethinking Schools, 30.* Retrieved from www.rethinkingschools.org/special/RS30-1_bale1.shtml

Ballantyne, K. G., Sanderman, A. R., & Levy, J. (2008). Educating English language learners: Building teacher capacity. Roundtable Report. *National*

Clearinghouse for English Language Acquisition & Language Instruction Educational Programs.

Berman, P., McLaughlin, M., Bass, G. V., Pauly, E., & Zellman, G. (1977). Federal programs supporting educational change, Vol. VII: *Factors affecting implementation and continuation, The RAND Corporation.* R-1589/7-HEW, April.

Bronfenbrenner, U. (1979). *The ecology of human development.* Cambridge, MA: Harvard University Press.

Bronfenbrenner, U. (1989). Ecological systems theory. *Annals of Child Development, 6,* 187–249.

Butler, F. A., & Stevens, R. (2001). Standardized assessment of the content knowledge of English language learners K-12: Current trends and old dilemmas. *Language Testing, 18,* 409–427.

Butvilofsky, S. A., & Sparrow, W. L. (2012). Training teachers to evaluate emerging bilingual students' biliterate writing. *Language and Education, 26*(5), 383–403.

Caprara, G. V., Barbaranelli, C., Borgogni, L., & Steca, P. (2003). Efficacy beliefs as determinants of teachers' job satisfaction. *Journal of Educational Psychology, 95,* 821–832.

Caprara, G. V., Barbaranelli, C., Steca, P., & Malone, P. S. (2006). Teachers' self-efficacy beliefs as determinants of job satisfaction and students' academic achievement: A study at the school level. *Journal of School Psychology, 44,* 473–490.

Collaborative for Academic, Social, and Emotional Learning (CASEL). (2013). Effective social and emotional learning programs. Preschool and Elementary School Edition.

Darling-Hammond, L. (2000). How teacher education matters. *Journal of Teacher Education, 51,* 166–173.

Darling-Hammond, L., & Bransford, J. (Eds.). (2005). *Preparing teachers for a changing world: What teachers should learn and be able to do.* San Francisco: Jossey-Bass.

Echevarria, J., & Graves, A. (2010). *Sheltered content instruction: Teaching students with diverse abilities* (4th ed.). Boston: Allyn & Bacon.

Faltis, C., & Valdés, G. (2016). Preparing teachers to teach in and advocate for linguistically diverse classrooms: A vade mecum for teacher educators. In D. H. Gitomer & C. A. Bell (Eds.), *Handbook of research on teaching* (5th ed., pp. 549–592). Washington, DC: American Educational Research Association.

Flores, B. B. (2001). Bilingual education teachers' beliefs and their relation to self-reported practices. *Bilingual Research Journal, 25,* 275–299.

Gándara, P., Maxwell-Jolly, J., & Driscoll, A. (2005). Listening to teachers of English language learners: A survey of California teachers' challenges, experiences, and professional development needs. Santa Cruz, CA: The Regents of the University of California. Retrieved from http://files.eric.ed.gov/fulltext/ED491701.pdf

Gándara, P., & Santibañez, L. (2016). The teachers our English language learners need. *Educational Leadership, 73,* 32–37.

García, O. (2009). Emergent bilinguals and TESOL: What's in a name? *Tesol Quarterly, 43*(2), 322–326.

Gay, G. (2005). Politics of multicultural teacher education. *Journal of Teacher Education, 56,* 221–228.

Genesee, F., Geva, E., Dressler, C., & Kamil, M. (2008). Cross-linguistic relationships in second language learners. In D. August & T. Shanahan (Eds.), *Developing reading and writing in second language learners* (pp. 61–94). Mahwah, NJ: Lawrence Erlbaum.

Goldenberg, C. (2013). Unlocking the research on English learners: What we know—and don't yet know about effective instruction. *American Educator, 37,* 4–11.

Grant, S., Hamilton, L. S., Wrabel, S. L., Gomez, C. J., Whitaker, A. A., Leschitz, J. T., Unlu, F., Chavez-Herrerias, E. R., Baker, G., Barrett, M., Harris, M., & Ramos, A. (2017). Social and emotional learning interventions under the Every Student Succeeds Act: Evidence review. RAND Corporation. Retrieved from https://www.wallacefoundation.org/knowledge-center/Documents/Social-and-Emotional-Learning-Interventions-Under-ESSA.pdf

Guskey, T. R., & Passaro, P. D. (1994). Teacher efficacy: A study of construct dimensions. *American Educational Research Journal, 31,* 627–643.

Hakuta, K. (1990). Language and cognition in bilingual children. In A. Padilla, C. Valdez, & H. Fairchild (Eds.), *Bilingual education: Issues and strategies* (pp. 47–59). Newbury Park, CA: Sage Publications.

Halle, T. G., Whittaker, J. V., Zepeda, M., Rothenberg, L., Anderson, R., Daneri, P., Wessel, J., & Buysee, V. (2014). The social-emotional development of dual language learners: Looking back at existing research and moving forward with purpose. *Early Childhood Research Quarterly, 29,* 734–749.

Harper, C. A., & de Jong, E. J. (2009). English language teacher expertise: The elephant in the room. *Language and Education, 23,* 137–151.

Hollins, E., & Torres-Guzman, M. E. (2005). Research on preparing teachers for diverse populations. In M. Cochran-Smith & K. Zeichner (Eds.), *Studying Teacher Education: The Report of the AERA Panel on Research and Teacher Education.* Mahwah, N.J.: Lawrence Erlbaum Associates.

Hopkins, M. (2013). Building on our teaching assets: The unique pedagogical contributions of bilingual educators. *Bilingual Research Journal, 36*(3), 350–370.

Judge, T. A., Thoresen, C. J., Bono, J. E., & Patton, G. K. (2001). The job satisfaction–job performance relationship: A qualitative and quantitative review. *Psychological Bulletin, 127,* 376–407.

Karabenick, S. A., & Noda, P. A. C. (2004). Professional development implications of teachers' beliefs and attitudes toward English language learners. *Bilingual Research Journal, 28,* 55–75.

Klassen, R. M., & Chiu, M. M. (2011). The occupational commitment and intention to quit of practicing and pre-service teachers: Influence of self-efficacy, job stress, and teaching context. *Contemporary Educational Psychology, 36,* 114–129.

Kumar, R., & Hamer, L. (2013). Preservice teachers' attitudes and beliefs toward student diversity and proposed instructional practices: A sequential design study. *Journal of Teacher Education, 64,* 162–177.

Lillie, K. E., Markos, A., Arias, M. B., & Wiley, T. G. (2012). Separate and not equal: The implementation of structured English immersion in Arizona's classrooms. *Teachers College Record, 114,* 1–33.

Loeb, S., & Miller, L. C. (2006). A review of state teacher policies: What are they, what are their effects, and what are their implications for school finance? IREPP Working Paper, Stanford University.

López, F. (2010). Identity and motivation among English language learners in disparate educational contexts. *Education Policy Analysis Archives, 18*(16). Retrieved from http://epaa.asu.edu/ojs/article/view/717

López, F. (2017). Altering the trajectory of the self-fulfilling prophecy: Asset-based pedagogy and classroom dynamics. *Journal of Teacher Education, 68,* 193–212.

López, F., & Santibañez, L. (2018). Teacher preparation to teach English learners and policy implications. *Education Policy Analysis Archives, 26.*

López, F., Scanlan, M., & Gundrum, B. (2013). Preparing teachers of English language learners: Empirical evidence and policy implications. *Education Policy Analysis Archives, 21.* Retrieved from http://epaa.asu.edu/ojs/article/view/1132

Lucas, T., Villegas, A. M., & Freedson-Gonzalez, M. (2008). Linguistically responsive teacher education preparing classroom teachers to teach English language learners. *Journal of Teacher Education, 59,* 361–373.

Master, B., Loeb, S., Whitney, C., & Wyckoff, J. (2012). *Different skills? Identifying differentially effective teachers of English language learners.* Palo Alto, CA: Center for Education Policy Analysis.

McKown, C., & Weinstein, R. S. (2002). Modeling the role of child ethnicity and gender in children's differential responses to teacher expectations. *Journal of Social Psychology, 32,* 159–184.

Menken, K., & Antunez, B. (2001). *An overview of the preparation and certification of teachers working with limited English proficient (LEP) students.* Washington, DC: National Clearinghouse for Bilingual Education. Retrieved from http://files.eric.ed.gov/fulltext/ED455231.pdf

Menken, K., Kleyn, T., & Chae, N. (2012). Spotlight on "long-term English language learners": Characteristics and prior schooling experiences of an invisible population. *International Multilingual Research Journal, 6,* 121–142.

Milner, H. R. (2010). What does teacher education have to do with teaching? Implications for diversity studies. *Journal of Teacher Education, 61,* 118–131.

Morrison, K. A., Robbins, H. H., & Rose, D. G. (2008). Operationalizing culturally relevant pedagogy: A synthesis of classroom-based research. *Equity & Excellence in Education, 41*, 433–452.

Niehaus, K., & Adelson, J. L. (2014). Academic and social-emotional outcomes for English language learners. *American Educational Research Journal, 51*, 810–844.

Peal, E., & Lambert, W. E. (1962). The relation of bilingualism to intelligence. *Psychological Monographs, 76*, 1–23.

Potowski, K., & Shin, N. L. (2018). Gramática española: variación social. Routledge.

Pray, L., & Marx, S. (2010). ESL teacher education abroad and at home: A cautionary tale. *The Teacher Educator, 45*, 216–229.

Raudenbush, S. W., Rowan, B., & Cheong, Y. F. (1992). Contextual effects on the self-perceived efficacy of high school teachers. *Sociology of Education, 65*, 150–167.

Rotter, J. B. (1966). Generalized expectancies for internal versus external control of reinforcement. *Psychological Monographs: General and Applied, 80*, 1–28.

Sandstrom, H., & Huerta, S. (2013). *The negative effects of instability on child development: A research synthesis.* Washington, DC: Urban Institute.

Santibañez, L., & Gándara, P. (2018). Teachers of English language learners in secondary schools: Gaps in preparation and support. The Civil Rights Project/Proyecto Derechos Civiles, UCLA.

Santibañez, L., & Snyder, C. (2018). Teaching English learners in California: How teacher credential requirements in California address their needs. Technical Report (with peer review) for Getting Down to Facts II. September 2018. Stanford University and PACE. Retrieved from http://gettingdowntofacts.com/sites/default/files/2018-09/GDTFII_Report_Santibanez.pdf

Santos, M., Darling-Hammond, L., & Cheuk, T. (2012). Teacher development to support English language learners in the context of Common Core State Standards. Palo Alto, CA: Stanford University Understanding Language Initiative. Retrieved from http://ell.stanford.edu/sites/default/files/pdf/academic-papers/10-Santos%20LDH%20Teacher%20Development%20FINAL.pdf

Skaalvik, E. M., & Skaalvik, S. (2007). Dimensions of teacher self-efficacy and relations with strain factors, perceived collective teacher efficacy, and teacher burnout. *Journal of Educational Psychology, 99*, 611–625.

Tenenbaum, H. R., & Ruck, M. D. (2007). Are teachers' expectations different for racial minority than for European American students? A meta-analysis. *Journal of Educational Psychology, 99*, 253–273.

Tschannen-Moran, M., & Hoy, A. W. (2001). Teacher efficacy: Capturing an elusive construct. *Teaching and Teacher Education, 17*, 783–805.

Tschannen-Moran, M., Woolfok Hoy, A. W., & Hoy, W. K. (1998). Teacher efficacy: Its meaning and measure. *Review of Educational Research, 68*, 202–248.

Valdés, G. (2005). Bilingualism, heritage language learners, and SLA research: Opportunities lost or seized?. *The Modern Language Journal, 89,* 410–426.

Valenzuela, A. (Ed.). (2016). *Growing critically conscious teachers: A social justice curriculum for educators of Latino/a youth.* New York: Teachers College Press.

Walker, A., Shafer, J., Iiams, M. (2004). "Not in my classroom": Teacher attitudes towards English language learners in the mainstream classroom. *NABE Journal of Research and Practice, 1,* 130–160.

Wright, M., & Masten, A. S. (2005). Resilience processes in development. *Handbook of Resilience in Children,* 17–37.

Zúñiga, V., & Hamann, E. T. (2009). Sojourners in Mexico with US school experience: A new taxonomy for transnational students. *Comparative Education Review, 53,* 329–353.

Chapter 9

From *Plyler* to Sanctuary

U.S. Policy on Public School Access and Implications for Educators of Transnational Students

Julie Sugarman

At a time of great uncertainty in U.S. immigration policy, the long-standing principle of equal access to education provides a bedrock of protection for school-age children from an immigrant background seeking to enroll in and obtain an education from the country's public elementary and secondary schools. In fact, the K-12 education system stands out among public institutions for the strength of its legal framework prohibiting schools from taking immigration status into account in enrollment or denying immigrant-background or English learner (EL) children meaningful access to schooling. This decades-old framework has taken on heightened importance as the anti-immigration sentiment that was a cornerstone of the Trump presidential campaign—which propelled a slew of rapid policy changes in the first two years of his administration—has deeply disrupted the lives of many transnational families and their communities.

In 1982, the U.S. Supreme Court ruled in *Plyler v. Doe* that all children—including unauthorized immigrants—have the right to a free, public education in keeping with the definition of primary and secondary schooling in each state. In the years since, this decision has been interpreted to mean not only that districts must not charge tuition or bar enrollment on the basis of immigration status, but that schools must not engage in "practices that may chill or discourage the participation, or lead to the exclusion, of students based on their or their parents' or guardians' actual or perceived citizenship or immigration status" (U.S. Department of Justice and U.S. Department of Education, 2014a, p. 1). While policies developed to comply with *Plyler* tend to concern procedures related to school registration, many educators have applied it more generally and avoid asking about immigration status at any time. The decision also reverberates in the efforts undertaken in some districts after the 2016 election to establish schools as "sanctuaries" or "safe havens" in response to stepped-up immigration enforcement activity.

Despite the enduring influence of the *Plyler* ruling, the real work of providing access to education is done by educators and administrators who implement the procedures that protect immigrant families' privacy and make them feel safe and welcome in schools. This on-the-ground work takes place in communities that vary widely in terms of their attitudes toward immigration and immigrant families. Further, states vary in the extent to which they disseminate information about and monitor compliance with *Plyler*, resulting in uneven awareness and mindfulness of these issues at the local level. And when it comes to day-to-day decision making, some school leaders and other staff who know the rules still may not abide by them or make sure they are implemented. For these reasons, it sometimes falls to the teachers who work directly with immigrant-background and EL children to ensure that schools are meeting their obligations and to remind their colleagues that they have a professional stake in ensuring students enroll and come to class and parents can participate in their children's education.

This chapter reviews how the Supreme Court decision in *Plyler v. Doe* informs school enrollment policies and practices, as well as how it relates to the declaration of sanctuary or safe haven districts in dozens of communities following the election of President Trump. Policies related to *Plyler* and to sanctuary declarations help schools systematize nondiscrimination by setting expectations for how immigrant children and their families are to be welcomed into and supported in the school community. These issues are also increasingly relevant to Mexican educators, as parents deported or returning from the United States have encountered similar challenges registering their children for Mexican schools to ones experienced by U.S. immigrants. With immigration policy affecting the lives of large shares of U.S. schoolchildren in diverse communities across the country—and more than half a million U.S.-born children in Mexico—it is critical for educators working with such children on both sides of the border to understand how laws and regulations can pave a smooth path to educational access for transnational children in otherwise tumultuous times.

The Sociodemographic Context

The share of U.S. schoolchildren from linguistically and culturally diverse families has been growing for many years. However, many schools and districts have yet to ensure they provide equal access and equitable services to all students. Many educators—especially those in so-called "new destination" states—may not be aware of the number of children and families in their community whose immigration status is relevant to their relationship with schools.

Policies that concern the treatment of immigrants and refugees affect a substantial share of U.S. children. Just over one quarter of school-age children (age three to 17)—about 15.6 million—live with one or more foreign-born parents (see Table 9.1). Nevertheless, only 13% of those children—3% of school-age children overall—are themselves foreign-born (see Table 9.2). Educators may be more likely to be aware of the number or share of ELs in their school, because those figures are reported for performance accountability purposes, but there actually are three times more children of immigrants than there are ELs, who number 4.9 million nationally (National Center for Education Statistics, 2017). As of 2016, about 26% of the foreign-born population in the United States was from Mexico, making them the largest foreign nationality by a wide margin

Table 9.1. Nativity of Parents of U.S. Children Age 3 to 17—2016

	Number	Share of Population %
Children between 3 and 17 with	59,241,000	100.0
Only native-born parents	43,678,000	73.7
One or more foreign-born parents	15,563,000	26.3

Note: Migration Policy Institute tabulation of the U.S. Census Bureau's 2016 American Community Survey.

Table 9.2. Nativity of U.S. Children of Immigrants Age 3 to 17—2016

	All Children		Children with One or More Mexican-Born Parents	
	Number	Share of Population (%)	Number	Share of Population (%)
Children between 3 and 17 with one or more foreign-born parents	15,563,000	100.0	6,282,000	100.0
Child is native born	13,529,000	86.9	5,795,000	92.2
Child is foreign born	2,035,000	13.1	487,000	7.7

Note: Migration Policy Institute tabulation of the U.S. Census Bureau's 2016 American Community Survey.

(Zong, Batalova, & Hallock, 2018). What is more, Table 9.2 shows that children with at least one Mexican parent make up 40% of children from an immigrant background. It also shows that a larger share of children of Mexican-born parents are U.S.-born (92%) than children of immigrants of all nationalities (87%).

Since the 1990s, there has been a marked decrease in the degree to which immigrant families are clustered in traditional receiving states and metropolitan areas. As of 2016, 57% of children of immigrants lived in the top five states (California, Florida, Illinois, New York, and Texas), compared to 66% in 2000 and 69% in 1990. However, the fastest-growing shares of children of immigrants are primarily in the southern and midwestern states, which have arguably had less time to develop robust systems related to immigrant and EL students (see Figure 9.1). Between 2007 and 2016, North Dakota tripled and Wyoming doubled the number of school-age children with one or more foreign-born parents; rates for Kentucky, Mississippi, and South Dakota were all more than 80%.[1] At the community level, although the number of immigrants living in cities has increased over time, their share decreased from 41% in 1980 to 33% in 2010, and the share of immigrants living in suburbs grew from 43% to 51% over that time period (National Academies of Sciences, Engineering, and Medicine, 2015).

The group of immigrants who are most affected by Trump-era changes to immigration policy are those who are unauthorized immigrants, a

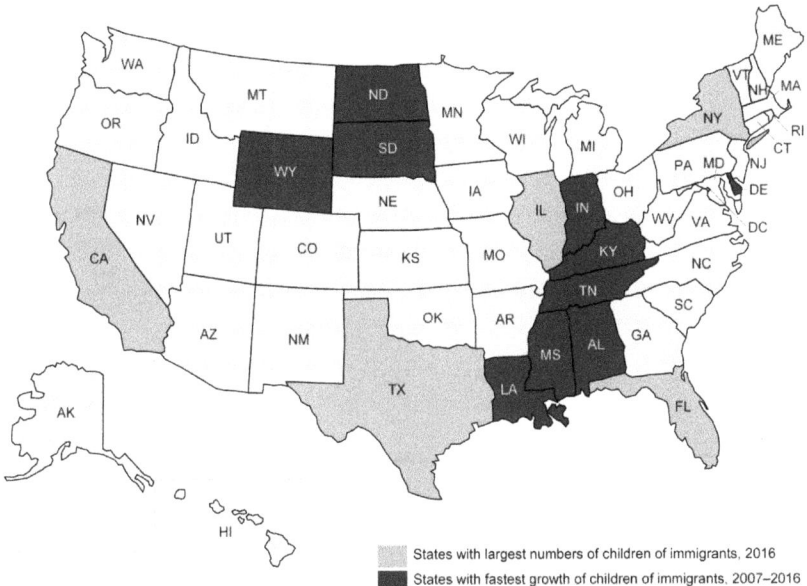

Figure 9.1. States with the Largest Numbers and Fastest-Growing Populations of Children of Immigrants.

group that includes those who enter the country illegally as well as those who entered lawfully but overstayed their visas. According to estimates by the Migration Policy Institute, about 4.3 million children age 3 to 17 lived with at least one unauthorized parent in 2016, but only 18% of these children were unauthorized themselves (see Table 9.3). This means that most children of the unauthorized were in mixed-status families, where some family members are unauthorized while others are legal immigrants or U.S. citizens. Including both children and adults, Mexican immigrants make up the largest share of the unauthorized population (56%). The next-largest shares of the unauthorized come from Guatemala (7%), El Salvador (4%), and Honduras (3%) (Zong et al., 2018). However, Table 9.3 shows that children of Mexican heritage make up 68% of all children of unauthorized immigrants. Children of unauthorized Mexican parents are slightly less likely to be unauthorized immigrants themselves (16%) than children from other countries (24%).

Given the implications for students' academic success, it is important for educators to understand the local context in which immigrant and

Table 9.3. Citizenship and Legal Status of Children Age 3 to 17 Living with One or More Unauthorized Immigrant Parents—2016

	All Children		Children with One or More Mexican-Born Parents	
	Number	Share of Population (%)	Number	Share of Population (%)
Children with at least one unauthorized parent	4,266,000	100.0	2,920,000	100.0
Child is U.S. citizen	3,328,000	78.0	2,389,000	81.8
Child is legal immigrant	162,000	3.8	78,000	2.7
Child is unauthorized immigrant	776,000	18.2	453,000	15.5

Notes: Migration Policy Institute tabulation of the U.S. Census Bureau's pooled 2012–16 American Community Survey, and the 2008 Survey of Income and Program Participation, drawing on a methodology developed in consultation with James Bachmeier of Temple University and Jennifer Van Hook of The Pennsylvania State University, Population Research Institute.

culturally diverse communities live. For example, as these populations have dispersed to states in the Midwest and South and into suburban and rural settings, they have had considerable cultural, economic, and demographic impacts on their communities that have brought benefits—especially in areas previously marked by population declines—but also challenges such as strains on the provision of social and educational services (National Academies of Sciences, Engineering, and Medicine, 2015). The process of immigrant integration, then, is not just marked by national politics—although this phenomenon is well illustrated in the other chapters in this volume—but by the characteristics and the response of the communities into which they settle.

The experience of the children of immigrants and the response of the schools in which they spend a large share of their waking hours is of considerable importance to the individual children and families in question but also—not least because 87% of such children are U.S. citizens—to their communities. As addressed in Chapter 2, years of research have demonstrated the ways in which the children of unauthorized immigrants (whether citizens or not) are a particularly vulnerable population. In addition to the developmental risk factors associated with poverty and low parental education—experienced disproportionately by unauthorized immigrant families—children also may suffer from high levels of stress, the effects of frequent moves and switching schools, and lack of access to government benefits. U.S. citizen children in mixed-status households may suffer from the same fear and stress as children who are unauthorized themselves (Yoshikawa, Suárez-Orozco, & Gonzales, 2016). Even children of lawful immigrants may face such challenges because of changes to the "public charge" rule proposed by the Trump administration in 2018. Under such rules, foreign nationals applying for permission for short-term admission and for green cards would be penalized for use of certain public benefits such as the Supplemental Nutrition Assistance Program (food stamps), and advocates reported that even the rumor of this proposed change caused immigrant families to cancel or not to apply for benefits to which they were otherwise entitled (Blitzer, 2018). In this context, access to school and the associated resources schools provide to families may be a critical factor in lessening the effects of the known risk factors to academic success for children from an immigrant background.

The *Plyler* Decision

The U.S. Supreme Court decision that protects all students' rights to attend primary and secondary school has its roots in the history of Mexican immigration to the United States. Throughout much of the 20th century, there were no caps on the number of people who could migrate from other Western Hemisphere countries to the United States. Further, with a labor shortage during World War II, the United States and Mexico instituted a guest worker program—known widely as the Bracero Program—which gave Mexican agricultural workers very favorable terms for their labor. By the mid-1960s, lawmakers ended that program and signed the *Immigration and Nationality Act of 1965* (INA), which prioritized family reunification over other selection criteria and established caps for the number of immigrants that could be accepted from each country.

By the 1970s, legal permanent residents seeking to sponsor the immigration of family still in Mexico began to feel INA's constraints on legal immigration options. Additionally, demographic, economic, and political conditions in Mexico and Central America were pushing workers to seek employment in the United States, which was eager for low-wage workers. Between 1970 and 1980, both the number of Mexican immigrants and their share of the total U.S. immigrant population more than doubled. By the early 1970s, federal policy makers and labor and civil rights groups were starting to express significant concerns about the impact of unauthorized immigration (Migration Policy Institute, n.d.; Rosenblum & Brick, 2011).

As these dynamics were unfolding, in 1975, Texas state lawmakers—at the request of border-area school superintendents—included a provision in a routine education bill stating that school districts were only obligated to provide free, public education to U.S. citizens and authorized immigrants. Once adopted, some districts used the law to deny enrollment to students whose families could not prove legal immigration status, while others—such as Houston Independent School District (ISD) and Tyler ISD—enrolled such students but charged their families $1,000 annual tuition. Seeing an opportunity to draw attention to ways that Mexicans had been subjugated in American schools and other institutions, the Mexican American Legal Defense and Educational Fund (MALDEF) spearheaded the effort to raise legal challenges to this law. Following the loss of a similar case brought by a local lawyer against the Houston ISD, MALDEF attorneys successfully sued Tyler ISD—led by Superintendent James Plyler, for whom the case is named—on behalf of a family with both U.S. citizen and undocumented children (Olivas, 2005).

As additional cases and appeals mounted against Houston, Tyler, and the state of Texas, these cases were eventually consolidated in order to be heard by the U.S. Supreme Court under the *Plyler* heading. In 1982, the Court ruled against Texas and the two districts, stating that denying free education to one class of people violated the equal protection clause of the Fourteenth Amendment to the U.S. Constitution (Olivas, 2005). In so doing, the court indicated that the state was obliged to treat all persons within its jurisdiction equally under the law, regardless of how they came to be there (Ofer, 2012).

In its arguments, the state of Texas had asserted that preserving state education dollars for lawful residents would have a positive effect on education, charging tuition would discourage illegal immigration, and the children of unauthorized immigrants were unlikely to stay in the United States long enough to justify the investment made in their education. In the opinion for the majority, Justice Brennan rejected those arguments, saying that the state had failed to justify how denying education to a group of children furthered a substantial state interest. Instead, the Court held that while education was not a fundamental right under the U.S. Constitution—as determined in the 1973 *San Antonio Independent School District v. Rodriguez* decision—schooling played a critical role in a democratic society and is different from other government benefits. Justice Brennan wrote, "it is difficult to understand precisely what the State hopes to achieve by promoting the creation and perpetuation of a subclass of illiterates within our boundaries, surely adding to the problems and costs of unemployment, welfare, and crime" (as quoted in Olivas, 2005, p. 209). Although a lower court hearing the *Plyler* case had ruled the Texas law was unconstitutional because only the federal government and not the states had the right to regulate immigration, the Supreme Court did not take up this aspect of the case in its ruling (Olivas, 2005, 2010).

Challenges to *Plyler*

In the following decades, the federal government and several states made attempts to single out unauthorized immigrants or exclude them entirely from public schools despite the ruling in *Plyler*. The first major challenge to the ruling was Proposition 187 passed by California voters in 1994. This statute denied any state-funded public services—including education—to unauthorized immigrants. It also required schools to report unauthorized parents and required local authorities to cooperate with federal agencies in identifying and detaining unauthorized immigrant children. Several organizations—including MALDEF and the American Civil Liberties Union (ACLU)—filed suit, and most of Proposition 187, including sections relevant to education, was declared unconstitutional by a federal district court in 1995 (Ofer, 2012).

In response to the overturning of Proposition 187, its Republican supporters—including then-governor of California Pete Wilson—appealed to the federal government to pass federal legislation allowing states to deny education to unauthorized immigrant students. In 1996, representative Elton Gallegly (R-CA) introduced an amendment to the *Illegal Immigration Reform and Immigrant Responsibility Act* allowing states to deny public education to unauthorized immigrants or charge them tuition. Although the amendment passed in the House of Representatives, the amendment was withdrawn before the immigration reform act was enacted because of opposition from key Republicans, President Clinton, and educators (Ofer, 2012; Olivas, 2010).

In the early 2010s, there were efforts in Alabama, Arizona, Maryland, and Texas to track and report the number of unauthorized immigrants enrolling in public schools, ostensibly to determine the cost of educating those students. Although these measures did not go so far as to charge tuition or deny enrollment, critics charged they would have had the effect of discouraging unauthorized families from enrolling and thus violate the Fourteenth Amendment (Ofer, 2012). The measures in Arizona, Maryland, and Texas were never enacted, and the relevant portions of the Alabama law were overturned in the courts (LegiScan, n.d.; Ofer, 2012; Open States, n.d.-a, n.d.-b; Southern Poverty Law Center, 2013).

Violations and Responses

With the failure of the abovementioned state and federal efforts to sidestep *Plyler*, the ruling was solidified as the law of the land. However, it has taken many years for some schools, districts, and states to implement meaningful policies to comply with the ruling. The Education Law Center reported in 2008 that one-third of school districts in Pennsylvania maintained enrollment practices in violation of federal and state law. These included requiring children or parents to provide a social security number or a passport, green card, or visa. The same year, the ACLU of New Jersey likewise found that 20% of state districts inquired about immigration status in enrollment, and two years later, the New York Civil Liberties Union released similar findings, with 20% of New York districts in violation (Ofer, 2012; see Text Box 9.1).

TEXT BOX 9.1
Enrollment Barriers and Responses in New York State

In 2009, the New York Civil Liberties Union (NYCLU) received a complaint about enrollment practices in a New York State school district. After several letters to the New York State Education Department (NYSED) failed to result in corrective action, the NYCLU surveyed enrollment policies and practices across the state and found violations of *Plyler*-related guidelines in at least 20% of school districts. After release of this information to the media and the affected school districts attracted significant publicity, NYSED issued a memo to district superintendents describing the implications of the *Plyler* ruling and detailing alternative documentation that districts may accept as proof of age, residence within district boundaries, and for other data collection purposes (King, 2010; Ofer, 2012).

Following complaints in 2014 that students on Long Island were being turned away from schools due to their immigration status, the NYCLU reexamined enrollment practices at the original offending districts. It found that more than half still employed practices that may discourage immigrant family enrollment (requiring social security numbers or birth certificates), including 16 districts that required proof of immigration status (New York Civil Liberties Union, 2014).

Then in fall 2014, NYSED and the state attorney general responded to complaints by NYCLU and other groups that immigrant students were prevented from enrolling in school or were being denied educational opportunity, particularly in suburban districts that had recently received a large influx of unaccompanied minors. In order to ensure consistent application of enrollment procedures, NYSED released new regulations, training materials, and information for parents—translated into ten languages—that explained district obligations under *Plyler* and alternative documentation that may be accepted for enrollment (New York State Education Department, 2014a, 2014b, 2015). The new policy was described as "admit first, ask questions later" (Tenenbaum & Drummond, 2016).

The attorney general's 2014–15 investigation of the NYCLU complaint initially focused on four counties in the greater New York City area but later expanded to the whole state. The investigation resulted in agreements with 20 school districts to amend their enrollment policies. Hempstead Union Free School District was a particular focus of the attorney general's investigation (and media coverage). In that Long Island district, dozens of students saw their enrollment delayed due to strict policies on required documentation or were put on a "wait list." Some newly enrolled students were told to sign in for attendance but were then sent home, as their school said there was no room to accommodate them. In a 2015 agreement with the attorney general, the district was required to modify enrollment procedures (including required documentation), train staff, and hire an enrollment ombudsperson and independent monitor (Mueller, 2015; New York State Office of the Attorney General, 2015).

In a similar case, the Utica City School District was sued by the NYCLU and Legal Services of Central New York on behalf of six older adolescent refugees who alleged that they were denied admission to the district's comprehensive high school and were sent to what they described as an inferior alternative educational program. The settlement of the lawsuit called for the Utica district to contact school-age refugees who were not enrolled to explain their educational options (Tenenbaum & Drummond, 2016).

In response to complaints from across the country about discriminatory enrollment practices, the U.S. Department of Justice and the U.S. Department of Education jointly issued guidance in 2011 underscoring the basic message of *Plyler* that schools and districts cannot deny children access to free, public K-12 education on the basis of their immigration or citizenship status or that of their parents or guardians. Additionally, the guidance stated that practices that discourage or prohibit the enrollment of students based on actual or perceived immigration status may violate federal law, including the *Civil Rights Act of 1964*. The guidance—released as a "Dear Colleague" letter and accompanying fact sheet and question and answer document—was updated in 2014 (U.S. Department of Justice and U.S. Department of Education, 2014a, 2014b).

The 2014 guidance spells out what information may and may not be requested of families enrolling their children in primary or secondary schools. These cover four main areas:

- **Proof of residency.** Districts may ask for proof that a family lives within its borders but may not inquire into citizenship or immigration status. Types of documents that may be accepted as proof include utility bills or lease agreements. Districts cannot require families to produce state-issued identification such as a driver's license.

- **Proof of age.** Districts may also require proof that children are within age limits to attend school but may not require a birth certificate or reject a foreign birth certificate to do so. Types of documentation that may be accepted include hospital or adoption records, an entry in a family bible, or an affidavit from a parent.

- **Social security number.** Districts must not require children or their parents or guardians to provide a social security number. If they request this information, they must state that it is voluntary to provide it, under what authority they are requesting it, and for what purpose the social security number will be used.

- **Race or ethnicity.** Districts may request race and ethnicity data but may not refuse enrollment if parents or guardians do not provide this information or based on their answer.

The guidance suggests that districts review their enrollment procedures and documents for impermissible questions, provide lists of alternative forms of evidence to enrolling families, and ensure staff comply with federal law. It also points out that schools may create a more welcoming atmosphere if they wait until after a student is enrolled to collect additional demographic information (for example, race and ethnicity data), some of which must be reported annually to the federal government. Schools must also follow guidelines under the *McKinney-Vento Homeless Assistance Act* regarding documentation of residence and guardianship (U.S. Department of Justice and U.S. Department of Education, 2014a, 2014b).

Despite this federal guidance, some districts continued to struggle to meet their obligations. In 2017, attorneys identified 40 school districts in California that asked about students' or parents' citizenship status on enrollment forms and five that required parents to bring a child's birth certificate and/or social security card to registration (Lawyers' Committee for Civil Rights of the San Francisco Bay Area and California Rural Legal Assistance, 2017). In July 2018, the ACLU of New Jersey filed a lawsuit against 11 school districts and a charter school for requiring inappropriate documentation for enrollment (Mooney & O'Dea, 2018).

In addition to districts that ask about immigration status for enrollment, immigrant and refugee advocates and civil liberties organizations have recently drawn considerable attention to the problem of students being denied enrollment or referred inappropriately to alternative educational programs. The problem seems to have intensified between 2014 and 2016 when a large number of unaccompanied youth—primarily from El Salvador, Guatemala, and Honduras—arrived in the United States and were released to families or other sponsors in communities across the country. Many of those young people arrived overage and undercredited—older than the traditional age to begin high school and without evidence of high school credits to transfer—and with significant deficits in their prior schooling. Families reported being turned away because of a lack of required documents to prove the student's age, relationship to their guardian, or residence within the district. In other cases, personnel improperly referred students to alternative or adult education programs that offered only high school equivalency, not a regular diploma (Booi, et al., 2016; Burke & Sainz, 2016). In fact, young people are entitled to enroll in district high schools until the maximum age set by each state, which is 20 or 21 in most cases (Diffey & Steffes, 2017). Referring students to adult education because of their (perceived) language ability or educational background violates students' rights under the *Equal Educational Opportunity Act of 1974* and Title VI of the *Civil Rights Act of 1964* forbidding discrimination based on race, color, or national origin (Booi, et al., 2016).

In trying to understand why families continue to face difficulties in the school enrollment process, it is reasonable to assume that outright discrimination and racism play a part in some cases. However, regarding the older newcomers who were discouraged from enrolling or referred to alternative programs, there are several systemic issues that could also be relevant to understanding why administrators responded as they did. First, making new seats available midyear for an unexpectedly large influx of newcomers may be a financial challenge because school budgets are usually set the previous year. With unanticipated midyear enrollment, districts might not have the financial resources—or the flexibility—to hire new teachers and make additional space available. There is federal funding available for districts that experience an increase in enrollment of recent immigrants to support the additional learning needs that many of these students have, but those funds are also allocated based on previous-year trends. Second, performance accountability provisions tied to standardized test scores and four-year high school graduation rates may make administrators wary of taking on students they judge to be unable to meet the state benchmarks and timelines, because low performance by these students would likely lead to penalties for schools and districts that enroll them. Third, administrators may feel that an alternative school placement is truly a better option for some students, as these programs are often more flexible and may better fit some students' learning goals. For example, administrators may believe it is not in an older immigrant student's best interest to enroll in a traditional high school program if she or he has little chance of accumulating enough credits to graduate before reaching the maximum age of enrollment. They may then refer such students to adult education where they may learn English and earn a high school equivalency credential (Booi et al., 2016; Sugarman, 2017).

Finally, implementing guidelines related to *Plyler* may be particularly challenging for school districts because of the inherent subjectivity in determining what makes an atmosphere "chilled." As discussed more below, it is not enough simply to avoid inappropriate questions on a form, as students and families draw on the totality of their experience to judge whether they feel targeted based on their immigration status.

Protecting Attendance in a Restrictionist Climate

Policies related to *Plyler v. Doe* seek to ensure that students make it through the schoolhouse door. However, following the election of President Trump in 2016, schools and districts faced new challenges to ensuring that children from immigrant backgrounds experienced equitable access to schools. From the very beginning of the campaign, then-candidate Trump focused heavily in his public remarks on unauthorized immigration and the presence of Mexican immigrants in the United States—including a promise to build a wall to keep them out of the country. Once president, his earliest actions included issuing a series of high-profile executive orders related to immigration. Although some of those orders were delayed by the courts, there was an almost immediate change in interior enforcement. Whereas President Obama's administration had prioritized the deportation of recent border crossers and unauthorized immigrants with criminal convictions, the new policy was to detain and deport anyone without legal status. Stepped-up immigration enforcement and heightened expressions of racism and xenophobia created a sense of fear in many communities. For some, this anxiety made immigrant families reluctant to go out in public and to avail themselves of resources from police departments, courts, and government benefits (McHugh, 2018; Pierce, Bolter, & Selee, 2018).

Deportation of unauthorized immigrants was nothing new, and localities around the country had for many years expended considerable energy in protecting health and safety, for example, by spending state and local funds on health and social benefits denied to immigrants by federal programs and ensuring that immigrants knew they could report crimes without being reported to Immigration and Customs Enforcement (ICE). Despite assurance from the Trump administration that the policy of avoiding enforcement activity in schools was still in place (see below), many educators worried that immigrant parents would be afraid to bring their children to school and participate in parent engagement activities because of the risk of running into enforcement agents, and that community attitudes might make them feel unwelcome. Indeed, some media outlets reported a drop in attendance among immigrant-background students— especially immediately following immigration raids in their communities (see, e.g., Blitzer, 2017). Students also reported an increase in bullying and harassment, affecting their ability to participate in school (Costello, 2017).

A number of school districts moved quickly after the election to declare their support to students, family, and staff, and, as one superintendent wrote, to reassure the community that schools "will continue to be safe places where students and families will be welcome without fear of harm" (as quoted in St. George, 2016). Taking more official steps, from late 2016 through 2017, several school boards declared their district schools as "sanctuaries," "safe havens," or "safe zones" (see Text Box 9.2). The specifics of each declaration differed, but most included a policy that schools would not cooperate with immigration enforcement officers unless officers had a judicial warrant, subpoena, or court order; outlined processes for school staff to obtain permission to share information about students with law enforcement; and limited the kinds of information related to immigration status that can be collected (Jones, 2017).

TEXT BOX 9.2
Safe Haven School Districts in California

Five weeks after the election of Donald Trump, California State Superintendent of Public Instruction Tom Torlakson issued a letter urging school districts to pass resolutions declaring themselves "safe havens." In his letter, Superintendent Torlakson outlined schools' obligations to follow existing laws regarding enrollment and family privacy, to maintain a safe environment, and to ensure "the prospect of the deportation of undocumented students and their families will not interfere with helping our students succeed" (Torlakson, 2016, para. 9). He also noted the importance of parent engagement in the learning process, which could be hampered if parents feel unwelcome in schools. As of March 2018, 117 California districts (about 11%) had made such declarations (California Department of Education, 2018).

In October 2017, the legislature passed the California Values Act, which forbid the use of local law enforcement resources in federal immigration enforcement (McHugh, 2018). Later that fall, California passed Assembly Bill (A.B.) 699, which codified several policies outlined in the superintendent's letter. These included a rule not to collect any information about immigration status even after the enrollment process (thus going beyond the *Plyler* guidance released by the federal government) and a requirement that school or district personnel report any inquiry related to immigration enforcement to their school board. Additionally, A.B. 699 instructs schools to avoid referrals to Child Protective Services if a students' parents are detained due to immigration enforcement, and it requires districts to inform immigrant parents and guardians of their legal rights and to educate students on the negative impact of bullying (EdTrust West, n.d.).

The following year, the attorney general of California released guidance and model school policies related to A.B. 699. The guide described the relevant federal

> and state laws and regulations that govern policies such as gathering information from families and maintaining privacy. It also provided sample documents that schools might receive from federal agents, such as Immigrations and Customs Enforcement warrants and judicial subpoenas (Becerra, 2018).

The act of declaring a district as a safe zone or sanctuary has no specific legal meaning, although the principles behind it are well supported by existing law. Many of the sanctuary policies adopted by school boards reinforce existing statutes such as *Plyler* and anti-discrimination laws. Additionally, clauses regarding whether school staff comply with ICE requests are based on constitutional protections in the Fourth Amendment to the U.S. Constitution—which, like most constitutional protections, apply to all people in the country, not just citizens. The Fourth Amendment requires law enforcement to have a judicial warrant to investigate or detain a person who is in a location where he or she has an expectation of privacy. ICE had generally operated with administrative (not judicial) warrants and counted on other agencies to voluntarily cooperate with them. Although no U.S. institution (including schools and churches) can prevent law enforcement from carrying out judicial warrants, such institutions may establish procedures to verify the legitimate claim of any visitor to come on campus (Hanson, Cheer, & Broder, 2017).

These school board declarations were also in line with the stated intentions of the federal government. The Department of Homeland Security indicated in 2016 that its agencies would continue to honor the sensitive locations policy enacted in 2014. This policy said that that federal agents would avoid immigration enforcement actions at schools (including preschools, daycares, universities, educational events, and bus stops when children are present), hospitals and other medical facilities, places of worship, and public gatherings such as ceremonies or demonstrations. However, actions may take place in such locations with approval from an "appropriate supervisory official" or exigent circumstances (U.S. Customs and Border Protection, 2016).

Some sanctuary district policies also reaffirm the rights that families have under the *Family Educational Rights and Privacy Act of 1974* (FERPA), which prevents schools from releasing student information to a third party (including immigration enforcement) without the consent of a parent (for minors) or the student him- or herself if over age 18. One concern advocates have noted is that FERPA does not protect "directory information." Districts can choose what categories of student information to classify as directory information, but the list suggested in federal FERPA guidance—and adopted by many districts—includes name, address, and date and place of birth, all of which could be useful to ICE for enforcement purposes. Whereas all other information requires affirmative family permission to release, directory information works on an opt-out basis. Schools must provide public notice for families to opt out of sharing such information, but after a "reasonable time" to allow families to do that, it is within schools' discretion to provide directory information to other agencies (Hanson et al., 2017).

Despite the sensitive locations policy and the assurance from sanctuary districts that schools will not voluntarily cooperate with immigration enforcement officials, there are limits to how safe unauthorized immigrants are in and near those locations. In one well-publicized example, ICE arrested a father blocks from the school where he had just dropped off one daughter and was on his way to dropping off another daughter at a different school (Sanchez, 2017). Further, although schools have the obligation not to voluntarily comply with policies that would result in disruption to the school environment, they do not have the authority to interfere with immigration enforcement actions that are otherwise lawful.

By declaring themselves as safe zones or sanctuaries, districts send a message to immigrant parents and students that they are welcome and will be protected within the boundaries of the legal system. They also send a message to educators and staff about what is expected of them to meet the legal and ethical mandates of the U.S. educational system. As a statement of values, many sanctuary declarations also reinforce the values of multiculturalism that those districts have established as a key characteristic of their community.

Discussion

With the *Plyler* decision in 1982, significant pushback against legal challenges and district noncompliance throughout the 1990s and 2000s, and the release of 2011 federal guidance on enrollment practices, it would be easy to assume that the matter of immigrant students' access to public K-12 schooling had been settled. Instead, responses to the surge of unaccompanied minors between 2014 and 2016 exposed—at best—systemic failures in training and inflexibility in accommodating older immigrant newcomers. Additionally, although many highly impacted school districts declared themselves as sanctuaries following the 2016 election, many other districts elected not to make a statement even in support of existing law and policy at a time when many immigrant families were uncertain of their rights. These events expose how the implementation of seemingly straightforward education policy becomes symbolically charged when it intersects with immigration policy, which has become one of the country's most politically divisive issues.

Plyler Themes Across Immigration and Education

At the surface level, the *Plyler* decision regulates a very narrow slice of schooling: registration and enrollment. However, *Plyler* has come to stand for more than the finding in a specific case. Indeed, it "has become an important case for key themes, such as fairness for children, how we guard our borders, how we constitute ourselves, and who gets to make these crucial decisions" (Olivas, 2005, p. 197). One of the ruling's strongest messages—called out explicitly by Justice Brennan in his opinion—asserts that children should not be punished for decisions made by their parents. This theme recurs in other policies related to immigration. For example, it is one of the justifications for the Deferred Action for Childhood Arrivals (DACA) program, enacted by President Obama in 2012, which grants work permits and relief from deportation to eligible unauthorized immigrants brought to the United States as children. Likewise, while non-emergency government benefits (such as Medicaid and Supplemental Security Income) are unavailable to unauthorized immigrants and to many authorized immigrants for their first five years in the country, there are numerous exceptions for benefits for children, including free and reduced-price school meal programs and the Special Supplemental Nutrition Program for Women, Infants and Children (WIC).

Another prominent theme of Justice Brennan's opinion is the idea that education is different from other social services or civic institutions because of its importance to individuals, communities, and a democratic society more broadly. As post-secondary education has come to be seen as more of a necessity than a luxury, increasing access of traditionally underserved populations has become a widespread concern of advocates and higher education administrators. The question then arises as to whether *Plyler* should apply beyond K-12 education—this would support policy-making efforts to open state university enrollment to unauthorized immigrant youth and allow them to pay in-state tuition (Olivas, 2010).

Some themes in the *Plyler* ruling are also relevant to educational debates beyond immigrant education; for example, shared responsibility for educating other people's children. In *Plyler*, the question was whether unauthorized families counted as members of the community and as such had the right to benefit from a public good. That issue resonates today in philosophical differences over whether tax dollars spent on education belong to the community and its public institutions or whether they belong to the child (in which case families may use vouchers or tax credits to move those dollars out of the public school system and to private schools).

For fifty years, the federal government has played a central role in establishing the rights of immigrant-background students to access education—through the provisions discussed in this chapter—and to a meaningful educational experience—through various provisions including the 1974 Supreme Court decision *Lau v. Nichols* requiring appropriate accommodations for EL students. Nevertheless, the events of the Trump era demonstrated the important role states and localities play in the daily experience of immigrants navigating civic life. This has been particularly evident with declarations of sanctuary districts as well as the broader sanctuary cities movement, which directs local agencies to limit cooperation with ICE and provide unauthorized immigrants access to services such as driver's licenses and legal aid.

State and local policies that protect immigrant-background students' meaningful access to education may take on extra weight if past interpretations of the equal protection clause are reconsidered, a prospect whose likelihood may have increased with former President Trump's significant success in adding new judges to the federal courts during his years in office. It is also possible that the U.S. Department of Education could attempt to reinterpret Plyler if future presidents favored policies that limit immigration.

Implications for Educators

Given the central role local actors play in policy implementation, many educators find themselves serving as advocates in addition to instructors.

The professional standards for EL teachers published by TESOL International (the association of teachers of English to speakers of other languages) include expectations for educators to be familiar with the laws related to ELs and to be able to serve as advocates and sources of information for students and their families (TESOL International Association, 2010). Educators in many different fields engage in this type of work, but it is a unique imperative for EL teachers, because they work with students and families who frequently lack the language skills and systems knowledge to advocate for themselves, and because teachers and administrators outside the field are generally not trained to understand the needs of EL students and families (Staehr Fenner, 2014). In fact, many administrators come to count on EL specialists to serve as a kind of watchdog for the needs of linguistically and culturally diverse students and families.

As a result, as described in Chapter 8 of this book, EL professionals have an important part to play to ensure that schools follow federal laws that protect the rights of students from an immigrant background. Educators can learn about these rights and how they should be implemented using the many resources available online—especially the English Learner Tool Kit and the Newcomer Tool Kit, published by the U.S. Department of Education in 2015 and 2016, respectively.[2] Educators can then take steps to review their district's policies and practices and raise concerns with administrators, if, for example, enrollment forms include impermissible questions or staff have not been trained on what documentation may be accepted for school registration. Some educators may feel comfortable taking a more active role as a community liaison or to work directly with community groups to help immigrant communities understand their rights and navigate school systems.

Educators and other community members can also ask local school district leaders to consider enacting sanctuary or safe haven resolutions. Indeed, the sanctuary schools movement may provide a new opportunity for schools to develop and implement more holistic policies to support their immigrant-background students. These could include policies related to school registration, data collection, student privacy, and interacting with federal immigration agencies, as discussed in this chapter, but also more generally in terms of academic and social support. EL instructors are well placed to describe to administrators—especially those who are reluctant to deal with what they see as politically charged issues—how these practices impact students' academic, linguistic, and social development. Educators could also gather evidence of the efficacy of these practices. With a significant number of geographically and demographically diverse districts taking on sanctuary policies, there is ample opportunity for researchers to investigate the role of these declarations in stimulating greater system supports for immigrant-background students and families and whether there are observable effects of sanctuary policies at the student, classroom, or community level.

Researchers and policy makers might also be interested in comparing the experiences of schools in the United States with those in Mexico working to implement new policies intended to facilitate the enrollment of U.S. citizen children returning with their families to Mexico. Those families have experienced obstacles similar to those enumerated in this chapter, including parents arriving without key U.S. school records, families given incorrect information about the enrollment process, and schools that continue to require an apostille (endorsement) on foreign birth certificates and officially translated student records in spite of new regulations eliminating those requirements (Jacobo & Jensen, 2018). Clearly, the dissemination of information about such policies has proven challenging on both sides of the border. The suggestions above for U.S. educators who advocate for immigrant children in the United States are applicable to Mexican teachers working with newcomer American Mexican children, as discussed in Chapter 5.

Despite the Trump administration's restrictionist approach, there is no doubt that immigration is a permanent feature of modern life. By becoming aware of and encouraging the implementation of policies related to *Plyler v. Doe* and sanctuary districts, educators can ensure that immigrant families continue to experience welcoming and safe school environments, as required by law, that foster immigrant children's academic success and the longer-term civic and economic vitality of their communities.

Notes

1. Data from Migration Policy Institute tabulation of the U.S. Census Bureau's 2007 and 2016 American Community Surveys.

2. See https://www2.ed.gov/about/offices/list/oela/resources.html for links to these and other resources from the Office of English Language Acquisition, U.S. Department of Education.

References

Becerra, X. (2018). Promoting a safe and secure learning environment for all: Guidance and model policies to assist California's K-12 schools in responding to immigration issues. Retrieved from the State of California Department of Justice website: https://www.oag.ca.gov/sites/all/files/agweb/pdfs/bcj/school-guidance-model-k12.pdf

Blitzer, J. (2017, March 23). After an immigration raid, a city's students vanish. *The New Yorker.*

Blitzer, J. (2018, September 28). Trump's public-charge rule is a one-two punch against immigrants and public assistance. *The New Yorker.*

Booi, Z., Callahan, C., Fugere, G., Harris, M., Hughes, A., Kramarczuk, A., Kurtz, C., Raimy, R., & Swaminathan, S. (2016). *Ensuring every undocumented student succeeds: A report on access to public education for undocumented children.* Washington, DC: Georgetown Law Human Rights Institute.

Burke, G., & Sainz, A. (2016, May 2). Migrant children kept from enrolling in school. *AP News.*

California Department of Education. (2018, March 27). *California safe haven school districts list.* Sacramento, CA.

Costello, M. B. (2017). *The Trump effect: The impact of the presidential campaign on our nation's schools.* Montgomery, AL: Southern Poverty Law Center.

Diffey L., & Steffes, S. (2017). *Age requirements for free and compulsory education.* Retrieved from Education Commission of the States website: http://www.ecs.org/wp-content/uploads/Age_Requirements_for_Free_and_Compulsory_Education-1.pdf

EdTrust West. (n.d.). Safe schools for immigrant students: AB 699 (O'Donnell)—Implementation fact sheet. Retrieved from https://west.edtrust.org/wp-content/uploads/2015/11/AB-699-Fact-Sheet-Implementation-.pdf

Hanson J., with Cheer, S.-M., & Broder, T. (2017). The legal authority for "sanctuary" school policies [Practice advisory]. Los Angeles, CA: National Immigration Law Center.

Jacobo, M., & Jensen, B. (2018). *Schooling for US-citizen students in Mexico* [Working paper]. Los Angeles: Civil Rights Project, UCLA.

Jones, C. (2017). What it means when a school district declares itself a "safe haven" or "sanctuary": A quick guide. Retrieved from EdSource website: https://edsource.org/2017/what-it-means-when-a-school-district-declares-itself-a-safe-haven-or-sanctuary-a-quick-guide/584273

King, J., Jr. (2010, August 30). *Student registration guidance* [Memorandum]. Albany, NY: New York State Education Department.

Lawyers' Committee for Civil Rights of the San Francisco Bay Area & California Rural Legal Assistance. (2017, March 27). Complaint concerning discriminatory enrollment practices denying immigrant youth their right to enroll in school [Letter]. Retrieved from https://www.crla.org/sites/all/files/u6/2017/pr/BecerraResCmplnt.pdf

LegiScan. (n.d.). Texas House Bill 22. Retrieved from https://legiscan.com/TX/bill/HB22/2011

McHugh, M. (2018). *In the age of Trump: Populist backlash and progressive resistance create divergent state immigrant integration contexts.* Washington, DC: Migration Policy Institute.

Migration Policy Institute. (n.d.). Mexican-born population over time, 1850-present [Graph]. Retrieved from https://www.migrationpolicy.org/programs/data-hub/charts/mexican-born-population-over-time

Mooney, J., & O'Dea, C. (2018, July 27). ACLU-NJ sues school districts for asking about immigration status. *NJ Spotlight.*

Mueller, B. (2015, February 18). New York compels 20 school districts to lower barriers to immigrants. *The New York Times.*

National Academies of Sciences, Engineering, and Medicine. (2015). *The integration of immigrants into American society.* Washington, DC: The National Academies Press.

National Center for Education Statistics. (2017). Digest of education statistics—Table 204.27. Retrieved from https://nces.ed.gov/programs/digest/d17/tables/dt17_204.27.asp?current=yes

New York Civil Liberties Union. (2014, October 30). NYCLU survey: NY school districts illegally denying education to immigrant children. Retrieved from https://www.nyclu.org/en/press-releases/nyclu-survey-ny-school-districts-illegally-denying-education-immigrant-children

New York State Education Department. (2014a). New York State Board of Regents passes emergency regulation concerning school enrollment following joint review by State Education Department and the Attorney General's Office [Press release]. Retrieved from http://www.nysed.gov/news/2015/new-york-state-board-regents-passes-emergency-regulation-concerning-school-enrollment

New York State Education Department. (2014b). Residency. Retrieved from http://www.p12.nysed.gov/sss/pps/residency

New York State Education Department. (2015). A guide to understanding the new rules for school registration. Retrieved from http://www.p12.nysed.gov/sss/documents/EnrollmentBrochure_English.pdf

New York State Office of the Attorney General. (2015, March 3). A. G. Schneiderman secures agreement with Hempstead Union Free School District to ensure equal educational opportunities for students regardless of immigration status [Press release]. Retrieved from https://ag.ny.gov/press-release/ag-schneiderman-secures-agreement-hempstead-union-free-school-district-ensure-equal

Ofer, U. (2012). Protecting *Plyler*: New challenges to the right of immigrant children to access a public school education. *Columbia Journal of Race and Law, 1*(2), 187–226.

Olivas, M. A. (2005). *Plyler v. Doe*, the education of undocumented children, and the polity. In D. Martin & P. Schuck (Eds.), *Immigration stories* (pp. 197–220). New York: Foundation Press.

Olivas, M. A. (2010, September 9). Plyler v. Doe: Still guaranteeing unauthorized immigrant children's right to attend U.S. public schools. *Migration Information Source*. Retrieved from https://www.migrationpolicy.org/article/plyler-v-doe-still-guaranteeing-unauthorized-immigrant-childrens-right-attend-us-public

Open States. (n.d.-a). Arizona HB 2382. Retrieved from https://openstates.org/az/bills/49th-2nd-regular/HB2382

Open States. (n.d.-b). Arizona SB 1097. Retrieved from https://openstates.org/az/bills/49th-2nd-regular/SB1097

Pierce, S., Bolter, J., & Selee, A. (2018). *U.S. immigration policy under Trump: Deep changes and lasting impacts*. Washington, DC: Migration Policy Institute.

Rosenblum, M. R., & Brick, K. (2011). *U.S. immigration policy and Mexican/Central American migration flows: Then and now*. Washington, DC: Migration Policy Institute.

Sanchez, R. (2017, March 3). ICE arrests undocumented father taking daughter to California school. Retrieved from CNN website: https://www.cnn.com/2017/03/03/us/california-father-ice-arrest-trnd/

Southern Poverty Law Center. (2013, October 28). SPLC victorious against Alabama anti-immigrant law. Retrieved from https://www.splcenter.org/news/2013/10/29/splc-victorious-against-alabama-anti-immigrant-law

St. George, D. (2016, December 26). Schools warn of increased student fears due to immigration arrests, Trump election. *Washington Post*.

Staehr Fenner, D. (2014). *Advocating for English learners: A guide for educators*. Thousand Oaks, CA: Corwin Press.

Sugarman, J. (2017). *Beyond teaching English: Supporting high school completion by immigrant and refugee students*. Washington, DC: Migration Policy Institute.

Tenenbaum, L., & Drummond, D. (2016, September 5). NYS school districts enter second year of new approach to enrollment—District concerns and strategies. Retrieved from New York State School Boards Association website: https://www.nyssba.org/news/2016/09/01/on-board-online-september-5-2016/nys-school-districts-enter-second-year-of-new-approach-to-enrollment-district-concerns-and-strategies

TESOL International Association. (2010). *Standards for the recognition of initial TESOL programs in P–12 ESL teacher education*. Retrieved from https://www.

tesol.org/docs/default-source/advocacy/the-revised-tesol-ncate-standards-for-the-recognition-of-initial-tesol-programs-in-p-12-esl-teacher-education-(2010-pdf).pdf

Torlakson, T. (2016, December 21). Public schools remain safe havens for California's students [Letter]. Retrieved from California Department of Education website: https://www.cde.ca.gov/nr/el/le/yr16ltr1221.asp

U.S. Customs and Border Protection. (2016). Sensitive locations FAQs. Retrieved from https://www.cbp.gov/border-security/sensitive-locations-faqs

U.S. Department of Justice and U.S. Department of Education. (2014a, May 8). *Dear colleague letter: School enrollment procedures.* Retrieved from U.S. Department of Education website: https://www2.ed.gov/about/offices/list/ocr/letters/colleague-201405.pdf

U.S. Department of Justice and U.S. Department of Education. (2014b, May 8). *Information on the rights of all children to enroll in school: Questions and answers for states, school districts and parents.* Retrieved from U.S. Department of Justice website: https://www.justice.gov/sites/default/files/crt/legacy/2014/05/08/plylerqa.pdf

Yoshikawa, H., Suárez-Orozco, C., & Gonzales, R. G. (2016). Unauthorized status and youth development in the United States: Consensus statement of the Society for Research on Adolescence. *Journal of Research on Adolescence* *27*(1): 4–19.

Zong, J., Batalova, J., & Hallock, J. (2018, February 8). Frequently requested statistics on immigrants and immigration in the United States. *Migration Information Source.* Retrieved from https://www.migrationpolicy.org/article/frequently-requested-statistics-immigrants-and-immigration-united-states

Chapter 10

Binational Policies for the Students We Share and the Teachers We Need

Patricia Gándara and Bryant Jensen

Even educators working with immigrant students and in bilingual classrooms are often surprised, even shocked, to hear that more than 600,000 U.S. citizen students are attending schools in Mexico or that 2 million young people have spent part of their young lives in both Mexico and the United States. For the most part, the movement of Mexican-origin families and children has been framed as a one-way northerly journey. Some have even pressed to build a wall to shut these children and their families out. However, the fact is that now more Mexican-origin individuals and families are leaving the United States than entering it. There is an exodus occurring among U.S.-citizen children of Mexican families, creating new challenges for which Mexico is not prepared and the United States does not acknowledge.

The chapters in this volume form the contours of a relatively new scholarship on the educational, social, and emotional needs of binational students, and the characteristics of a teaching force we need to support these students. As we saw in Chapters 3, 5, and 7, the transition into Mexican schools can be challenging when students have never been educated in Spanish and do not read and write in the language, have no foundation in Mexican history and schooling practices, and when they are unfamiliar with the routines of the classroom and the pedagogy and expectations. While there are now hundreds of thousands of U.S.-citizen children in Mexican schools, we have no idea how many have simply found the transition too difficult, the schools too crowded, or the bureaucratic impediments to enrolling too insurmountable, and have dropped out. We also don't know how many others, because the family was deported and without resources, have gone to work instead of to school to help support the family. These numbers may also be in the tens of thousands or more. And, because these young people are U.S. citizens, they can, and many will, return whether they are prepared for the U.S. economy and civic life or not.

While there is now an emerging scholarship on this phenomenon, for the most part it has occurred under the educational radar, and so policies have not been developed to address these students' needs or to prepare educators to teach them. Meanwhile, in spite of the exodus of Mexican-origin families, the percentage of U.S. students who are Latino and speak Spanish at home continues to grow. In some parts of the United States, such as New Mexico, Texas, and California—and soon Nevada and Arizona—these students are already the numerical majority in the public schools. Moreover, while the phenomenon is not new, the solutions to providing these students with an equitable education that will prepare them to participate meaningfully in civic life and the economy are still wanting. It seems that too many policy makers have thought that if they just ignored the problem, it would go away.

As this book was being finalized, the world was hit by the coronavirus pandemic, and schools in both the United States and Mexico were closed. Students on both sides of the border have lost many months of school, and it remains unclear when schools will open again. Students have been sent home to be schooled through distance learning on devices that many of the most disadvantaged students do not have via Wi-Fi to which they do not have regular access (Esquivel et al., 2020). Moreover, their migrant parents in the United States are both disproportionately represented among those being felled by the virus and also, because of lack of access to public benefits, are often required to go to essential jobs in the food industry and in hospitals and care facilities, at great risk, to put food on their own tables (Oppel Jr. et al., 2020).

In Mexico, the widespread lack of digital resources in students' homes has forced the Secretary of Public Education to put school lessons on television, a strategy that does not allow for interaction with teachers or even monitoring of attendance. Moreover, many of the poorest students do not have televisions (Linthicum, 2020). Not surprisingly, we hear daily about students in the United States and in Mexico giving up on distance education. Many of these families on both sides of the border simply cannot also take on the job of homeschooling their children. The stress on these migrant (as well as other poor) families is extraordinary, and there is mounting evidence that students are being traumatized with potentially long-term effects (Kelly et al, 2020). So these students we share are multiply disadvantaged by the pandemic and are being seriously left behind. Among the strategies being suggested to address this problem, once the world leaves the pandemic behind, is additional instructional time for these students. But where the funds and human resources will come from is not at all clear. Projections for the economies of the United States and Mexico are dire; they are both likely to be in a serious recession, with social services severely cut back. The teachers of the students we share will be asked to step up to find ways to narrow the educational gaps that were once large and are now worse. The knowledge and strategies shared in the preceding chapters will form a baseline for the task ahead. What we once might have argued should begin to be introduced in teacher preparation will become urgent. And we cannot lose sight of the fact that teachers, too, have been struggling with the effects of the virus on them and their families. It will require a collaboration between countries, school systems, and educators of unprecedented proportions.

Wall or no wall, the United States and Mexico are inexorably linked. Mexico and the United States are one another's most important trading partner. The two economies are deeply interdependent. If one falters, so will the other. And falter they will unless something is urgently done about raising the education level of these Mexican-origin young people on both sides of the border and attacking the yawning gaps in achievement and the mental health challenges that have resulted from the pandemic. For example, if the region including Los Angeles, San Diego and Tijuana—a region we call *Lasanti* (Mordechay & Orfield, 2017)—were a nation, it would be the 11th largest economy in the world. Yet the average education level of the region is actually declining. A recent study by the Public Policy Institute for California has warned that within a decade, the whole state of California will be more than a million college degrees short of those needed to fill existing jobs (Johnson, Cuellar Mejia, & Bohn, 2015). This is primarily because Mexican-origin youth are an increasing percentage of the school-age population, yet they are not being prepared for college. They are the least likely of all subgroups to graduate college (Gándara & Mordechay, 2017). At the same time, the average education level on the Mexican side of the border is only the equivalent of ninth grade—far short of a high school diploma. If this continues, many U.S.-citizen young people will return to the United States without sufficient educational preparation to participate meaningfully in civil society, contribute to the economy, or even sustain a family. The stakes are incredibly high.

Policies We Need

Some of the solutions to these challenges are fairly obvious. Bilingual instruction would allow students to thrive in both U.S. and Mexican classrooms and would allow students to get on track academically in a relatively seamless fashion. The popularity of two-way dual-language programs that not only teach in both Spanish and English, but can also integrate primarily Spanish-speaking and primarily English-speaking students in stronger schools is a relatively recent development that holds enormous promise in the United States. Yet misguided language education policies have proliferated in the states, focusing on English-only instruction, leaving little reason for bilingual individuals to prepare themselves as bilingual teachers (Gándara & Escamilla, 2017). Why invest all the extra effort and costs to prepare for a job that may not exist? And why continue to teach as a bilingual teacher when the job requires twice the work with no additional compensation or support? There has been limited recruitment of bilingual teachers, and few school districts provide any economic incentive to take on the job. Thus, we have seen the numbers of bilingual teachers shrink in key states (see López & Santibañez, Chapter 8) even while the numbers of students needing these teachers has grown. As several studies have shown, bilingually prepared teachers simply have many advantages over English monolingual teachers regardless of the type of language program being offered. They can monitor students' learning, adjust lessons when students aren't learning, encourage students and listen to their concerns, welcome them, ease their transitions, and make them feel like they DO belong. All of these functions will be particularly critical coming out of the pandemic. Parents are also more likely to confide important information about their children to a teacher who speaks their language.

In Mexico, where federal education policy requires that English be taught and students graduate as competent bilinguals, only about 5% of the teachers actually speak English, and only about half of English teachers actually have the level of competency expected of their students. So there are few teachers to meet the linguistic needs of English-dominant American Mexican students. Bilingual education is virtually unheard of in the public schools. The state of Baja California—a state with a higher percentage of English speakers than any other in Mexico—has recently opened its first two bilingual public schools. In Guanajuato, for example, promising initiatives have emerged to recruit "American Mexican" young adults to English teacher preparation programs (Mora Pablo et al., 2015). While bilingual education is an obvious response to the students we share, it is a challenge to mount in large numbers in both countries because of the dearth of adequately prepared bilingual teachers. Language, however important, is not the only impediment that these students experience in the United States or in Mexico.

Students' Migrant Experiences

The decision for a family to leave their home and migrate is fraught with fear, anxiety, and a deep sense of loss (Suarez-Orozco & Suarez-Orozco, 1995). Most who arrive at the U.S. border are also desperately poor and traumatized by the journey. Only dire circumstances would prompt families to leave all behind to take a chance in another country where they are considered illegal or unwelcome. Falicov (2002) describes the response to migration as grief or mourning, not unlike losing a loved one. For children this can be especially stressful if the family migrates in stages with one parent going and one staying behind or if children are separated from their parents at the border (as has occurred under Trump administration policies in 2018). These separations can have damaging lifelong psychological and physical health consequences, including alterations in brain development (SRCD, 2018). Even U.S. citizen children are affected by family separations resulting from immigration enforcement, increasing the risk for these children's mental health, including anxiety, depression, behavior problems, and symptoms of post-traumatic stress disorder (Rojas-Flores, Clements, Hwang Koo, & London, 2017; Yoshikawa & Kholoptseva, 2013; Zayas, Aguilar-Gaxiola, Yoon, & Rey 2015).

Compounding the typical stress of immigrant families are the draconian immigration enforcement policies of the former Trump administration. The children of immigrants in the United States are an especially vulnerable group, particularly if they are Latinos. While most are U.S. citizens, an estimated 5.9 million (American Immigration Council, 2018) have at least one unauthorized family member, which put them at risk for sudden deportation or family loss of livelihood. Not all the undocumented are Latinos, or more specifically Mexican, but they have been the targets of ICE.[1] While undocumented immigrants come from all over the world, individuals perceived to be Mexican (such as Central Americans) have been at highest risk (Shan, 2018, p. 9).

These immigration policies have created a near-impossible learning situation for "English learners," almost all of whom are the children of immigrants. Between October 2017 and January 2018, the Civil Rights Project at the University of California at Los Angeles conducted a survey of school personnel in approximately 750 schools in 24 districts, urban, suburban, and rural, in 13 states, attempting to investigate the degree to which these policies were affecting the nation's schools (Ee & Gándara, 2019). Approximately 3,600 educators responded that they had observed an impact of heightened immigration enforcement on their students. It is important to note as well that 90% of educators responding were working in schools designated by the federal government as Title I—schools that serve high percentages of poor and low-income students and that are already challenged often beyond their limits.

Across all respondents who had noted some impact of immigration policy on their schools, 80% responded that they had observed behavioral or emotional problems among immigrant youth, and more than a fourth reported that these problems were "extensive." Likewise, nearly 85% of respondents reported that their immigrant students had talked openly about fearing ICE, and almost 40% said that this was extensive. An issue that is not widely reported but that was mentioned repeatedly is the increasing housing and food insecurity of immigrant students, in addition to the psychological trauma they suffered. Even very young children are suffering on many levels. One little first grader asked her teacher, "How are we going to eat?"

Not surprisingly, almost two-thirds of respondents reported that as a consequence of the enforcement regime, their immigrant students were experiencing a decline in academic performance, and many educators commented that even their most outstanding college-bound students were giving up on school because their futures were now so uncertain. Although most of these students are U.S. citizens, deportation of a parent can mean they too will be leaving the country (Jensen & Jacobo, 2019) or that they will no longer have the resources to continue their education and may need to leave school to help support the family, as the primary breadwinner or caregiver has been deported. Deciding to stay or go is a wrenching decision for these young people—to follow a parent to a country they do not know, giving up their dream of an education, or carrying the guilt of staying behind while other family members leave to an uncertain future. Of course, there is also the challenge of figuring out a way—and place—to live if one decides to remain. Students are also anxious for their friends and classmates even when they are not directly affected, and the loss of students from the classroom creates a pall over the whole class (Minikwu, 2017). The image of empty desks where classmates and friends sat haunts the other students, as frequently no one knows what has happened to them.

Teachers' Experiences with Immigration Enforcement

Teachers, too, are deeply affected by the impact on their students. They reported having to interrupt lessons to deal with students crying or acting out in class. But perhaps the greatest impact on the schools has been the declining sense of trust and community among educators. Some teachers reported that they didn't know whom they could trust among their colleagues with information about a student's immigration situation. Revealing information about a student's family situation to the wrong person could result in severe consequences for that family. In addition to the concerns about trust in the school, teachers also worry about how they are perceived by parents who may hold strong negative views on immigration. An Arizona teacher lamented that "[the students] want to know about what's going on but anytime it is discussed in class I get an upset parent phone call." It was clear from educators' responses that many feel pressured from all sides and unsure about where to turn for support.

Little has been reported in the popular press or in the academic literature about the tremendous impact immigration enforcement has had on teachers in both countries of the students we share, but this has placed an additional layer of stress and responsibility that weighs on most of these teachers, and for which they are essentially unprepared. However, as evidenced in this book, a number of researchers and practitioners have been actively working to study the issues and develop projects and collaborations to begin to address the needs of the teachers of the students we share. Much more is needed. What has been learned by the research must be put into practice urgently.

Binational Policy Dialogue

A major impediment to greater progress in this area, in addition to inadequate attention, is the failure to see this as a joint challenge with responsibility for these students and their teachers shared equally by both Mexico and the United States. Clearly, U.S.-born citizens are the responsibility of the United States, and these students should have access to every educational benefit that all American students have. As Sugarman points out in Chapter 9, the U.S. Constitution has also been found to include the education of all minor children in the country up through high school graduation. What is to happen to them after that remains a vexing, unresolved problem (Gonzales, 2011). But when parents are deported, or otherwise return to Mexico with their children—U.S. citizens or not—Mexico is faced with providing these students with a basic education. However, as Santibañez notes in Chapter 1, Mexico is poorly prepared to address their needs without Spanish as a second language programs or other newcomer strategies.

The two education systems—U.S. and Mexico—have rarely met to sort out responsibilities or design policies to address educational issues, and when this does happen, agreements are usually forgotten in subsequent administrations. It would seem that the policy response must begin with a clear statement of our shared responsibility to provide an equitable education for these students. We do have some precedent for binational collaboration. The U.S.-Mexico Binational Commission, established through the U.S. Department of State by Presidents Reagan and López Portillo in 1981, provides precedent and a framework for binational policy dialogue in education (Escobar, Martin, & Lowell, 2013). We recommend reviving this effort to improve teacher preparation and school quality for the students we share. In the 1980s, the U.S. Department of Education, the *Secretaría de Educación Pública*, and the *Secretaría de Relaciones Exteriores* worked together to develop educational programs to support Mexican immigrants and their children in the United States (Martínez-Wenzl, 2013). Administered through Mexican consulates in the United States, programs included a teacher exchange, transfer document, textbook donation, online secondary education, adult education, scholarships, and community computing centers. Lack of resources and careful planning in addition to weak supervision by the Mexican consulates rendered most of these activities as only modestly effective (Gándara, 2008).

Though woefully underresourced, understudied, and with limited support by recent administrations, the organizational framework provided by previous policy dialogues can be helpful to address the educational needs of these students. One of the primary challenges that must be confronted is the fact that each state in the United States enjoys autonomy with respect to its educational programs and funding, and creating partnerships with Mexico necessarily requires a state-by-state commitment. This sometimes confounds the efforts of the Mexican education system, which is much more centralized. Still, the U.S. Department of Education can work with Mexican institutions to redesign programs and evaluate their effectiveness and collaborate with state education offices in this regard. Indeed, Alfaro and Gándara show in Chapter 2 how the recently signed memorandum of understanding between the California Department of Education, the University of California, and the Mexican *Secretaria de Educación Pública* can be a useful tool that could be replicated elsewhere. The document provides a framework whereby one U.S. state (California) can enter into agreements with various Mexican states, with the imprimatur of the Mexican federal government, to build and fund joint programs. While the document does not guarantee that such programs will be established, it removes certain bureaucratic impediments and makes these efforts possible.

Enact Existing Laws

There must be a serious consideration in these dialogues and related agreements of the resources needed to meet shared challenges and how those resources should be deployed. It is also clear that teachers and schools will not be able to adequately meet the learning needs of the children of immigrants until the reign of terror on immigrant families in the United States has been completely halted. Until that time, it may simply be asking too much of teachers to provide effective lessons for students who are psychologically traumatized and unable to focus attention on learning, without also having resources to support those students and their teachers emotionally. But we must begin to prepare teachers in both the United States and Mexico who at the very least understand these students and their circumstances and have pedagogical strategies designed for those circumstances. While it is beyond the scope of the schools to intervene in immigration policy, schools must understand the ways these policies have affected their students, the things they can do to support them, and raise their voices in their defense.

Part of this understanding is how laws already in place are designed to protect the educational rights and well-being of the students we share.

In Chapter 9, for example, Sugarman identifies what rights K-12 administrators, teachers, and other school personnel ought to understand from the *Plyler* ruling by the U.S. Supreme Court in 1982. Educators can and should take measures to make sure their schools are following federal law by guaranteeing free and appropriate education for all students regardless of their or their parents' immigrant or documented status. Moreover, civil rights lawyers have argued that a "free and appropriate" education for children in these circumstances must include the support services necessary for them to access education. This can include counselors, social workers, and psychologists. Sugarman highlights that the online "English Learner Tool Kit," by the Office of English Language Acquisition in the U.S. Department of Education, is an excellent resource to review school and district policies and practices in relation to federal law.

There are also legal protections for the students we share in Mexico. In 2015, for example, the *Secretaría de Educación Pública* (SEP) amended several regulations to facilitate school access for students with U.S. experiences. These changes removed the requirement to have a Mexican birth certificate, an Apostille certification, or a Spanish translation of school records to enroll a child in school. Though these are positive changes meant to benefit the students we share and their families, Jacobo (2017) finds that dissemination and implementation of these policies to local educators and officials vary greatly. The SEP has not trained state-level staff to guarantee proper policy implementation. Many, including parents, are still unaware of these changes. We recommend a bold campaign to communicate school access rights for transnational students throughout Mexico, targeting especially those states with large non-urban populations.

Asset-Oriented Teacher Preparation

A great irony is that while these students are often viewed as problems or burdens on the schools, the students we share have unique and highly valuable assets that should be acknowledged, developed, and taken advantage of in both countries. Children of immigration are *resilient*. Most have experienced, either first- or secondhand, tremendous privations and insecurity, having to adapt to new circumstances from day to day with little guidance. Yet they persevere, they show up at school, they often work before and after school to help the family, and in the United States they overwhelmingly graduate from high school. They are also *optimistic*—true believers in the American dream—even when they find themselves on the opposite side of the border. Many continue to believe that they will one day realize that dream back in the United States. Many Mexican-origin students, raised to be *bien educados*, are *collaborative learners*; they often prefer learning in groups or teams and are less individualistic than most other American students (see Chapter 6 by Jensen), something that employers consistently say they want in employees. They are *bilingual* and potentially biliterate if provided the instruction. Bilingualism is a clear asset in the workplace as well as in society as a whole (Callahan & Gándara, 2014). And their *multiple cultural perspectives* lead them to the realization that there is more than one way to see a problem or a solution. It is multiple (cultural) perspectives that so often lead to innovation and creativity, breakthroughs in addressing seemingly intractable problems (see for example Page, 2007). There is every reason we should be investing in these talented, promising young people. And, as we have argued in this book, that investment must begin with teachers.

Chapters 1, 4, and 5 of this book also highlight how students' knowledge and experiences associated with migration itself can be assets that educators should appreciate and incorporate to meet the educational needs of students we share. Gallo in Chapter 5 recommends that teachers provide opportunities for transnational students in Mexico to share their lived experiences abroad as a way of getting to know them better and sharing their acquired knowledge and assets. Teachers also need to modify, or at least explain classroom practices, such as *el dictado*, to meet the developmental needs of American Mexican students. Teachers in both countries, she argues, need specific training to position the migration experiences of students we share as assets to support classroom learning. In Chapter 1, Santibañez argues that English proficiency is a particularly important asset of American Mexican students to leverage in Mexican classrooms, and that training to enhance teachers' biliteracy should address the significant differences between U.S. and Mexican public-school systems and practices. One way in which the English skills of many American Mexican students can be acknowledged and built upon is through the extension of the Seal of Biliteracy into Mexican schools, a practice that has gained support at both the federal and local levels. A project is currently underway in Baja California to provide the Seal of Biliteracy to those students who are able to demonstrate strong biliteracy skills upon graduation from secondary school. The objective is to (a) encourage students to maintain their English skills; (b) encourage teachers to focus on English instruction, and (c) provide a formal validation of biliteracy that can be used for college and job applications.

Mexican and U.S. academics have also been engaged in developing programs to provide a pathway for American Mexican students finding themselves in Mexico to gain a college degree in English language instruction and help fill the ranks of English teachers. The *Universidad de Guanajuato*, for example, has a highly touted program that recruits U.S.-born and return migrants into undergraduate and graduate programs to become English teachers in various settings, including in public primary and secondary schools (Mora Pablo et al., 2015). To foster an asset-based approach, the program has changed its design based on British English to incorporate the American genres that new recruits come to class speaking. And the *Universidad Pedagógica Nacional* (UPN) is now engaged in developing a degree program that would offer the *licenciatura* (undergraduate degree) in English pedagogy that would qualify graduates to become English teachers in the public school system. There is growing interest in providing pathways for students we share in Mexico to pursue a career in teaching English. Given the growth in teacher salaries in Mexico (see Santibañez, Chapter 1), this can be an important option for English-speaking students who remain in Mexico.

Local Education Policies

Not surprising, the learning needs of students, the professional needs of their teachers, and the extent to which these needs are currently being met vary by region within and between countries. Urbanicity is an especially important factor underlying school quality in Mexico, where material and human resources tend to be stronger in urban than in rural or semi-rural settings. Similar variation can be seen among regions in the United States. Given historic decentralization of school governance to states and school districts, local policies are critical to consider when seeking to meet the needs of Mexican-origin students in the United States. In Chapter 8, López and Santibañez find discrepancies in state licensure requirements of teachers to meet the cultural and linguistic needs of "emergent bilingual" students, most of whom come from immigrant families. They find that teacher education requirements for developing cultural and linguistic knowledge are stronger in Texas, with its long-term commitment to bilingual instruction in the early grades, than in Arizona, which has all but banned bilingual instruction. This translates into higher teacher efficacy, job satisfaction, and academic achievement for transnational students in Texas.

Thoughtful local policies are also needed in Mexico to meet teacher and student needs. Chapters 3 and 7 in this book argue, for example, for pre- and in-service training to help teachers in Central Mexico (state of Morelos) to learn how to incorporate the experiences and developmental strengths of children from immigrant families into school and classroom life, especially students with U.S. experiences. Bybee and his colleagues (Chapter 3) demonstrate how teacher candidates in *escuelas normales* need coursework and practicum experiences focused explicitly on equity (fairness) rather than equality (sameness) in order to shake existing deficit views of transnational students and their families. Román González and Sánchez García (Chapter 7) argue for providing Morelos' teachers with bilingual materials to support American Mexican students, as well as learning about the organization of schooling in the United States to help children and their families transition to the norms of schooling in Mexico.

Local policy efforts should be binational as well, as in the teacher preparation program in California and Baja California, described in Chapter 2 by Alfaro and Gándara. Partnerships between U.S. and Mexican local educational agencies can facilitate school access, appropriate placement, and curricular transitions for the students we share. Reviving and revising the "transfer document" (Martínez-Wenzl, 2013) can assist with this. This effort can help schools and districts in the United States provide parents and their children with information they need to experience as smooth a transition as possible to U.S. or Mexican schools. Of course, when families leave without notice, which is often the case in deportations and detentions, it isn't possible to acquire a transfer document. Nonetheless, in some Mexican states, PROBEM (*Programa Binacional de Educación Migrante*) operates effectively to track down school documents for students arriving suddenly in Mexico and facilitates accurate school placement.

Fund Collaborative Improvement

There is much we need to know about teaching and learning for the students we share and the development, support, and well-being of their teachers. Future research should address exactly what teachers should know, be able to do, and become, to meet the learning potential and life aspirations of the students we share in time and space. Supportive policies can be designed and implemented with stronger evidence regarding teacher recruitment, state requirements for certification, enactment of requirements in preparation programs, and ongoing supports for teacher learning in situ (National Research Council, 2010). We recommend that U.S. funding agencies—e.g., National Science Foundation, Institute of Education Sciences (Dept. of Education), National Institutes of Health—collaborate with Mexican institutions—e.g., *Comisión Nacional para la Mejora Continua de la Educación (MejorEdu)*, *Consejo Nacional de Ciencia y Tecnología (CONACYT)*—on joint requests for proposals about teaching and teacher preparation and development. The focus should be on research for the improvement of teaching and student learning, and this can be especially helpful if it focuses on educational recovery from the pandemic. Some research topics include (a) differences in academic achievement opportunity between groups of transnational students and their peers; (b) comparing alignment between U.S. and Mexican curricular content and standards; and (c) design and testing of professional learning teams to build capacity for durable implementation of improved teaching practices (Gallimore, Ermeling, Saunders, & Goldenberg, 2009), in addition to strategies to help students recover from educational losses. If the findings from these research efforts are to be as fruitful as we would all hope, there needs to be a concerted effort by both U.S. and Mexican academic publishers to establish a program of publication and dissemination in both languages so that educators on both sides of the border have access to this work.

Time to Learn

In Chapter 6, Jensen identifies low-hanging fruit for policy makers and researchers to improve opportunities for shared students. For example, the gap between intended and actual classroom learning time, especially poignant in (semi-) rural Mexican schools, should be addressed. Policy makers should fund evaluations to ensure implementation of intended instructional hours and consider lengthening the school day in Mexico (currently less than five hours in most primary schools). As noted earlier, this is likely to be a critical resource for students who have lost many months of instructional time. He also suggests more research on teacher learning for instructional improvement, leading to products (e.g., curricula, instructional guides, teacher collaboration protocols, practical measures of teaching) that can be tested for effectiveness at scale. This, too, requires that teachers be given time outside of instructional time, still uncommon in the United States and novel in Mexico. The *Programa Escolar de Mejora Continua* (PEMC), a federal professional development program launched in 2019 in Mexico (SEP, 2019), has tremendous potential to make collaborative, close-to-practice teacher learning in Mexico a reality.

Gándara (2017) has pointed out that students who are still learning a language require more time to successfully complete schoolwork. It is simply mathematically impossible for a student who has the dual tasks of acquiring a new language while also keeping up with the regular curriculum to be able to accomplish this in the same time as other students who must accomplish only one task. Moreover, it has been shown that in U.S. schools, English learners actually have *less* time than other students because of bureaucratic and logistical factors such as time spent waiting for the teacher to explain what cannot be understood, or being shuttled among aides to provide language support (Gándara et al, 2003). It is imperative that schools on both sides of the border acknowledge that these students we share need extra learning time to be successful, and this should not normally be in the form of holding students back. There are a number of ways to approach this, but one cost-effective way is to create peer-tutoring networks. Peer tutors can receive second language practice at the same time they are helping a migrant student strengthen language skills or better understand an assignment.

Conclusion

While our understanding of what binational students need is growing rapidly, this is a challenging moment in which to suggest policy options dealing with these students. The United States has been in a period of heightened anti-immigrant sentiment and both the U.S. and Mexico have suffered economic upheaval from the pandemic. Moreover, Mexico is at a critical juncture in determining the degree to which the government will retain control of education policy or the teachers' union will seize it. Significant reforms that aimed to improve the preparation of teachers were underway, but they have been largely dismantled in the current administration. The *Instituto Nacional para la Evaluación de la Educación* (INEE) was closed down in 2019, and with it all national testing of students. It may be some time before the recommendations we make will be seriously considered. Nonetheless, we are calling for federal, state, local, and, yes, bilateral policies to better reflect and respond to the transnational realities of the more than 9 million students we share between the United

States and Mexico. The benefits are mutual. Mexico is now a net destination rather than a sending country for immigrants, meaning that the fastest-growing groups of "students we share" are U.S.-born children and youth now in Mexico, whether their families were deported or returned voluntarily. Education is a sector in which we cannot afford to allow partisanship to cloud or misconstrue reality. Many of these students can cross the border legally at will. They see their futures not in one country or the other, but in both. Our policies can be more responsive by reviving substantive dialogues between countries, taking measures to enforce existing laws that protect the rights of transnational students, developing asset-oriented teacher preparation programs, innovating at local levels, and by funding and disseminating problem-focused research to enhance teaching, learning, and teacher learning in various settings.

We see educators—i.e., teacher candidates, teachers, teacher educators, school administrators, and para-educators—as intimate partners in this work. We are hard-pressed to identify a task more complex than teaching (Shulman, 1987). Policy makers should invest in solutions *with* rather than *for* educators to better serve their students. Teachers need support to improve their craft, not incentives that pit schools against each other, or counterproductive initiatives like the recent 2015 *desempeño docente* policy in Mexico, which threatened teachers with job loss rather than prioritizing support to improve their teaching. Preparing the teachers we need for the students we share will require thoughtful engagement and collaboration across multiple borders. The possibilities are as thrilling as the demands are pressing.

Note

1. Immigration and Customs Enforcement: the federal agency charged with policing immigration.

References

Alfaro, C., & Gándara, P. (2021). Binational teacher preparation: Constructing pedagogical bridges for the students we share. In P. Gándara & B. Jensen (Eds.), *The students we share*. Albany, NY: State University of New York Press.

American Immigration Council (2018). *U.S. citizen children impacted by immigration enforcement*. Washington, DC: American Immigration Council.

Bybee, E. R., Jensen, B., & Johnstun, K. (2021). *Normalista* perspectives on preparing Mexican teachers for American-Mexican students. In P. Gándara & B. Jensen (Eds.), *The students we share*. Albany, NY: State University of New York Press.

Callahan, R., & Gándara, P. (Eds). (2014). *The bilingual advantage: Language, literacy, and the US labor market*. Bristol, UK: Channel View/Multilingual Matters.

Ee, J., & Gándara, P. (2019). The impact of immigration enforcement on the nation's schools. *American Educational Research Journal*. doi.org/10.3102/0002 831219862998

Escobar, A., Martin, S., & Lowell, L. (2013). *Binational dialogue on Mexican migrants in the US and in Mexico—Final report*. Washington, DC: Georgetown University/CIESAS.

Esquivel, P., et al (2020, August 13). A generation left behind? Online learning cheats poor students, Times survey finds. *Los Angeles Times*. Retrieved from https://www.latimes.com/california/story/2020-08-13/online-learning-fails-low-income-students-covid-19-left-behind-project

Gallimore, R., Ermeling, B. A., Saunders, W. M., & Goldenberg, C. (2009). Moving the learning of teaching closer to practice: Teacher education implications of school-based inquiry teams. *The Elementary School Journal, 109*(5), 537–553.

Gallo, S. (2021). Preparing educators for asset-based pedagogies: The case of recently arrived transnational students in Central Mexico. In P. Gándara & B. Jensen (Eds.), *The students we share*. Albany, NY: State University of New York Press.

Gándara, P. (2017). English learners, immigrant students and the challenge of time. In M. Saunders, J. Ruiz de Velasco, & J. Oakes (eds). *Learning Time. In Pursuit of Educational Equity*. Cambridge MA: Harvard University Press. Pp. 145–160.

Gándara, P. (2008). A preliminary evaluation of Mexican-sponsored educational programs in the United States: Strengths, weaknesses, and potential. Libro de Recursos, Southwest Center for Education Equity and Language Diversity, Arizona State University. (Also available through Instituto de Mexicanos en el Exterior [IME], Secretaria de Relaciones Exteriores, Mexico City.)

Gándara, P., & Escamilla, K. (2017). Bilingual education in the United States. In O. García, A. Lin, & S. May (Eds.), *Bilingual and multilingual education* (pp. 1–14). New York: Springer International Publishing.

Gándara, P., & Mordechay, K. (2017). Demographic change and the new (and not so new) challenges for Latino education. *The Educational Forum, 81*, 148–159.

Gándara, P., Rumberger, R., Maxwell-Jolly, J., & Callahan, R. (2003). English learners in California Schools: Unequal resources; unequal outcomes. *Educational Policy Analysis Archives, 16*.

Gonzales, R. (2011). Learning to be illegal: Undocumented youth and the shifting legal contexts in the transition to adulthood. *American Sociological Review, 76*, 602–619.

Jacobo, M. (2017). De regreso a "casa" y sin apostilla: Estudiantes mexicoamericanos en México. *Sinéctica, 48*, 1–18.

Jensen, B. (2021). Equitable teaching enhances achievement opportunity for the students we share. In P. Gándara & B. Jensen (Eds.), *The students we share*. Albany, NY: State University of New York Press.

Jensen, B., & Jacobo, M. (2019). Integrating American-Mexican students in Mexican classrooms. *Kappa Delta Pi, 55*(1), 36–41.

Johnson, H., Cuellar Mejia, M., & Bohn, S. (2015). *Will California run out of college graduates?* San Francisco: Public Policy Institute of California.

Kelly, M. S., Astor, R. A., Benbenishty, R., Capp, G., & Watson, K. R. (2020). Opening schools safely in the COVID-19 era: School social workers' experiences and recommendations. Technical Report. UCLA Luskin School of Public Affairs, Department of Social Work.

Linthicum, K. (2020, August 4). Instead of returning to school this fall, Mexican students will watch TV. *Los Angeles Times*. Retrieved from https://www.latimes.com/world-nation/story/2020-08-04/instead-of-returning-to-school-mexican-students-will-watch-class-on-tv

López, F., & Santibañez, L. (2021). Language and cultural skills of U.S. teachers: Informing policy to meet the needs of transnational bilingual students. In P. Gándara & B. Jensen (Eds.), *The students we share*. Albany, NY: State University of New York Press.

Martinez-Wenzl, M. (2013). Bi-national education initiatives: A brief history. Regarding educacion: Mexican-American schooling, immigration and binational improvement. In B. Jensen & A. Sawyer (Eds.), *Regarding educación: Mexican American schooling, immigration, and binational improvement*. New York: Teachers College Press.

Minikwu, J. (2017). *Lessons from Postville: How an immigration raid changes a small town and its school*. Retrieved from Colorín Colorado website: http://www.colorincolorado.org/article/lessons-postville-how-immigration-raid-changed-small-town-and-its-schools

Mora Pablo, I., Rivas Rivas, L. A., Lengeling, M. M., & Crawford, T. (2015). Transnationals in Mexico: Effects of language brokering and identity formation. *Gist: Education and Learning Research Journal, 10*, 7–28.

Mordechay, K., & Orfield, G. (2017). Demographic transformation in a policy vacuum: The changing face of U.S. metropolitan society and challenges for public schools. *The Educational Forum, 81*(2), 193–203.

National Research Council (2010). *Preparing teacher: Building evidence for sound policy*. Washington, DC: The National Academies Press.

Oppel Jr., R., et al. (2020, July 5). The fullest look yet at the racial inequity of the coronavirus. *New York Times*, online, July 5. https://www.nytimes.com/interactive/2020/07/05/us/coronavirus-latinos-african-americans-cdc-data.html

Page, S. (2007). *The difference: How the power of diversity creates better groups, firms, schools, and societies*. Princeton, NJ: Princeton University Press.

Rojas-Flores, L., Clements, M. L., Hwang-Koo, J., & London, J. (2017). Trauma and psychological stress in Latino citizen children following parental detention and deportation. *Psychological Trauma, 9*(3), 352–361.

Román González, B., & Sánchez García, J. (2021). Mirroring students' and teachers' classroom experiences to address the challenges of transnationalism in Mexican schools. In P. Gándara & B. Jensen (Eds.), *The students we share*. Albany, NY: State University of New York Press.

Santibañez, L. (2021). Contrasting realities: How differences between the Mexican and U.S. education systems affect transnational students. In P. Gándara & B. Jensen (Eds.), *The students we share*. Albany, NY: State University of New York Press.

Secretaría de Educación Pública (SEP). (2019). *Orientaciones para elaborar el Programa Escolar de Mejora Continua*. México, DF: Secretaría de Educación Pública, Subsecretaría de Educación Básica.

Shan, J. (2018, July). Asians are the fastest growing undocumented group. And ICE tends to leave them alone. *The California Sunday Magazine, Los Angeles Times*.

Shulman, L. (1987). Knowledge and teaching: Foundations of the new reform. *Harvard Educational Review, 57*(1), 1–23.

Suárez-Orozco, C., & Suárez-Orozco, M. M. (1995). *Transformations: Immigration, family life, and achievement motivation among Latino adolescents*. Palo Alto, CA: Stanford University Press.

Yoshikawa, H., & Kholoptseva, J. (2013). *Unauthorized immigrant parents and their children's development*. Washington, DC: Migration Policy Institute.

Zayas, L. H., Aguilar-Gaxiola, S., Yoon, H., & Rey, G. N. (2015). The distress of citizen-children with detained and deported parents. *Journal of Child and Family Studies, 24*(11), 3213–3223.

Contributors

Editors

Patricia Gándara is Research Professor and Co-director of the Civil Rights Project at UCLA. Gándara is an elected fellow of the American Educational Research Association (AERA) and the National Academy of Education. In 2011, she was appointed to President Obama's Commission on Educational Excellence for Hispanics. Her most recent publications include *The Bilingual Advantage: Language, Literacy, and the U.S. Labor Market* with Rebecca Callahan (2014) and "The Students We Share: Falling through the cracks on both sides of the US-Mexican border" (Ethnic and Racial Studies, 2020).

Bryant Jensen is Associate Professor of Teacher Education at BYU. He works with educators and researchers to support teacher learning to implement effective and meaningful practices to enhance learning opportunities for marginalized children and youth in the United States, Mexico, Central America, and beyond. With colleagues, he developed the Classroom Assessment of Sociocultural Interactions (CASI). He examines uses of measures like the CASI to sustain improvements in teaching and learning across school and classroom settings. He has been a Fulbright Scholar and Fellow at the Institute for Education Sciences.

Authors

Cristina Alfaro is Professor and Associate Vice-President for Global Affairs at San Diego State University. She is recently chaired the Dual Language and English Learner Education Department in the College of Education at

SDSU, where she has championed and led the largest bilingual-binational teacher education program in the state of California. She is the Director of the Formadores de Docentes Binacionales, a project that addresses the needs of the "students we share" between Mexico and the United States. As a researcher, she has examined and published on the role of pedagogical practices to situate equity at the core of bilingual education across borders.

Sarah Gallo is Associate Professor of Language Education and Urban Social Justice Education at Rutgers University. She conducts ethnographic research across children's schools, homes, and communities to critically promote school-based learning that better recognizes and leverages children's mobile and heterogeneous resources in the United States and Mexico. She is particularly interested in understanding the intersections of immigration and education policies for children from mixed-status Mexican heritage families on both sides of the border. In 2016 Sarah was a Fulbright Scholar in Mexico, and in 2016–2018 she received a postdoctoral fellowship from the National Academy of Education and Spencer Foundations.

Edmund 'Ted' Hamann is an anthropologist of education and a Fulbright Garcia-Robles U.S. Scholar who spent the fall of 2019 in Tijuana, Mexico, examining binational cooperation for initial and continuing teacher professional development related to "The Students We Share." He has studied school and school system responses to transnationally mobile youth in both the United States and Mexico for 25 years. He is a Professor at the University of Nebraska-Lincoln.

Kevin Johnstun recently completed a master's degree in Instructional Psychology and Technology at Brigham Young University. He currently works for The Office of Education Technology in the U.S. Department of Education, examining the ways technology can be leveraged to improve learning for teachers and students alike.

Francesca López is Professor and Waterbury Chair of Equity Pedagogy in the Department of Curriculum and Instruction at Pennsylvania State University. She began her career in education as a bilingual (Spanish/English) elementary teacher and later as a high school counselor in El Paso, Texas. Her research is focused on the ways asset-based pedagogy promotes achievement and identity for Latinx youth. Her work has been funded by the American Educational Research Association Grants Program, the Division 15 American Psychological Association Early Career Award, the National Academy of Education/Spencer Postdoctoral Fellowship, and the Chan Zuckerberg Initiative.

Betsabé Román González is a Professor at El Colegio de Sonora in Hermosillo, Mexico. A current member of the Sistema Nacional de Investigadores, her work focuses on educational and migratory trajectories of migrant children between the United States and Mexico. She uses child-centered methodologies to capture children's experiences and perspectives on migration, schooling, and family, and writes their life stories. She currently leads a CONACYT-funded project on return child migrants in Sonora. She is interested in pre- and in-service teacher education, curriculum design for migrant students, welcome protocols in schools, and children migratory trajectories as funds of knowledge in schools.

Eric Ruiz Bybee is Assistant Professor of Teacher Education at Brigham Young University, where he teaches courses in multicultural education. Dr. Bybee's research interests include the social and cultural foundations of education; Latinx education; teacher education; and identity, agency, and social movements in education. He is particularly interested in issues of identity, cultural knowledge, belonging, and transnationalism as they relate to experiences of Mexican-heritage students and teachers in the United States and Mexico.

Juan Sánchez García is Director and Professor of Teacher Education at the Escuela Normal "Miguel F. Martínez," Centenaria y Benemérita in Monterrey, Nuevo León, Mexico. He has 39 years of teaching experience from primary to graduate school. A member of the Sistema Nacional de Investigadores in Mexico, he has written articles, book chapters, and reviews on several topics in education. Together with Víctor Zúñiga and Edmund T. Hamann, he received the Henry Trueba Award in 2018 from AERA for their pioneering research on transnational students in Mexico.

Lucrecia Santibañez is an Associate Professor at UCLA's Graduate School of Education & Information Studies. Her research focuses on how to improve teaching and learning for low-income, English learners, and other vulnerable populations in the United States, Latin America, and Southeast Asia. Her papers have been published by Economics of Education Review, Teachers College Record, Review of Educational Research, Education Policy

Analysis Archives, and other peer-reviewed publications. Her research has been funded by the Institutes of Education Sciences, the National Science Foundation, the Spencer Foundation, the W. K. Kellogg Foundation, the Inter-American Development Bank, and The World Bank.

Julie Sugarman is a Senior Policy Analyst at the Migration Policy Institute's National Center on Immigrant Integration Policy, where she focuses on policies related to immigrant and English learner students in elementary and secondary schools. Her areas of interest include state- and district-level policies that support effective programs for newcomer students and helping stakeholders understand key education policy issues. Previously, Dr. Sugarman was a senior research associate at the Center for Applied Linguistics, where she specialized in dual language education and program evaluation.

Victor Zúñiga is Professor of Sociology at Tecnológico de Monterrey. He is a tier 3 member of Mexico's Sistema Nacional de Investigadores and Editor of TRACE (Procesos Mexicanos y Centroamericanos) since 2012. His most recent articles and books have been published in Ethnic and Racial Studies, Migraciones Internacionales, Current Anthropology, Mondi Migranti, Sinéctica, Mexican Studies, Oxford University Press, Presses de l'Université Laval, and El Colegio de México. He was awarded the 2018 Henry T. Trueba Award by Division G of AERA for his research. Currently, he is leading a CONACYT-funded project about school exclusion and international migration.

Index

AACTE. *See* American Association of Colleges for Teacher Education
A.B. *See* Assembly Bill (A.B.) 699
Academic, Social, and Emotional Learning Act (2013), 212
access, to education, 3, 9n4, 224, 225
  SEP on, 258
  unauthorized immigrants and, 230–232, 242
accountability, 26–28
achievement opportunities, 163, 163n2
  equitable teaching and, 147–153, 155
  generic quality and, 151–152
  immigrant status and, 160–161
  migration and, 161–162
ACLU. *See* American Civil Liberties Union
activism
  normalista, 74, 76
  student, 76
Acuerdo Nacional para la Modernizaciónde la Educación Básica (ANMEB), 21
Adam (binational student), 134–135
adaptation problems, 186, 212
Addressing Diversity course (*Atención a la Diversidad*), 78

Addressing Educational Inclusion course (*Atención Educativa para la Inclusión*), 78
Adecuación Curricular (Curricular Adaptations course), 78, 80
  "imagined" approaches to, 81–83
adult education, 235, 236
advocacy, for students, 157
affective support, 151–152
age, proof of, 234
Agency, local quality domain, 154
Alina (ITEP graduate), 52
Alison (binational student), 119–120, 125, 130–131
  dictation and, 126–129
allied technocrats (*los científicos*), 74
American Association of Colleges for Teacher Education (AACTE), 205
American Civil Liberties Union (ACLU), 231
American Mexican students, 5, 71–72, 81, 94, 95n1
  inclusion and, 90–92
  needs of, 82–83
  visibility of, 83
Amistad (school pseudonym), 76
  mural at, 77, *77*
  research participants at, 78t

274 | Index

ANMEB. See *Acuerdo Nacional para la Modernizaciónde la Educación Básica*
anti-bilingual education legislation, 204
anti-immigrant policies, 135
anti-immigration sentiment, 223, 263
Arizona, 8, 255, 260–261
  LIEP in, 204, 214
aspirations. *See* future aspirations
Assembly Bill (A.B.) 699, 238–239
assessment, of DLLs, 207
asset-oriented teacher preparation, 258–259
assimilation, 213
Atención a la Diversidad (Addressing Diversity course), 78, 83–84
Atención Educativa para la Inclusión (Addressing Educational Inclusion course), 78
attacks, on immigrants, 55–56
attainment, educational, 23
attendance, protection of, 237–240
awareness, social, 157

Baja California, 46–49, 72, 259
BCLAD. *See* Bilingual Cross-Cultural and Language Academic Development
belonging, sense of, 53–54
benefits, government, 241
Beto (transnational student), 180, 183, 184–185
biculturalism, 63
bien educados, 147–149, 163, 259
Bilingual Cross-Cultural and Language Academic Development (BCLAD) credential, 50
bilingual education, 4, 38, 39, 54, 136
  anti-bilingual education legislation, 204
  for immigrant families, 141
  laws against, 160
  policies for, 252–253
  for teachers, 49–52
bilingual programs, transitional, 38, 217n4
bilingual schools, 47, 136
bilingual students, 120, 138, 260
bilingual teachers, 47, 49–52, 54, 111, 204, 211, 217n4
  ESL and, 216n3
  FDB project for, 46, 61–62
  incentive for, 252, 253
  study on, 48
bilingualism, 26, 62–63, 111, 139, 259
  in U.S. and Mexico, 27, 27t
biliteracy, 51, 259–260
binational education, 47, 52–53, 136
binational policy, 256–257, 261
binational students, 130, 139, 192, 249. *See also* transnational students
  asset-based pedagogies with, 123–124
  bullying of, 135
  club for, 140–141
  daily classroom experiences of, 122–123
  ethnographic study on, 120, 122–123
  exclusion of, 133–134
  social integration and, 133
  teachers and, 134
binational teachers, 46
  identifying KDS for, 59
Binational-Bilingual Teacher Education. See *Formadores de Docentes Binacionales*
blindness, moral, 177
border pedagogy, 52–53
border wall, 237, 249
borderland psychology, 52–53
borders, 105
  bridging, 99–100, 109–111, 112–113
Bracero program, 142n3, 229

Brennan, William (Justice), 230–231, 241
bridging borders, 99–100
  challenges and opportunities of, 112–113
  teachers, 109–111
buddy system, for binational students, 139
bullying, 130–131, 237
  of binational students, 135

California, 47, 61
  Latinx students in, 48
  SEL in, 215
California Commission on Teacher Credentialing (CCTC), 49, 50
California Department of Education, 47, 61
California school districts, as "safe havens," 238–239
California State University (CSU) system, 49
California Values Act (2017), 238
Camila (student), 54
Carlos (*normalista*), 81–82, 85–86
Carrera Magisterial, 28
El Caso de Juan, el Niño Triqui (The case of Juan, the Trique child), 84, *85*, 94
Catholic missions, 73
CCSS. *See* Common Core State Standards
CCTC. *See* California Commission on Teacher Credentialing
Central American children, 2, 4
challenges, in Mexican schools
  dictation, 124–130
  social isolation, 130–135
challenges and opportunities, of bridging borders, 112–113
children, of immigrants, *227*, 228–229
  citizenship of, 228t

children interviewed, in Morelos, 178t
los científicos (allied technocrats), 74
citizenship, 120, 228t
  of children with immigrant parents, 229t
  dual, 191–192
  status of, 235
Cívica (school pseudonym), 76, 77
  research participants at, 78t
Civil Rights Act of 1964, 234, 236
Civil Rights Project, 254
civil war, in Mexico, 20
Clinton, Bill, 231
club, for binational students, 140–141
code switching, 208
collaborative improvement, 262
collaborative learners, 259
collaborative organization, 154
college, 1, 47, 189, 251–252
college degree, 48, 260
  study on, 251–252
college degree programs (*licenciatura*), 48, 74, 260
Collins, Allan, 100
colonization, 213
  history of, 134
Common Core curriculum U.S., 100, 113n2
Common Core State Standards (CCSS), 207
communication
  intercultural, 138
  through social media, 110
communities, indigenous, 19, 26, 73, 139, 153
"community" schools, 19
community use, of schools, 35
Consejo Nacional de Ciencia y Tecnologia (CONACYT), 103, 104
Constitution U.S., 256
content, and language, 57

coronavirus pandemic, 2, 6
  immigrants disadvantaged by,
    250–251
Cortina, Regina, 101
Cristina (*normalista* student), 91–92
CSU. *See* California State University
cultural differences, *normalistas*
  discussing, 83
cultural diversity, 209
cultural learning, 51–52
cultural misunderstandings, 34–35
curricular adaptations course
  (*Adecuación Curricular*), 78, 80
  "imagined" approaches to, 81–83
curricular reforms and diversity, in
  escuelas normales, 75–76
curriculum
  Common Core U.S., 100
  for DLLs, 207
  for FDB Project, 63–64
curriculum map, for *escuelas
  normales*, 79
curriculum standards (*Planes y
  Programas de Estudio*), 26–28,
  99–100

DACA. *See* Deferred Action for
  Childhood Arrivals
daily classroom experiences, of
  binational students, 122–123
Dalton, Georgia, 103
data collection
  with *normalistas*, 76–77
  race or ethnicity, 234
decentralization reform, 21, 260
  funding and, 25
declarations, sanctuary, 224, 239
Deferred Action for Childhood
  Arrivals (DACA), 241
demographics, of high school dropout
  rates, 25
denial, of education, 230–231, 233

Department of Education, California,
  47, 61
Department of Education, US, 216n3,
  234, 242, 256, 257
Department of Homeland Security,
  239
deportation, 4–5, 17–18, 108, 237, 264
  "safe havens" from, 238–239
  stress of, 254–255
desempeño docente (2015) (policy), 264
development, professional, 211
  for equitable teaching, 158
DeVos, Betsy, 242
Díaz, Porfirio, 20, 73–74
el dictado (dictation), 140, 259
  Alison and, 126–129
  challenges in Mexican schools with,
    124–130
digital age, 100–101
disability, 80, 93
  inclusion and, 90, 91–92
  Mexican educators on, 85–86
discrimination, 83, 87, 134, 139
  Civil Rights Act of 1964, 234
  *Equal Educational Opportunity Act
    (1974)*, 236
  against immigrants, 141, 216
  role-play on, 84
  school enrollment and, 234, 236
displaced students, 46
distance learning, 2, 250–251
  Telesecundarias, 19
diversity, 75–76
  cultural, 209
  "imagined" approaches to, 85–87
  Inclusiva para la Educación and,
    87–88
  linguistic, 138
  normalistas and, 85
  racial, 84
divided families, 180–181, 182. *See
  also* separation, of families

divorce, 107–108
DLLs. *See* dual language learners
Dolores (*normalista* student), 90–91, 92
double-shift schools, 20–21, 32
dual citizenship, 191–192
dual language learners (DLLs), 202–203, *204*
  assessment of, 207
  curriculum for, 207
  LIEP and, 213–214
  teacher self-efficacy and, 209–211
  teaching, 204–208
dual-language immersion programs, 39, 108, 138–139, 160, 252
dyslexia, 184

education. *See also* access, to education; binational education
  adult, 235, 236
  denial of, 230–231, 233
  migration facilitating, 110
  Plyler v. Doe and, 241–242
education bill, in Texas, 230
educational attainment, 23
  by race, 48t
educational funding, 35–36, 57–58, 103, 159
  in Mexico, 25–26
Educational Law Center, 232
educational laws, 257–258
educational needs, 99–100
educational policies, 159, 213, 215, 243. *See also* Language Instruction Educational Policies
  local, 260–261
  Mexican, 252–253
educational transitions, 183–184
  mirroring for, 188–189
  teachers on, 185–188
educator narratives, 109–111
educator preparation, 6

educators. *See also* Mexican educators; U.S. educators
  teacher, 156–157
  effectiveness, teacher, 30–33
EL teachers, 243–244
EL-authorization, 216n3
ELD. *See* English Language Development
Eleine (teacher), 186
Elementary schools, 18, 19, *24*
ELs. *See* English Learners
emotional trauma, 53–54
employment, in U.S., 230
English, 55, 86, 121, 130, 187–188
  tests in, 124
English as a second language (ESL), 55, 206–207
  bilingual teachers and, 216n3
  programs for, 27, 217n5
English classes, 136–137
English Language Acquisition, 258
English Language Development (ELD), 206, 216n3
English Learner Tool Kit, 243, 258
English Learners (ELs), 46, 47–48, 55, 202, 225, 243
  peer-tutoring networks for, 263
English proficiency, 54, 206, 207, 259
ENLACE program, 28
enrollment. *See* school enrollment
Equal Educational Opportunity Act (1974), 236
equality. *See* social justice and equality
equitable learning, 155, 158
equitable teaching, 145–146, 150t, 163. *See also* local quality, in teaching
  achievement opportunities and, 147–154, 155
  generic quality and, 153
  instructional time and, 151

equitable teaching *(continued)*
  professional development for, 158
  recommendation for, 154–159
  research on, 158
  transnational students and, 156
Escuela Normal Rural de Ayotzinapa, 74
escuelas normales (normal schools), 71, 72, 92, 261
  curricular reforms and diversity in, 75–76
  curriculum map for, 79
  history of, 73–75
  studies on, 76–79
ESL. *See* English as a second language
ethnic identity, 213
ethnographic study, on binational students, 120, 122–123
evaluation, student, 26–28
Every Student Succeeds Act, 215
EXCALE program, 28
exclusion, of binational students, 133–134
executive orders, immigration, 237
extracurricular activities, 23

families. *See also* immigrant families; transnational families
  divided, 180–181, 182
  mixed-status, 109, 180, 227
  returned, 179–180
  separation of, 176, 179, 182, 253
Family Educational Rights and Privacy Act of 1974 (FERPA), 239–240
family values, 148
FDB Project. *See Formadores de Docentes Binacionales* Project
FDB team, 62
Federal Education Ministry (*Secretaría de Educación Pública*), 20, 23, 50, 62
Federal government, of Mexico, 21, 26

FERPA. *See Family Educational Rights and Privacy Act of 1974*
first-generation immigrant students, 9n2
food stamps (Supplemental Nutrition Assistance Program), 229
forced immigration, 255
Formadores de Docentes Binacionales (FDB) (Binational-Bilingual Teacher Education), 46, 59–61
Formadores de Docentes Binacionales Project (FDB Project), 61–62
  curriculum for, 63–64
los 43 desaparecidos (43 missing students), 74
funding, educational, 35–36, 57–58, 103, 159
  in Mexico, 25–26
future aspirations
  migration and, 192
  mirroring for, 192–193
  recommendations for, 193–194
  teachers on, 191–192
  transnational students and, 189–190, 193

Gallegly, Elton, 231
García, Romero, 113
gender, 80
gender inequalities, 88
gender ratio, in schools, 72
generic quality, of teaching, 151–152, 154
  equitable teaching and, 153
Georgia Project, 103
Global California 2030, 47
goals
  of LIEP, 203t
  for literacy, 138
de Gortari, Salinas, 21
governance, school, 35–36

government benefits, 241
grades, 185
graduation, high school, 1, 19, 47
"Great Expulsion," 103
Great Recession, 5, 71
  return migration during, 176
group activities, 140
grupos (school groups), 148–149
guidance, for school enrollment, 234–235

health, mental, 251, 253
high school dropout rate, 24
  demographics and, 25
high school graduation, 1, 19
high schools (*preparatorias*), 19
history
  of colonization, 134
  of educational system in Mexico, 20–22
  of *escuelas normales*, 73–75
home language literacy, 206
home visits, 156
Houston Independent School District, 230
hypersegregation, 214

ICE. *See* Immigration and Customs Enforcement
identity, ethnic, 213
Illegal Immigration Reform and Immigrant Responsibility Act (1996), 231
"imagined" approaches, 94
  to curricular adaptation course, 81–83
  to diversity, 85–87
  to inclusion, 88–92
immersion Spanish programs, 26
immigrant families
  bilingual education for, 141
  locations of, 226

immigrant parents, 3, 37–38, 106–107, 147–148, 225
  citizenship of children of, 228t
  parental involvement and, 34–36
  undocumented, 4, 180–181
immigrant students, 53–54, 58, 102, 124, 233, 257. *See also* transnational students; *specific topics*
  second-generation, 9n2
immigrants
  attacks on, 55–56
  children of, 227, 228–229
  coronavirus pandemic disadvantaging, 250–251
  discrimination against, 141, 216
  integration of, 228
  Mexico returned to by, 71, 107–108
  unaccompanied youth, 235–236
  unauthorized, 226–227, 228–229, 228t
immigration, 71, 80
  anti-immigration sentiment, 223, 263
  executive orders for, 237
  forced, 255
  Plyler v. Doe and, 241–242
Immigration and Customs Enforcement (ICE), 237, 239–240, 242, 254, 264n1
Immigration and Nationality Act of 1965 (INA), 229–230
immigration policies, 216
immigration policy, U.S., 223–225
  impacts of, 254
  Trump, 253–254
immigration status, 223–224, 225
  achievement opportunity and, 160–161
  school enrollment and, 232, 233
impacts
  of ITEP, 51–52
  of U.S. immigration policies, 254

improvements
  collaborative, 261–262
  instructional, 156
INA. See *Immigration and Nationality Act of 1965*
incentives, teacher, 32–33
inclusion, 87–88
  American Mexican students and, 90–92
  disability and, 91–92
  imagined approaches to, 88–92
Inclusive Education (*Inclusiva para la Educación*), 87–92
inclusive learning, 84
indigenous communities, 19, 26, 73, 139, 153
indigenous languages, 23, 87
indigenous populations, migration of, 106
indigenous students, 38, 59, 84, 87, 93, 106
"Indigenous-intercultural and bilingual" schools, 19
INEE. See *Instituto Nacional para la Evaluación de la Educación*
INEGI. See *Instituto Nacional de Estadística y Geografía*
inequalities
  gender, 88
  social, 84
inequities, structural, 159–162, 163
Instituto Nacional de Estadística y Geografía (INEGI), 122
Instituto Nacional para la Evaluación de la Educación (INEE), 28, 263
instructional improvement, 156
instructional support, 152
instructional time, 151, 155, 262–263
integration, immigrant, 228
intercultural communication, 138
international migrant students, 105, 113

International Teacher Education Program (ITEP), 49–51, 57–58, 64
  borderland psychology and, 52–53
  impact of, 51–52
interpersonal skills, 212
interviews, with *normalistas*, 81–82
involvement, parental, 34–36, 38, 39, 188–189
isolation, in Mexican schools, 130–135
issues, policy, 159
ITEP. See International Teacher Education Program

Jacobo, Mónica, 136
Javier (ITEP graduate), 53
Jefferson, Thomas, 100
Jiménez, R., 124–125
Jocelyn (binational student), 131–134, 136
José Antonio (teacher), 186
Julián (binational student), 134

Kalman, J., 100–101
KDS. See knowledge, disposition, and skills
key term frequency, across three curricula, 79t, 80
knowledge, disposition, and skills (KDS), 55, 58
knowledge, of pedagogy, 205–208

language, 100, 111, 208. See also English; Spanish
  content and, 57
  dual-language immersion programs, 39, 108
  indigenous, 23, 87
  second, 18
  teaching, 56–58
  U.S. teachers and, 202–205

Language Instruction Educational
  Policies (LIEP), 203–204
  in Arizona, 214
  DLLs and, 213–214
  goals of, 203t
Lasanti (Los Angeles, San Diego and
  Tijuana region), 251
Latino U.S students, 250
Latinx students
  in California, 47
  in Dalton, Georgia, 103
Lau v. Nichols (1974), 242
LAUSD. See Los Angeles Unified
  School District
laws, against bilingual education, 160
laws, educational, 257–258
learners, collaborative, 259
learning
  distance, 2, 19, 250
  equitable, 155
  inclusive, 84
  SEL, 201–205, 211–213, 214–215
  virtual, 62
legislation, anti-bilingual education,
  204
licenciatura (college degree programs),
  48, 74, 260
LIEP. See Language Instruction
  Educational Policies
Life Applications, local quality
  domain, 153
linguistic diversity, 138, 209
  of Mexico, 87
linguistics, knowledge of, 208
literacy, 20, 83
  goals for, 138
  home language, 206
  Spanish, 120, 121–122, 126, 140
  transnational, 101
local educational policies, 260–261
local quality, in teaching, 152
  Agency, 154

Life Applications, 153
  Self in Group, 153–154
López Obrador, Andrés Manuel, 22
Los Angeles, San Diego and Tijuana
  region (Lasanti), 251
Los Angeles Unified School District
  (LAUSD), 211
low income parents, 23, 36
Lulú (transnational student), 180, 184

Maestra Elena (normalista), 82, 89–90
MALDEF. See Mexican American
  Legal Defense and Educational
  Fund
marginalized students, 75, 88, 93, 209
Maricruz (teacher), 186–187, 191–192
Martínez-León, N., 124–125
material wealth, 121
McKinney-Vento Homeless Assistance
  Act, 235
meekness, 157
mental health, 251, 253
Mexican American Legal Defense and
  Educational Fund (MALDEF),
  230, 231
Mexican Americans, 3
Mexican educational policies, 252–253
Mexican educational system, 18–19,
  37–39
  history of, 20–22
  parents in, 33–36
  quality of, 23–25
  recommendations for, 136–139
  reforms for, 20–22
  U.S. students in, 49
Mexican educators, 58, 60, 72, 103,
  135, 181
  on disability, 85–86
  recommendations for, 139–141
Mexican federal education policy,
  252–253
Mexican migration, 103

282 | Index

Mexican Revolution, 20, 74
Mexican schools
   dictation challenges in, 124–130
   isolation in, 130–135
   learning from students and teachers in, 120–123
   transnationalism in, 175, 194
   U.S. schools compared with, 23, 39, 121, 147, 185–186
Mexican teachers, 31–33, 37, 40n7, 191–193
   FDB project and, 62
   learning from, 120–123
   pedagogical content knowledge of, 23
   salaries for, 29–30, 30t
Mexican-origin parents, 148, 226
Mexican-origin students, 1–2, 46, 55, 102–103, 107, 259
Mexico, 61
   bilingualism in, 27, 27t
   citizenship in, 120
   civil war in, 20
   educational funding in, 25–26
   educational system in, 18–22
   federal government of, 21, 26
   high school dropout in, 24
   immigrants returning to, 71, 107–108
   linguistic diversity of, 87
   migration to, 103, 104
   political bureaucracy in, 60
   rural schools in, 120, 122, 123, 161, 162, 260
   School Trajectory (1990–2012) in, *24*
   teacher shortage in, 73
   teachers in, 20, 21–22, 28–30, 29t
   urbanicity, 161, 260
   U.S. citizen students in, 249–250
   U.S. meeting with, 256–257
   U.S. teachers traveling to, 58
   wages in, 121

Mexico City, 50
Meyers, Susan, 101, 109–110
Michoacán, Mexico, 109–110
Middle school, 19
Mientras Llego a Mi Escuela (García and Stoopen), 113
migrant children, 112
   in two systems, 102–105
migrant students, 78, 94
   experience of, 253–255
   international, 105, 113
migration, 5, 103, 109
   achievement opportunities and, 161–162
   education facilitated by, 110
   future aspirations and, 192
   of indigenous populations, 106
   to Mexico, 103, 104
   from Puebla, 120–121
   return, 71, 141, 176
   stress of, 253
   study on, 162
Migration Policy Institute, 227
minoritized youth, 213
mirroring, 175
   for educational transitions, 188–189
   for future aspirations, 192–193
   for transnational students, 182–183, 194–195
misunderstandings, cultural, 34–35
mixed-status families, 109, 180, 227
mobility
   teacher, 31–32
   transnational, 185–186
monolingualism, 111
Mrs. Monserrat, 181–182, 187, 192
"moral blindness," 177
Morelos, Mexico, 181, 261
   children interviewed in, 178t
motivation, student, 210
murals, at *Amistad*, 77, *77*

NAEP. *See* National Assessment of Educational Progress
Nahuatl language, 86
narratives, educator, 109–111
National Assessment of Educational Progress (NAEP), 202
National Board for Professional Teaching Standards, 55
nativity
   of parents, 225t
   of U.S. children, 226t
needs
   of American Mexican students, 82–83
   educational, 99
new curricular map, for SEP, 76–77
"new destination" states, 225
"New Latino Diaspora," 103
New York, school enrollment in, 232–233
New York Civil Liberties Union (NYCLU), 232
New York State Education Department (NYSED), 232–233
Newcomer Tool Kit, 243
Next Generation Science Standards (NGSS), 207
normal school educators and students. *See normalistas*
normal schools (*escuelas normales*), 71
normalista activism, 74, 76
normalistas (normal school educators and students), 72–74, 92
   cultural differences discussed by, 83
   data collection with, 76–78
   diversity and, 85
   interviews with, 81–82
   recommendations for preparation of, 93–94
Northern Triangle, 4
nuestro sueño (our dream), 64

Nuevo León, Mexico, 103–104
Nuevo Modelo Educativo, 113n1
NYCLU. *See* New York Civil Liberties Union
NYSED. *See* New York State Education Department

"Oaxacalifornia," 106
Obama, Barack, 237, 241
opportunities. *See* achievement opportunities
oracy, 125, 140
organization
   collaborative, 154
   generic quality and, 152
Ortiz, Andrea, 142n1
"el otro lado" (the other side), 111
our dream (*nuestro sueño*), 64

Paloma (student), 45–46
pandemic, coronavirus, 2, 6
   immigrants disadvantaged by, 250–251
parental involvement, 34–36, 38, 39, 48, 188–189
parents. *See also* immigrant parents
   low income, 23, 36
   in Mexican educational system, 33–36
   Mexican-origin, 148, 226
   nativity of, 225t
payroll, 25
pedagogical content knowledge, of Mexican teachers, 23
pedagogies, 205–208
   binational students asset-based, 123–124
   border, 52–53
   dictation, 125
peer-tutoring networks, for ELs, 263
PEMC. See *Programa Escolar de Mejora Continua*

Plan de Estudio (2012), 75
PLANEA program, 28
Planes y Programas de Estudio (curriculum standards), 26–28, 99–100
Plyler, James, 230
Plyler v. Doe (1982), 108, 223–224, 229–230, 258
   attendance protected under, 237–240
   challenges to, 231–232
   education and, 241–242
   Immigration and, 241–242
   violations and responses to, 232–236
policies
   anti-immigrant, 135
   bilingual education, 252–253
   binational, 256–257, 261
   desempeño docente, 264
   educational, 159, 213, 215, 243, 252–253
   immigration, 216
   LIEP, 203–204, 213–214
   sanctuary, 244
   U.S. immigration, 223–225
policy issues, 159
political bureaucracy, in Mexico, 60
"Porfiriato," 74
pregnancy, teenage, 25
preparation. *See also* teacher preparation
   educator, 6
preparatorias (high schools), 48, 74
pre-service teachers, 75–76, 77, 157, 214
private schools, 19
privilege, 145, 153
   study on, 160
PROBEM. *See Programa Binacional de Educación Migrante*
problems, adaptation, 186, 212
professional development, 211
   for equitable teaching, 158

professional learning, teacher preparation and, 55–56
proficiency, English, 54, 206, 207, 259
Programa Binacional de Educación Migrante (PROBEM), 178, 195n2, 261
Programa Escolar de Mejora Continua (PEMC), 263
programs. *See also* International Teacher Education Program
   Bracero, 142n3, 229
   dual-language immersion, 39, 108, 138–139, 160, 252
   ENLACE, 28
   for ESL, 27, 217n5
   EXCALE, 28
   immersion Spanish, 26
   PLANEA, 28
   Supplemental Nutrition Assistance Program, 229
   transborder, 58, 61
proof
   of age, 234
   of residency, 234
Proposition 187, 231
protection, of attendance, 237–240
Proyecto 2030, 47
psycholinguistics, 208
psychology, borderland, 52–53
"public charge" rule, 229
public schools, 19
Puebla, Mexico, 120–121, 142n3
Purépecha, 106, 107

quality, of educational system in Mexico, 23–25
Quique (transnational student), 181, 184, 190

race, educational attainment by, 48t
race or ethnicity data, 234
racial diversity, 84

racialized students, 46, 51, 54
  teaching language to, 56–58
racism, 236
reading, teaching, 57
Real Academia Española (Jiménez, Smith, & Martínez-León), 124–125
recommendations
  for equitable teaching, 154–159
  for future aspiration, 193–194
  for Mexican education system, 137–139
  for Mexican educators, 139–141
  for preparation of *normalistas*, 93–94
  for teacher learning, 156, 262–264
  for U.S. educators, 141–142
Reforma Educativa (teacher accountability reform), 21–22, 30
La Reforma Integral de la Educación Básica, 80
reforms, for Mexican educational system, 20–22
Rendón, V., 100–101
repatriation, 17
research, on equitable teaching, 158
research participants, at *Amistad* and *Cívica*, 78t
residency, proof of, 234
resources
  for return migration, 141
  sharable, 137
  for teachers, 257
return migration
  during Great Recession, 176
  recourses for, 141
  study on, 71
returned families, 179–180
role-play, on discrimination, 84
rural schools, in Mexico, 120, 123, 162, 260
  urban schools compared with, 122, 161

"safe havens," 241, 243
  California school districts as, 238–239
salaries, teacher, 29–30, 30t, 260
San Antonio Independent School District v. Rodriguez (1973), 231
San Diego State University (SDSU), 50
sanctuary declarations, 224, 239. *See also* "safe havens"
sanctuary policies, 244
Sarah (researcher), 131
school boards, 36
school enrollment
  discrimination and, 234, 236
  guidance for, 234–235
  immigration status and, 232, 233
  in New York, 232–233
school governance, 35–36
school groups (*grupos*), 148–149
school size, 183
School Trajectory, in Mexico (1990–2012), 24
schooling, transnational, 176–177
schools. *See also* Mexican schools; U.S. schools
  access to, 3
  bilingual, 47, 136
  "community," 19
  community use of, 35
  double-shift, 20–21, 32
  gender ratio in, 72
  "Indigenous-intercultural and bilingual," 19
  private, 19
  public, 19
  as "safe havens," 238
science, teaching, 57
Scottish Freemason academies, 73
SDSU. *See* San Diego State University
Seal of Biliteracy, 47, 259
second-generation immigrant students, 9n2

Secretaría de Educación Pública (Federal Education Ministry) (SEP), 20, 23, 50, 62, 99–100, 104
   on access to education, 258
   on English classes, 136–137
   new curricular map for, 76–77
Secretaríade Instrucción Pública (SIP), 20
Secundaria (middle school), 19
segregation, 4, 145, 159–160, 213
SEL. *See* socioemotional learning
selection, teacher, 31
Selena (student), 86–87
Self in Group, local quality domain, 153–154
self-efficacy, teacher, 203, *204*, 209–211
sense of belonging, 53–54
SEP. *See Secretaría de Educación Pública*
separation, of families, 176, 179, 182, 253
SES. *See* socioeconomic status
sharable resources, 137
Sindicato Nacional de Trabajadores de la Educación en México (SNTE), 22
single parents, 107–108
SIP. *See Secretaríade Instrucción Pública*
Sistema Nacional de Coordinación Fiscal, 40n6
size, of school, 183
skills, interpersonal, 212
SLs. *See* Spanish Learners
Smith, P., 124–125
SNTE. *See Sindicato Nacional de Trabajadores de la Educación en México*
social awareness, 157
social inequality, 84
social integration, and binational students, 133
social justice and equality, 60–61
social media, communication through, 110
social security number, 234
social-behavioral strengths, 147
sociocultural dimension, of FDB curriculum, 63
socioeconomic status (SES), 154
socioemotional dimension, of FDB curriculum, 63
socioemotional learning (SEL), 201–205, 211–215
sociolinguistics, 63, 208
sociopolitical dimension, of FDB curriculum, 63
Sofía (transnational student), 185, 190
sojourners, 201. *See also* transnational students
Spanish, 108, 111, 126, 138
   immersion programs for, 26–27
   teaching, 49
   transnational students learning, 184, 187
Spanish as a second language (SSL), 55
Spanish Learners (SLs), 26
Spanish literacy, 120, 121–122
   dictation and, 126
   tutoring for, 140
Spanish writing, 125
special education students, 89–90
Special Supplemental Nutrition Program for Women, Infants and Children (WIC), 241
SSL. *See* Spanish as a second language
standardized tests, 33
status. *See also* immigration status
   of citizenship, 235
Stoopen, Morfín, 113
stresses
   of deportation, 254–255
   of migration, 253
structural inequities, 159–162, 163

struggles, social-emotional, 45–46
student activism, 76
student assessment, 26–28
student motivation, 210
students. *See also* American Mexican students; binational students; migrant students; transnational students; *specific topics*
  advocacy for, 157
  bilingual, 120, 138, 260
  displaced, 46
  indigenous, 38, 59, 84, 87, 93, 106
  international migrant, 105, 113
  Latinx, 47, 103
  marginalized, 75, 88, 93, 209
  Mexican-origin, 1–2, 46, 55, 102–103, 107, 259
  special education, 89–90
  traumatized, 257
  undocumented, 4, 191
  in United States, 3–4
studies
  on agency, 154
  on bilingual teachers, 48
  on binational students, 120, 122–123
  on college degrees, 251–252
  on *escuelas normales*, 76–79
  on instructional time, 151
  of LAUSD teachers, 211
  in Michoacán, 109–110
  on migration, 162
  on privilege in Mexico, 154
  on return migration, 71
  on transnational students, 177–179, 178t, 179t
Supplemental Nutrition Assistance Program (food stamps), 229
support
  affective, 151–152
  instructional, 152
Supreme Court U.S., 108, 223–224, 230, 242

switching, code, 208

taxes, and educational funding, 26, 40n6
TDLLs. *See* transnational dual language learners
teacher accountability reform (*Reforma Educativa*), 21–22
teacher characteristics, in Mexico and U.S., 29t
teacher educators, 156–157
teacher effectiveness, 30–33
teacher incentives, 32–33
teacher learning, 156, 262–264
teacher mobility, 31–32
teacher preparation, 56–57, 74–75, 181, *204*, 209
  asset-oriented, 258–260
  on the job, 156
  in Mexico, 5–6, 18, 39
  professional learning and, 55–56
  trust relationships and, 59
  "two-way" reciprocal program for, 58–61
  in United States, 5–6, 18
teacher selection, 31
teacher self-efficacy, 203, *204*, 209–211
teacher shortage, in Mexico, 73
teachers, 2, 216. *See also* bilingual teachers; binational teachers; Mexican teachers; U.S. teachers
  bilingual instruction for, 49–52, 138
  binational, 46, 59
  binational students and, 136
  bridging borders, 109–111
  on educational transitions, 185–188
  EL, 243–244
  forced immigration and, 255
  on future aspirations, 191–192
  pre-service, 157
  resources for, 257
  salaries for, 29–30, 30t, 260

teachers *(continued)*
   tenure received by, 22, 32
   on transnational families, 181–182
   of transnational students, 177
teacher's union, Mexico. See *Sindicato Nacional de Trabajadores de la Educación en México* (SNTE)
teaching. *See also* equitable teaching
   of DLLs, 204–208
   generic quality of, 151–154
   instructional time and, 151, 155
   local quality in, 152–154
   quality of, 5–6
   virtual, 6
teaching language, to racialized students, 56–58
teenage pregnancy, 25
Telesecundarias (technical school), 19, 23
tenure, teachers receiving, 22, 32
TESOL International, 243
tests
   in English, 124
   standardized, 33
Texas, 87, 214, 230–232, 260–261
   education bill in, 230
   SEL in, 215
three curricula, key term frequency across, 79t, 80
time, instructional, 151, 153, 262–263
Tomás, Leco, 106
Torlakson, Tom, 47, 238
transborder activities, 62
transborder programs, 58, 61. *See also Formadores de Docentes Binacionales* Project
transitional bilingual programs, 38, 217n4
transitions. *See* educational transitions
transnational dual language learners (TDLLs), 202, 212–213, 214–216

transnational families, 179–183
   teachers on, 181–182
   types of, 179–181
transnational literacy, 101
transnational mobility, 185–186
transnational schooling, 176–177
transnational students, 2–3, 9n1, 38–39, 46, 105, 201. *See also* transnational dual language learners
   equitable teaching and, 156
   future aspirations and, 189–190, 193
   mirroring for, 182–183, 194–195
   Spanish learned by, 184, 187
   study on, 177–179, 178t, 179t
   teachers of, 177
transnationalism, 8, 79, 87, 104, 176, 193
   in Mexican schools, 175, 194–195
trauma, emotional, 53–54
traumatized students, 257
Trump, Donald, 135, 190, 224, 226, 237, 238, 242
   immigration policies, 253–254
   "public charge" rule, 229
trust relationships, teacher preparation and, 59
tutoring, for Spanish literacy, 140
two systems, migrant children in, 102–105
"two-way" reciprocal teacher preparation program, 58–61
Tyler Independent School District, 230

unaccompanied youth immigrants, 235–236
unauthorized immigrants, 226–227, 228–229
   access to education and, 230–232, 242
   citizenship of children of, 228t
undocumented immigrant parents, 4, 180–181

undocumented students, 4, 191
United States (U.S.)
  bilingualism in, 27, 27t
  children of immigrants populations in, 227
  citizenship in, 120
  Common Core curriculum, 100, 113n2
  Constitution, 256
  Department of Education, 216n3, 234, 242, 256, 257
  employment in, 230
  immigration policy in, 223–225, 253–254
  Mexico meeting with, 256–257
  students in, 3–4
  Supreme Court, 108, 223–224, 230, 242
Universidad de Guanajuato, 260
Universidad Pedagógica Nacional (UPN), 260
urban schools, rural schools compared with, 122, 161
urbanicity, in Mexico, 161, 260
U.S. *See* United States
U.S. children, nativity of, 226t
U.S. citizen students, in Mexico, 249–250
U.S. educators, recommendations for, 141–142
U.S. schools
  Mexican schools compared with, 23, 37, 121, 147, 185–186, 188
  as "safe havens," 239–240
U.S. students
  Latino, 250
  in Mexican educational system, 49

U.S. teachers, 107, 210
  language and, 202–205
  salaries for, 29–30, 30t
  traveling to Mexico, 58
"Use before know-how" (Kalman and Rendón), 100–101
Utica City School District, 233

Valdés, Guadalupe, 34–35
values, family, 148
Vanessa (student), 131–133, 134
Víctor (*normalista*), 87
Una Vida Dos Paises (film), 113
violations and responses, to *Plyler v. Doe*, 232–236
Virginia (teacher), 185–186, 191
virtual learning, 62
virtual teaching, 6
visa papers, 189–190
visibility, of American Mexican students, 83

wages, in Mexico, 121
wall, border, 237, 249
wealth, material, 121
WIC. *See* Special Supplemental Nutrition Program for Women, Infants and Children
Wilson, Pete, 231
World Languages-ELD credential, 216n3
writing, Spanish, 125

youth, minoritized, 213

Zacatecas, Mexico, 103–104
Zúñiga, Víctor, 131

www.ingramcontent.com/pod-product-compliance
Ingram Content Group UK Ltd.
Pitfield, Milton Keynes, MK11 3LW, UK
UKHW041916140426
5217IPUK00013B/178